HOPE AND FRUSTRATION

HOPE AND FRUSTRATION

Interviews with Leaders of Mexico's Political Opposition

Edited by
Carlos B. Gil

SR
BOOKS

A Scholarly Resources Inc. Imprint
Wilmington, Delaware

#24067844

The paper used in this publication meets the minimum requirements of the American National Standard for permanence of paper for printed library materials, Z39.48, 1984.

© 1992 by Scholarly Resources Inc.
All rights reserved
First published 1992
Printed and bound in the United States of America

Scholarly Resources Inc.
104 Greenhill Avenue
Wilmington, DE 19805-1897

Library of Congress Cataloging-in-Publication Data

Hope and frustration : interviews with leaders of Mexico's political
    opposition / edited by Carlos B. Gil.
      p. cm. — (Latin American silhouettes)
    Includes bibliographical references (p.   ) and index.
    ISBN 0-8420-2395-X. — ISBN 0-8420-2396-8 (pbk.)
    1. Mexico—Politics and government—1970–1988. 2. Mexico—
Politics and government—1988– 3. Opposition (Political science)—
Mexico. 4. Politicians—Mexico—Interviews. I. Gil, Carlos B.
II. Series
F1236.H67 1992
320.972—dc20

91-25303
CIP

May Carlos Anthony Gil live to a ripe old age.

About the Editor

Carlos B. Gil, a native of southern California, received his bachelor's degree from Seattle University and his master's degree from Georgetown University. He then joined the U.S. Foreign Service and worked in connection with cultural affairs in Honduras and Chile. Upon resigning, he attended the University of California at Los Angeles, where he obtained a Ph.D. in history. He has been teaching at the University of Washington since 1974.

Contents

Preface

In a never-to-be-forgotten September night in 1985, my wife and I, along with thousands of *damnificados,* fled Colonia Roma in Mexico City, because it was devastated by the savage earthquakes that had killed thousands of people there and throughout the city a couple of days before. We found refuge in a middle-class home in the southern outskirts of the city, and, after a cup of warming and reassuring Mexican chocolate and some *pan dulce,* we began a friendship that will endure for a long time. *Doña* Ana and her grown children shared with us what life is like under an authoritarian system and in one of the largest *urbes* in the world. They answered many questions and often gave us directions and invaluable tips. The possibility of this book was discussed many evenings in *doña* Ana's kitchen; she and her family watched sympathetically as we learned to cope with the city, and we reciprocated by listening to their views about local and national affairs.

Like our friendship with *doña* Ana and her children, this book developed as a result of the devastation. I had intended another study, which was not carried out because of the terrible emergency. As happened with others in the city, our plans were twisted beyond recognition, but something valuable was salvaged in the end.

In addition to taking a "crash course" in earthquakes, Barbara Ruth Deane, my wife and colleague, devoted many hours to the early planning and fieldwork that produced the pages that follow. We sometimes drove our vehicle through incredibly congested avenues to our appointments, but more often than not we used the crowded metro and interconnected with various *peseros* to reach our destination on time. She never flagged. She also helped me establish a newspaper file to assist my fashioning of questions about contemporary Mexico to be used in the interviews. She took notes at the interviews and managed the technical aspects of recording, while I posed the questions and kept track of the ongoing discussion. Her help was crucial.

I appreciate the assistance of Richard M. Hopper, editorial director at Scholarly Resources, for making this book possible. Others who firmly supported the concept behind this book and indicated the many places where the manuscript needed strengthening and polishing include William H. Beezley, North Carolina State University; Judith Ewell, the College of William and Mary; and Carolyn J. Travers, Scholarly Resources. Also, I thank Lorenzo Meyer, who took time from his summer teaching schedule while visiting Seattle to edit Chapters 1 and 2 and suggest ways to fortify the bibliography with Mexican works.

At the University of Washington, I am indebted to the Francis Keller Endowment, which helped defray some of the costs involved in producing this book, and the Department of History, which provided time off to finish the project. Maggie Miller stands in for several students who helped me prepare this book. She spent many hours on final revisions and additions; having done so will surely aid her when she writes her own book in the not-too-distant future.

I am indebted especially to the interviewees themselves. Entrapped by their own political, organizational, and administrative vortices, they nonetheless found time to be interviewed without losing one iota of generosity or graciousness. Their kindness and cooperation are worthy of imitation. However, not all of the leaders interviewed appear in this volume. Inevitable cuts were made, and I hope that the men and women whose words did not fit into the final version will understand.

Finally, while the reader will find in the interviews references to trends that evolved and to individuals who played important roles in the mid- and late 1980s, he also will discover, I hope, that the opposition leaders raise issues that will remain important well into the 1990s. The interview material is enduring in this sense because fundamental change is always a slow process.

                                                                          CBG

CHAPTER 1

Introduction: The Historical Roots of Today's Issues

Six of the most important opposition leaders in Mexico from 1985 to 1990 are given the spotlight in this book. Next to the president of the republic and a handful of his cabinet officers, the men interviewed here enjoyed a high profile in the Mexican media during these years, although the media, especially television, reported on them and other members of the opposition with great reluctance and partiality. This biased coverage reflects the government's practice of denying the opposition the right to compete effectively in elections and of otherwise keeping it in the political shadows. Despite such hindrances, recent indications are that most Mexicans favor the men of the opposition, who have traditionally been excluded from the government, rather than those in the administration. Specifically, in the presidential election of July 1988, Mexico's ruling party, which has been in office for sixty years, retained power by manipulating the vote count. The world watched the country's political system intently to see if it would unravel during the hotly contested election; it did not. However, the leaders who speak out in this book probably will play an even more important role in the affairs of state than they have until now.

Since 1929 the Mexican people have lived under a political system controlled by the leaders of the Partido Revolucionario Institucional (PRI), the official party that has won all presidential elections without exception. While the system has permitted the election of opposition leaders to congress, especially since the 1970s, the official party had won all state governorships and an overwhelming majority of municipal elections until June 1989. The PRI also has enjoyed a near monopoly on public sector jobs, particularly the important, highly visible ones. Some jobs, however, have been available to members of the opposition—the less significant the jobs, the more open the appointments. The literature analyzing Mexican political phenomena has focused largely on the official party system and its various dimensions. This volume, on the other hand, offers the reader a glimpse at the opposition because Mexico's future is leaning in that direction.

Background information about the six leaders featured in this volume reveals social and economic patterns helpful in understanding these modern Mexican politicians. None hails from the peasantry or working class; all of them were born into middle-class, if not upper-class, families. Even though four were born in the provinces, all obtained the best education possible in Mexico, in part because they attended the nation's best grade schools, located in the capital; one of the leftist leaders claims that he attended the same school as Octavio Paz and Carlos Fuentes. All of the interviewees claim degrees from Mexico's biggest and most influential university, the Universidad Nacional Autónoma de México (UNAM). Indicative of the hegemonic role that *norteños* (northerners) have enjoyed in national politics in the twentieth century, four were born in the north, the remaining two in Mexico City.[1] However, four of the interviewees have spent their entire political lives battling the engulfing and irrepressible PRI; one of them was beaten unmercifully several times by politically appointed thugs in order to stifle his ideas and diminish his activism. Two of the six belonged to the PRI and fought for reform from within the official party to the extent that by 1989 they were considered pariahs. Three of the interviewees ran for the nation's presidency. Statements made by all six reflect the bitterness that thousands of politically active men and women in Mexico have felt because of the repression they have endured silently, and therein lies the reason for presenting the interviews themselves rather than a detached scholarly analysis. Given that the Mexican political system was hard pressed to change in 1988–1990, the words of leaders who have fought all their lives, including their feelings of hope and frustration, need to be enclosed in a book for the historical record. This is that book.

The editor has insisted on presenting the interviews because they are colored with a human dimension that coexists with all political phenomena yet rarely filters through onto the scholarly page. Recent analyses scrutinizing the "authoritarian" dimensions of Latin American politics are overlaid heavily with impersonal and scientific-sounding jargon. The reader will find many statements in this book that are personal and passionate, being free of the terminology of the social sciences. Repression engenders emotion, especially at the beginning. Some of it, however, may have been lost in the translating and transcribing even though the editor tried to let the interviewees' ideas come through clearly and simply. Translating from Spanish, which tends toward eloquence, to English, which tends toward simplicity, added to the difficulty.

The six leaders represent three positions on the spectrum of political opposition in Mexico in the late 1980s; none is on "the fringe." To compensate for party realignments occurring between the time of the first interviews and the final rewriting of the manuscript, the editor presents the leaders simply as representative of the oppositional Right, the Center, and the Left. The interviewees are named below, and the reader will find biographic notes preceding each interview.

Right
Jesús González Schmal
Pablo Emilio Madero Belden

Center
Cuauhtémoc Cárdenas Solórzano
Porfirio Muñoz Ledo

Left
Jorge Alcocer Villanueva
Heberto Castillo Martínez

Issues Raised by the Opposition Leaders

In the most general terms the six leaders disclose how their political organizations have been shackled by both the government and the PRI. They reveal the unfair tactics and the repression that the official party system has employed against them and their organizations in years past. In so doing, the interviewees offer a view of what life has been like for opposition politicians operating within the Mexican authoritarian regime in the 1980s and into the 1990s. On a private level, the reader will learn where the leaders studied, why they entered politics, and how they navigated past the obstacles that the government laid down to foil their work. The reader will see just how difficult it is for an opposition leader to keep going day after day. At the same time, the interviews unveil the level of intellectual complexity, or lack of it, that top politicians bring to the *problemas nacionales* that they address in their daily work. The six leaders reveal whether they are aware of the complexities and insights that scholars who specialize in Mexico churn out in book after book and article after article.

The details about control and repression that fill these pages should not convey the notion that political change has not been taking place in Mexico. Indeed, the prime argument that may be gleaned from the interviews is that the country's economic difficulties, including its indebtedness to the United States, have hastened discontent and criticism of the entire political and economic system. Indications abound that this condition led to what many observers consider the July 1988 defeat of the PRI candidate, Carlos Salinas de Gortari, even though he was pronounced "triumphant" to the world.

On July 6 the Mexican people went to the polls and found themselves, even by official tallies, split between Salinas de Gortari and two opposition candidates, Cuauhtémoc Cárdenas and Manuel J. Clouthier. All prior elections had produced a plurality on behalf of the PRI by about 85 percent. Despite what appears to have been heavy abstention, according to government figures, the PRI obtained only 55.4 percent of the popular vote, the lowest it has ever received. As much as 49.6 percent voted against the PRI by choosing other candidates, thus making the 1988 election truly a watershed.[2] This event explains why most of the interviewees recognize that profound changes occurred in the Mexican political arena in the 1980s and speculate about what it may mean for them and their fellow citizens in the future.

The questions raised by the political leaders featured in this book deal with most, if not all, of the primary issues that the opposition tried to address in the months prior to the crucial election of 1988. Even though the official party candidate won, these issues will continue to be relevant into the late 1990s. They will not go away easily. They may indeed constitute Mexico's national agenda for the first half of the twenty-first century. The more salient problems discussed by the interviewees include:

1) Mexico's indebtedness to the international banking community, especially American concerns, and the political and economic costs involved in making payments;
2) the role of state-owned enterprises in the nation's economy, particularly in light of the need to exert some control over natural resources threatened by foreign corporations;
3) the possible repercussions from Mexico's decision to throw open the nation's economy to international capital via its 1986 entry into the General Agreement on Tariffs and Trade (GATT) and its willingness to begin negotiating for free trade with the United States and Canada in 1991;
4) *presidencialismo* (presidentialism), or the PRI's symbiotic relations with the government, including the congressional dimensions of this interaction, and how it muzzles the opposition; and
5) questions on foreign policy, especially regarding Central America and the United States.

Four Legacies from Mexico's Past

Why and how were the official party and its political machine created? Why did it take on a monopolistic form? These questions already have been answered to a large extent by many authors who have contributed to our understanding of Mexico's early twentieth century, when the foundations of the official party were first laid. It was not the creation of anyone in particular but was rather the product of many factors present in Mexico in the 1910s and 1920s. The following summary, and the entire book, is offered to provide the nonacademic reader with a basic framework for understanding the current political situation.

Mexico's political system obviously differs from those operating in the United States and in other Western countries.
The main distinction lies in the degree to which governing
officials honor the demands of the citizenry. It is hard to
deny that citizen influence on the government appears limited, that the Mexican people have collectively assembled a
system that combines democracy with authoritarianism.[3] The
balance between one and the other cannot be said to be constant. Any analysis of Mexican history reveals that the political system has been moving away from the rigid
authoritarianism it inherited at the end of the Spanish colonial era. But the pace has been slow.

The need to distribute wealth more evenly helps explain
the sluggishness of the change. Although royal privilege was
outlawed in the 1820s, the advantages enjoyed by the ruling
former colonialists and their progeny were surrendered only
slightly in the nineteenth century and survived well into
the latter part of the twentieth. The distribution of wealth
in Mexico today is greatly tilted toward the national elites,
whose life-styles easily rival those of any other ruling class.
As a well-known observer has written, "The top 10 percent
of income-earners appropriates about 40 percent of the country's total income while the lower 40 percent receives barely
10 percent."[4]

Mexico's struggle toward modernity has brought
increased demands for nonelitist government, especially
during the latter half of the twentieth century. Since the
1960s more Mexicans than ever have demanded honest government, while many officials and ruling-party leaders have
resisted the pressure. The dynamic between those who seek
reform and those fighting it has become a large part of the
substructure of the country's contemporary history. The
words "authoritarianism" and "presidentialism" are used
synonymously to define the special blend of politics practiced in Mexico to resist full democracy.

This chapter offers selected concepts gleaned from
Mexico's turbulent history as keys to an understanding of its
presidential system in an effort to explain why the system
has been so hard to change. The concepts are drawn from
the nation's rich historiography, whose books and articles
may be consulted with great benefit. For those who cannot
do so easily, four legacies from Mexico's past are discussed at
length here; an understanding of them will help the reader

when the interviewees refer to individuals and events linked to the country's long-standing problems.

Mexico's Peculiar Industrialization

The country's economic situation in the 1980s and the way it became industrialized in the late nineteenth and twentieth centuries differ from that of the United States, Mexico's major commercial partner and most important political associate. The difference is said to hold the key to why Mexico became economically subordinate to its northern neighbor in the twentieth century, why its economy has not evolved beyond a certain point, and why its elites have been able to exploit the population they oversee. These ideas are inspired in the dependency school, composed of Latin American specialists, many of whom were trained in Latin American universities. Calling themselves *dependentistas,* they believe their role is to explain Latin America's troubled economic situation in the twentieth century in a way that U.S. intellectuals largely have ignored. The following characterization of Mexico's peculiar industrialization reflects the link between the country's economic development problems and the *dependencia* approach, which is upheld by many observers, especially those in the opposition.[5]

The Industrial Revolution began in England in the late 1700s, and many ideas and practices related to it were passed on to the United States in the early 1800s.[6] The introduction of mechanized labor-saving devices and, later, factory-style production using new energy forms such as steam played a dramatically important role in giving English speakers an international edge on capital accumulation and technical skill.

Full-strength industrialization was brought to Mexico during the dictatorship of Porfirio Díaz (1876–1911). There is no disagreement whatsoever among experts that the country's first industrial phase, based almost exclusively on mining and the building of railroads, was dominated by foreign capitalists, mostly Americans. Varying degrees of modernization took place only within certain enclaves, a condition that lasted into the 1940s.[7] An analyst of the period writes that "Mexico became El Dorado," especially for U.S. businessmen. In mining, the most dynamic sector of the economy, out of 1,030 companies registered, 882 (85.6 percent) were foreign owned, and, of these, 81.5 percent were owned by Americans. Of the 363 million pesos invested in Mexican mines (2 pesos were worth nearly U.S. $1), 335 million (92.2 percent) were owned by foreigners, and, of this amount, Americans controlled 81.5 percent.[8] American-built railroads, laid down on a north-south axis, accelerated the export of ores to the United States. Mexico's economy was thus tempered by "primary production" (that is, producing mostly raw materials) and a foreign orientation, and was, in effect, saturated with U.S. capital.

By the 1930s the Mexican economy was predisposed in such a way that the introduction of consumer-goods manufacturing during World War II did not appreciably alter its conditioning from the Díaz period.[9] Even when the economy grew with "miraculous" strides beginning in the 1950s,[10] it reached an invisible lid and failed to go further. Victor L. Urquidi has summarized this situation best:

> [Mexico's] industrial expansion took place under a highly protective system. . . . Much of the industry lacked cost-effectiveness and could not compete in international markets. Moreover, production was concentrated in large enterprises, many of them subsidiaries of multinational corporations, at the expense of small and medium-sized businesses. In addition, the growth of labor-saving technology contributed to a slower growth of industrial employment than might have been expected. . . . Many gaps developed in the industrial structure and dependence on imported intermediate products became larger than it had been before.[11]

Mexico gave the appearance of unbounded economic growth during these years mostly because progress took place in selected areas requiring limited amounts of unskilled labor. The provinces saw little change, if any, and the benefits of modernization were enjoyed by few. This unbalanced growth was further tilted by the decline of mortality rates and the rise of rural-to-urban migration, both of which contributed to accelerated unemployment and increasing misery, especially in the burgeoning cities. As discussed in Chapter 2, the government initiated special arrangements with most labor unions in order to control the unrest that would naturally arise. Spurred by the Bracero Program (Mexico furnished the United States with agricultural laborers during World War II[12]), emigration to the

United States, legal and illegal, began to mount. Social discontent grew during the 1950s, and political strife, which was difficult to contain, finally erupted in the 1960s.

When representatives of the Salinas de Gortari administration announced their willingness to engage in free-trade negotiations with U.S. officials in April 1990, many observers were simply astonished. The legacy of Mexico's peculiar industrialization, as presented here, was being overlooked with amazing aplomb. Some observers fear that the predominance of foreign ownership and control associated with the Díaz years serves as a precedent that may repeat itself. The countries of Latin America, including Mexico, engaged in "free trade" in the late 1800s and became subordinate to and dependent on the United States by the early 1900s. Mexico's revolution of 1910 arose mostly as a result of this condition.

The Mexican Revolution

The Mexican Revolution of 1910 is as pivotal in the consciousness of modern-day Mexicans as World War II is in the minds of most Americans. If the word "revolution" is used correctly to refer to a "sudden, radical, or complete change,"[13] one can be assured that revolutions do not take place in Latin America all the time, contrary to popular opinion. Although rebellions, coups, and other short-term events involving military force occur more frequently, they usually produce superficial change if any. "Real" revolutions have taken place only a handful of times in Latin America, and in Mexico only once in the twentieth century.[14]

The origins of the 1910 revolution go back to the fractured sense of nationhood that emerged out of the colonial period ending in 1821. Between 1821 and 1876 the nation's leaders, most of whom were descended directly from European families, fought wars among themselves in an effort to impose their views of what the new Mexican nation should be. Peasants, largely of Indian descent, acted as foot soldiers. Liberal leaders upheld various versions of democracy, while Conservatives rallied around a modified monarchical program. Little consensus was achieved. The civil wars and other internecine fighting are now referred to as *La Reforma*. Should the Indian peasants be permitted to

continue unchanged in their rural ignorance and depen-
dence on whites? Should communally owned lands be converted into private property? Could Indians become
independent yeoman farmers? Should the economic power of
the Roman Catholic church be curbed, and, if so, how?
Should the church continue as the nation's most important
educational institution and credit source? Should English
and U.S. capital be welcomed? These were some of the bitterly contested questions. While Liberals hunted down
Conservatives, and vice versa, both France and the United
States invaded Mexico with imperial ambitions. Half of the
nation's territory was lost as a result of the U.S. invasion,
and Mexico suffered trauma not yet forgotten.

The emergence of General Díaz as the nation's leader in
1876 brought both an end to the wars of *La Reforma* and
the opening of the country to foreign influence. As dictator
between 1876 and 1911, Díaz imposed law and order with legendary ruthlessness and laid the foundation for Mexico's peculiar industrialization, considered in the preceding section.

The countryside was changed forever during the years
now known as the *porfiriato*. Modernization came quickly
in some areas and more slowly in others. The ultimate effect
was the "transition from peonage to wage labor," with a
consequent loss of land by Indian villagers in particular.
Existing commercial-crop production (sugar and tobacco)
was reinforced with new crops (cotton, coffee, tomatoes, and
chick-peas), and haciendas specializing in exportable produce expanded exponentially at the cost of communal village lands.[15] Rural-to-urban migration was spurred. The
conditions that led to the revolution of 1910 were thus
linked to a period of rapid economic growth.

Such growth benefited a small segment of the population. A large percentage did not experience an improvement
in the standard of living. Pay increases failed to keep up
with rising prices during the entire nineteenth century, and
evidence shows that real wages during the *porfiriato* actually declined by at least 25 percent.[16] Contemporary
observers issued warnings that went unheeded. One critic,
Francisco Bulnes, observed that the Mexican people were
"moving toward death by starvation," while Andrés Molina
Enríquez censured the growing number of strikes in the
country.[17] The historiography of the period is filled with
many examples of oppression and repression. Moreover,

when the export-oriented economy dipped and faltered as a result of international market fluctuations and credit squeezes, many members of the middle and upper classes began to join the working classes in rejecting General Díaz and his "progressive" but highly vulnerable regime.[18] Some historians believe that old political differences within the upper class itself also contributed to the collapse of the Díaz dictatorship.[19]

Francisco I. Madero, the uncle of one of the leaders interviewed in this book, served as the lightning rod of the welling discontent. Although his wealthy family did not lose as much as others did in the Wall Street panic of 1907, Madero, hitherto a neophyte in politics, nonetheless strode into the thick of national campaigning. Running as a reformist opposition candidate in 1910 against Díaz, Madero was jailed in an attempt to halt his growing popularity. He escaped from his incarceration, fled to Texas, and called for the revolutionary overthrow of General Díaz. Thus the 1910 revolution slowly began to take form.[20] The accumulated unhappiness experienced by countless Mexicans, including many in the upper classes who were swept aside when the benefits of modernization were handed to foreigners, as well as workers who barely kept themselves clothed, vented itself in large-scale violence. The names Pancho Villa, Emiliano Zapata, Felipe Angeles, Alvaro Obregón, and many others began to echo from one community to another.

Lasting about ten years and severely straining U.S.-Mexican relations in the process,[21] the revolution succeeded in several ways. It brought down General Díaz in 1911 and weakened the old land-owning aristocracy responsible for the serflike conditions in which peasants had long lived, although land owners already had been injured by industrial competition for cheap labor. More subtly, the revolution helped the Indians and mestizos, both of whom had participated in its whirlwind of death and destruction, stamp onto the so-called revolutionary governments their own ethos, which had received little credit prior to 1910. *Lo indio* and *lo mestizo* were more openly recognized, especially in nonpolitical arenas such as art, literature, and song. Although most people of Indian descent would have to continue fighting to obtain a degree of respect for their heritage, the begrudged recognition would become one of the accomplishments of the revolution.[22] This acceptance was accompanied by several promises. One was to establish certain controls over foreign influence, especially in the economic sphere; others were to respect Mexico's agrarian tradition, specifically by giving or returning land to the small traditional farmer, and to create a welfare-sensitive state.

The revolutionary leaders, most of whom were bourgeois and later became government officials, agreed to give land to peasants who formally declared their need for it. This became the basis for Mexico's truly revolutionary land program, formally begun in 1917 but not at its zenith until the late 1930s. Communally owned land was distributed to entire villages in what was perceived as an affirmation of an ancient land tenure form known as the *ejido*.

The Constitution of 1917

Linked to the fruits of the 1910 revolution, the constitution of 1917 is still in effect and is one of the longest lasting in Latin America. Vital to an understanding of contemporary Mexico, the constitution has helped fashion a political viewpoint among Mexicans that places them, as a whole, to the left of most people in the United States. Mexican citizens often express deep pride in many of the provisions contained in their national charter. Substantial portions were written largely to counterweight the powerful economic presence that the United States already enjoyed when the members of the constitutional convention gathered in the colonial city of Querétaro.

In general terms, the Mexican constitution sets forth the legal bases for the radical transformation of the nation. In its most significant aspects, it specifies limits on foreign capital and foreign ownership of land and other key natural resources. Article 27 originally held that "the direct ownership of all minerals or [subsoil] substances [such as petroleum]" was "vested in the Nation" and could therefore never again be alienated to American or other foreign companies as had happened during the age of Díaz. Moreover, "only Mexicans" were permitted to acquire ownership of "land, waters, and their appurtenances, or to obtain concessions to exploit mines, water, or mineral fuels."[23] In this sense, the Mexican constitution buttresses the people's nationalistic intensity, which is sharpened by their need to guard their identity and interests in the shadow of the Northern Colossus.

The constitution also laid the foundation for an active federal government enjoying the authority to intervene in the various states if necessary. It has encouraged the government to play an overwhelming role in national education, to the exclusion of private or religious groups if it so wishes; the more conservative leaders featured in this book have called for a review of these provisions. The constitution allows the federal government to transform private property into "social" or public property if national conditions so merit. Given the strength enjoyed by the Catholic church before 1917, the constitution obligates the state to record vital statistics, and even goes to the extent of denying priests the right to vote (which again became a national issue in 1986) or otherwise express political views. The charter specifically grants workers the right to unionize and strike.

The full implementation of the document's provisions has been cushioned by the changing national conditions. Since 1917, Mexicans have pondered and debated which portions to enact, when, and how. The answers they gave to these questions, collectively speaking, form some stirring moments in the country's history since 1917. Most, if not all, of the six leaders featured in this volume make repeated references to Lázaro Cárdenas del Río. Most of his countrymen praise him and admire him because he tried to implement many aspects of the nation's revolutionary charter and in so doing became demonized by none too few. Opposition to the Cárdenas program gave rise to the Partido de Acción Nacional (PAN), one of the parties discussed later in this book. Meanwhile, the PRI has appointed itself as the guardian and executor of the constitution, and many opposition leaders bitterly censure this action.

The Official Party

Most of the social and economic conditions that gave rise to the 1910 revolution were unchanged by 1924, when much of the violence finally ended, and therefore helped lay the groundwork for the establishment of the official party. The nation's agrarian populace, hindered by rampant illiteracy, did not see any major alterations in their lives. Peasants, small-town artisans, workers in mines and on railroads, and their wives and children made up about 88 percent of the population.[24] Uneven industrialization of the kind already noted continued to limit the number of better-paying jobs. The conservative Catholic church, not yet tamed by the anticlerical provisions written into the constitution, kept preaching respect for the old ways; paternal authoritarianism inside the home and traditional stratification persisted unchanged everywhere. Powerful foreign firms, most of them American, continued to enjoy protection from the constitutional provisions that could jeopardize their pre-1917 investments. The job of honest and progressive leaders intent on changing Mexico for the better was a near-impossible one, despite the revolution. The growth of grass-roots democracy that could have acted as a steadying keel for officials of the new revolutionary governments remained stunted.

The revolutionary experience itself and its ready-made leaders also contributed to the rise of the official party. Years of violence encouraged instant decision-making; fast action at a local level was preferred to official determinations made far away in Mexico City long after they were needed. Acting in the public arena *a lo macho* (quickly and firmly, reflecting the male authority of the leader) was not entirely new, but it was undoubtedly strengthened by the violent years.

The taste for swift, strong direction encouraged the survival of "military" chieftains, or caudillos, spawned by the revolution. Such men enjoyed a certain moral authority because they had helped to overthrow the unpopular Díaz and to eliminate the equally unpopular pre-1910 army that had supported the general. The absence of this army directed from Mexico City in turn aided the chieftains' authority in their own bailiwicks because responsibility fell upon them to provide some semblance of law and order.[25] The image of revolutionary caudillos wreaking destruction everywhere they went is far too simple. They could fulfill both civil and military duties locally when not engaged in combat, and this ability helped them enjoy certain influence after the violence died down. As historian Romana Falcón has stated, "For the multitude of poor peasants who were already used to living under somebody's thumb, belonging to the clientele group of a powerful *cacique* was the only way to guarantee a minimal amount of security and the satisfaction of basic needs."[26] The official party arose from this state of affairs.

The chieftains were not confined to the provinces; they ruled the country from Mexico City as well. In the later 1910s and in the 1920s the nation's leaders were all caudillos—those who had survived the revolution. The presidential suites thus were occupied serially by a stern-looking rancher, Venustiano Carranza (1917–1920); a popular chickpea farmer, Alvaro Obregón (1920–1924); and a wily former schoolteacher, Plutarco Elías Calles (1924–1928).[27] All three were *norteños*. They served their country as the rough-and-ready leaders who literally shot their way to power during the tumult of the revolution, in contrast to the civilian presidents who would later peacefully take their place in the capitol without having bivouacked anywhere. The caudillo factor is essential to the foundation of the ruling party.

Specific events in 1928 helped to assure the final emergence of Mexico's official party. Although Calles firmly led the nation through a divisive four-year period (1924–1928), Obregón still enjoyed such popularity that his presence in the country proved to be decisive. Recognizing the critical importance of both men, some writers refer to these years as a diarchy.[28] The revered Obregón was reelected in 1928 but assassinated shortly thereafter by a religious fanatic who was protesting anticlerical measures that the outgoing Calles had imposed during his own term of office. Unrest bristled throughout the country; few people believed that a lone killer was responsible. An important contemporary participant in national politics wrote years later that many *obregonistas* quickly assumed that Calles, wanting to continue in office or select his own successor, had ordered Obregón's death. A handful of the murdered man's admirers actually visited Calles and asked him to step down from office immediately.[29]

To prevent the various disaffected caudillos—especially *obregonistas*—from shooting their way into the executive office, Calles acted quickly. He conceived the idea of a national party where none had existed before.[30] As he told a friendly critic, he wanted to create a political organization that would fuse all of the revolutionary groups interested in working toward democracy. Too much "sterile" struggling had been wasted on elections, he insisted, and the moment had finally come to set aside boundless aspirations and seek the right path.

> It would be possible to channel the ambitions of our undisciplined politicians into a program that could be approved beforehand. With an organism of this sort, the disorders that arise with each and every election could be avoided and, bit by bit, our institutions could become stronger with each democratic exercise; this way, democracy could be achieved in all its fullness some day.[31]

Calles evidently hoped that such a party would help maintain stability yet allow him to continue to keep watch over national affairs. Mexico's official party, then known as the Partido Nacional Revolucionario (PNR), was thus born, and Calles, in effect, controlled the country via the organization until 1934, when he was forced into exile in order to end his paternalistic control.

The new national party, which became the PRI in a later phase, was made up of various interest groups formed or strengthened by the revolution. These included existing small parties, labor unions, peasant organizations, and the various regional caudillos and their clannish adherents. In return for such groups' cooperation, all were probably rewarded by Calles. While evidence is not plentiful yet, indications are that the party head garnered support and loyalty in exchange for government help of one sort or another and the promise of little or no interference in local affairs. The caudillos were free to employ the machinery of state government in order to stay in command and maintain some order and stability.[32] This arrangement encouraged fraudulent elections, although the uniformity and consistency of misrepresentation is still sketchy.[33] A caudillo could organize his supporters in such a way that he, or someone loyal to him, could become state governor through a manipulated vote. The members of his *cacicazgo* (a caudillo's organization) could then be appointed to state cabinet positions, and all of them could receive lucrative state contracts. Calles benefited by creating an instrument for his guiding power and thereby securing national order; the regional caudillo benefited by feeling secure about his local power base. The country gave the appearance of democracy, and economic development was promoted once the effects of the Great Depression weakened.

The PNR thus became a cartel, or a national coalition, of revolutionary interest groups, which agreed to guarantee the nation's stability by renouncing participation in any type of coup against the central power in return for a degree of hegemony in their regions. The official party embodied crafty compromise and varying levels of co-optation from the start. Instead of allowing elections to become democratic exercises, the PNR erected and maintained a facade of representative government. Each succeeding president strengthened the power of the party, often by linking it ever more strongly with his administration. For example, Emilio Portes Gil, who served provisionally in 1929, decreed that each federal bureaucrat annually contribute seven days' pay to the party.[34] This action meant not only that the PNR was suddenly assured of much-needed revenue, but also that all bureaucrats were made party members by decree, since without this affiliation their appointments were not guaranteed.

In the 1930s, President Lázaro Cárdenas (1934–1940) moved the party beyond the initial coalition of varied interest groups by linking it intimately with popular organizations. This reorientation mirrored Cárdenas's social philosophy, which led him to impel Mexican workers to gain counterweighing power against employers. Even as he campaigned for the presidency in 1934, he exhorted workers "to organize yourselves in such a way that you stand ready to demand of national authorities, even of myself, that we comply with the promises the Revolution made to the working classes."[35] The net effect of his outlook was to make his six-year administration the eye of a storm by implementing as many aspects of the nation's constitution as circumstances allowed. When the dust settled, Cárdenas had successfully distributed to the landless more acreage than anyone before him, by exercising the constitutional clause that allowed the state to nationalize private property for "causes of public utility." Thus, he nationalized the railroads and the majority of foreign-owned oil companies, and he bolstered the formation of labor unions while tying them to the state.[36] He also gave the PNR a new organizational cast.

The reorganization of the official party, put into effect in 1938, enabled Cárdenas to accomplish two objectives. First, he reconciled conflicting political forces that demanded his exclusive support: the revolutionary Left, many of whose members were identified with Communist-led industrial

labor unions, and the revolutionary Center, which was connected with small farmers, businessmen, and bureaucrats.
Because the president's rhetoric and actions had been aimed
at implementing the socialist dimensions of the Mexican
constitution, one group strove to enlist him as an ally in the
outright abolition of private property, and the other sought
reforms that did not go so far. Cárdenas's answer was to
insert the state as mediator and thus prevent solutions from
the radical fringe. This intention was made clear in a speech
he delivered in the nation's cradle of industry, Monterrey,
at a time when strikes were proliferating:

> The campaign that workers' organizations have been waging
> recently does not have any other gist to it than a social one
> that adheres to the law and which does not alarm anyone in or
> out of the government because we all know that the workers'
> objective is to gain only that which is compatible with the pro-
> ductive and financial capacities of the companies.[37]

In other words, the abolition of companies and other forms
of private property would not proceed, but class conflict
would continue in the form of strikes, until the labor forces
of production acquired power equivalent to the employers'.[38]

Cárdenas's second objective was to promote among
workers self-organization as a means to achieve bargaining
power with employers, and it also became a reality. The
president apparently believed that, in order to nudge workers and peasants into a higher level of organizational self-
confidence, he had to encourage the formation of labor
unions and peasant leagues and to favor strikes. Organizing
and striking, however, could lead to excesses. Cárdenas
therefore incorporated most workers' groups into the party,
where controls could be exercised. This arrangement gave
rise to the corporative structure that Cárdenas imposed on
the official party in 1938. Industrial labor unions organized
around the Confederación de Trabajadores Mexicanos
(CTM), peasant leagues joined together in the Confederación
Nacional Campesina (CNC), and middle sector organizations
such as the Federación de Sindicatos de Trabajo al Servicio
del Estado (FSTSE) were all drawn into the official party.
Ideally, the interests of the nation's working classes were
now merged with the state, and they consequently would be
considered as factors in the distribution of publicly controlled resources.

The corruption of this ideal did not take long. The Mexican Left, which came around to supporting Cárdenas's programs (from which it received considerable support as well), began to disassemble. The much-maligned Right began to organize itself even while Cárdenas was still in office. The heady days of revolutionary nationalism came to an end when news filtered out, to the consternation of many, that the president had chosen a moderate military officer to succeed him, instead of the fiery former revolutionary Francisco Mújica, who stood ready to advance the *cardenista* program.

As president from 1940 to 1946, General Manuel Avila Camacho moderated the ideological direction of the government, and his successor, Miguel Alemán Valdés, yanked it further to the right from 1946 to 1952. The symbiotic structures that tied the state to labor unions and peasant leagues remained upright but were soon appropriated on behalf of capitalist production. The concept of countervailing power between unions and employers, or peasant leagues and plantation owners, was set aside. While the right to strike could not be voided easily, union leaders were co-opted when they were not assassinated. These measures gave the official party and the government a virtual monopoly over national politics by the 1950s, despite bloody confrontations with independent unions. Corruption flourished.

During the 1960s, with the president at their head, ruling-party leaders were in a position not only to fashion national and local policies but also to determine how they would be carried out. The inexorable tendency toward centralization provided by this system further guaranteed the party leadership the privilege of deciding who could become a government employee and thereby benefit from a myriad of advantages accruing from a government post.

The presidentialist system was alive and well in 1987. When the PRI candidate, Salinas de Gortari, visited the state of Nuevo León during one of his first campaign tours, in November 1987, local bureaucrats were clearly informed by the area PRI leader to do their duty and show their loyalty. He reminded them, in a memorandum, that "it is important that you, as a *priista* and a public servant participate in the ceremonies connected with Salinas de Gortari's campaign so that we may all show him our support and solidarity."[39] In line with the policy of enforcing loyalty on

behalf of a party head, a Nuevo León newspaper actually published a list of the members of the various PRI-controlled
labor unions, to make a review of their enforced presence
before Salinas an easier task.[40]

If the Mexican political system is compared with East
European systems before *glasnost*, many parallels immediately come to mind: The ruling party is the sole transmitter
of ideology, the consciousness of the party impels it to act as
a vanguard; it therefore decides on all affairs from the top,
and these decisions are binding.[41] It must be said, however,
that the Mexican system never created a gulag for dissident
political leaders, nor did it send millions of peasants to
Siberian oblivion, and often death, in order to force conformity. Nonetheless, it created an administrative-political system by which policy initiation always came from the top.
The system's implementation was vertical and required loyalty of a kind seldom experienced in the United States. As in
the Russian case, the reasons for Mexico's authoritarianism
are lodged in its conflictive history, and only the foolhardy
would make light of them or ignore them. Yet changes never
thought possible swept even the Soviet Union and Eastern
Europe in the late 1980s. Can this happen in Mexico?

On the eve of Mexico's 1988 presidential elections most
Mexicans held a deep and abiding distrust of their political
system, which they later expressed via the ballot box. As
measured by Miguel Basañez and other social scientists,
Mexicans' suspicions were greatest regarding people connected with the government, especially police officers, politicians, and labor leaders.[42] Mexican voters made a statement
in the summer of 1988. Clearly, they were unwilling to put
up with a system that may have been necessary in 1929 but
is no longer.

Notes

1. Roderic Ai Camp has carefully examined the social and economic backgrounds of many modern Mexican leaders. His most
recent works include *Entrepreneurs and Politicians in Twentieth
Century Mexico* (New York: Oxford University Press, 1989); and
Mexico's Leaders, Their Education and Recruitment (Tucson:
University of Arizona Press, 1980). Other works are cited in the
bibliography.

2. "Official" results from the *New York Times,* July 15, 1988:

PRI   9.64 million votes   50.4%
FDN   5.96 million votes   31.1%
PAN   3.27 million votes   17.1%
PDM ⎫
PRT ⎭ 0.23 million votes   1.4%

3. Without an appeal to arcane definitions, in their simplest forms democracy and authoritarianism may be defined as follows:

> *democracy*: rule of the majority . . . government in which the supreme power is vested in the people and exercised by them directly [or] indirectly through a system of representation [usually in the form of] periodically held free elections.
> *authoritarianism*: a political system which limits political pluralism, advocates a blind submission to authority . . . a government free of accountability favoring the concentration of power in a leader or an elite not constitutionally responsible to the people.

See *Webster's Third New International Dictionary of the English Language Unabridged* (Springfield, MA: G. and C. Merriam, 1971), 146, 600; and Juan J. Linz, "An Authoritarian Regime: Spain," in Erik Allardt and Yrjö Littumen, eds., *Cleavages, Ideologies, and Party Systems: Contributions to Comparative Political Sociology* (Helsinki: Transactions of the Westermarck Society, 1964), 291–341.

4. Victor L. Urquidi, "Economic and Social Development in Mexico," in Tommie Sue Montgomery, ed., *Mexico Today* (Philadelphia: Institute for the Study of Human Issues, 1982), 82.

5. For a recent discussion of *dependencia* and allied theories of Latin American economic development see Cristóbal Kay, *Latin American Theories of Development and Underdevelopment* (London: Routledge, 1989), esp. chaps. 5, 6.

6. The idea of a stock company as a vehicle to promote economic development and yield profits is an example of this intellectual legacy enjoyed by early Americans thanks to their English forebears. See, for example, a discussion of the first U.S. roads and turnpikes financed largely out of American stock companies, in George Rogers Taylor, *The Transportation Revolution, 1815–1860* (New York: Harper and Row, 1951), 24–26.

7. A clear expression of this concept is presented in René Villarreal, "The Policy of Import-Substituting Industrialization, 1929–1975," in José Luis Reyna and Richard S. Weinert, eds., *Authoritarianism in Mexico,* 67–107, Inter-American Politics Series (Philadelphia: Institute for the Study of Human Issues, 1977). See also James D. Cockcroft, "Social and Economic

Structure in San Luis Potosí," in his *Intellectual Precursors of the Mexican Revolution, 1900–1913* (Austin: University of Texas Press, 1976), 15–34; and idem, *Mexico: Class Formation, Capital Accumulation and the State* (New York: Monthly Review Press, 1983), 86–99.

8. Marvin D. Bernstein, *The Mexican Mining Industry, 1890–1950* (Albany: State University of New York Press, 1964), 74–77; Carlos B. Gil, ed., *The Age of Porfirio Díaz: Selected Readings* (Albuquerque: University of New Mexico Press, 1977), 103–5.

9. Villarreal argues this persuasively in "Import-Substituting Industrialization," 67–107.

10. See the discussion of the "Mexican Miracle," in Roger D. Hansen, *The Politics of Mexican Development* (Baltimore: Johns Hopkins University Press, 1974), 1–10.

11. Urquidi, "Economic and Social Development in Mexico," 79–80.

12. Ernesto Galarza, *Merchants of Labor: The Bracero Story* (Santa Barbara: McNally and Loftin, 1964), 41–57.

13. *Webster's Seventh New Collegiate Dictionary* (Springfield, MA: G. and C. Merriam, 1963), 736.

14. Historians generally agree that four revolutions have taken place in Latin America in the twentieth century: the Mexican Revolution (1910); the Bolivian Revolution (1952); the Cuban Revolution (1959); and the Nicaraguan Revolution (1979).

15. Cockcroft, *Mexico: Class Formation*, 91–92.

16. Hansen, *Politics of Mexican Development*, 21–23.

17. Francisco Bulnes, *El verdadero Díaz y la revolución* (Mexico City: Editora Nacional, 1952), 398; Andrés Molina Enríquez, *Los grandes problemas nacionales* (Mexico City: Imprenta de A. Carranza e hijos, 1909), 237; cited in Hansen, *Politics of Mexican Development*, 21–23.

18. The most useful analysis of the bourgeoisie's role in initiating a revolutionary climate in Mexico in 1908–1910 is Cockcroft, *Intellectual Precursors*, 35–46.

19. Lorenzo Meyer agrees with this political interpretation, which is also held by Stanley Ross among others. See Meyer and Héctor Aguilar Camín, *A la sombra de la revolución mexicana* (Mexico City: Cal y Arena, 1990), 26; and Stanley Ross, *Francisco I. Madero: Apostle of Mexican Democracy* (New York: Columbia University Press, 1955), 63–73.

20. There is a considerable amount of literature on the revolution of 1910. Recent reinterpretations include Meyer and Aguilar Camín, *A la sombra*; Alan Knight, *The Mexican Revolution* (Cambridge: Cambridge University Press, 1986); and Ramón E. Ruiz, *The Great Rebellion, 1905–1924* (New York: Norton, 1980). For information concerning Madero, see Ross, *Francisco I. Madero.*

21. See Clarence C. Clendenen, *Blood on the Border: The United States Army and the Mexican Irregulars* (London: Macmillan, 1969).

22. The themes of race, racism, and race relations in Mexico and elsewhere in Latin America are underexamined for the most part. See a refreshing reopening of these topics in Richard Graham, ed., *The Idea of Race in Latin America, 1870–1940* (Austin: University of Texas Press, 1990); and esp. Alan Knight, "Racism, Revolution, and *Indigenismo*: Mexico, 1910–1940," 71–113, in the same volume.

23. See E. V. Niemeyer, Jr., *Revolution at Querétaro: The Mexican Constitutional Convention of 1916–1917* (Austin: University of Texas Press, 1974), 257; Peter H. Smith, "The Making of the Mexican Constitution," in William O. Aydelotte, ed., *The History of Parliamentary Behavior* (Princeton: Princeton University Press, 1977), 186–224; and José Ovalle Favela, "Aspectos sociales y políticos de la Constitución mexicana de 1917," *Pensamiento Político* 20 (October 1975): 195–210.

24. James W. Wilkie and Paul D. Wilkins, "Quantifying the Class Structure of Mexico, 1895–1970," in James W. Wilkie and Stephen Haber, eds., *Statistical Abstract of Latin America, 1981* (Los Angeles: Latin American Center, UCLA, 1981), 21:584, Table 3605.

25. The elimination of the prerevolutionary army constitutes one of the major reasons why Mexicans have been free of the corrosive militarism seen in South America in the twentieth century. Even so, the revolutionary caudillos and their irregulars became the basis for the post-1910 army. See Guillermo Boils, *Los militares y la política en México 1915–1974* (Mexico City: Ediciones "El Caballito," 1975); and Edwin Lieuwin, *Mexican Militarism: The Political Rise and Fall of the Revolutionary Army* (Albuquerque: University of New Mexico Press, 1968).

26. Romana Falcón, *Revolución y caciquismo. San Luis Potosí, 1910–1938* (Mexico City: Colegio de México, 1984), 17.

27. Although Carranza almost always wore a military-style uniform and lived the life of an officer during the revolutionary years, some specialists insist that he was a civilian caudillo rather than a military one. See a new interpretation in Douglas W. Richmond, "Venustiano Carranza," in George Wolfskill and Douglas W. Richmond, eds., *Essays on the Mexican Revolution: Revisionist Views of the Leaders,* Walter Prescott Webb Memorial Lectures (Austin: University of Texas Press, 1979), 48–80.

28. See Rafael Segovia and Alejandra Lajous, "La consolidación del poder," in Lorenzo Meyer et al., *Historia de la revolución mexicana: Los inicios de la institucionalización, 1928–1934* (Mexico City: Colegio de México, 1978), 5.

29. According to Emilio Portes Gil, the governors of Sonora and Sinaloa delivered an ultimatum days after Obregón's death.

See Gil's *Quince años de política mexicana* (Mexico City: Ediciones Botas, 1954), 34. See also Ricardo J. Zeveda, *Calles el presidente* (Mexico City: Editorial Nuestro Tiempo, 1971).

30. Citing another source, Segovia and Lajous attribute the original idea of a revolutionary party to Obregón. Segovia and Lajous, "Consolidación del poder." However, Meyer believes that Calles long had the idea of such a party, but Obregón's "presence" prevented him from organizing it.

31. Portes Gil, *Quince años*, 228. Portes Gil attributes the word "sterile" to Calles, who probably used it to convey the idea that too many human lives had been lost to achieve certain political goals.

32. Dale Story, *The Mexican Ruling Party: Stability and Authority*. Politics in Latin America (A Hoover Institution Series) (New York: Praeger, 1986), 18–26.

33. See Falcón, *Revolución y caciquismo*, for the best interpretation available of *caciquismo*.

34. Story, *The Mexican Ruling Party*, 21.

35. Tzvi Medin, *Ideología y praxis política de Lázaro Cárdenas* (Mexico City: Siglo Veintiuno Editores, 1976), 4th ed., 76.

36. Story, *The Mexican Ruling Party*, 25.

37. Medin, *Ideología y praxis*, 80.

38. Ibid., 81.

39. *Proceso* 576 (November 16, 1987): 9.

40. Ibid.

41. See reports of the astonishing unraveling of the East European socialist system in the *New York Times* for November 1989. For a summary of the functions of an East European political system, see Barbara Wolfe Jancar, *Czechoslovakia and the Absolute Monopoly of Power: A Study of Political Power in a Communist System* (New York: Praeger, 1971), 14–29.

42. See a summary of this study, commissioned by the División de Estudios Económicos y Sociales del Banco de México, in Miguel Basáñez and Enrique Alducín, eds., "Valores, actitudes y opiniones," *Nexos* 11:129 (September 1988): 63–65. It is also discussed by Bertha Lerner de Sheinbaum, "El estado mexicano y el 6 de julio de 1988," *Revista mexicana de sociología* 51:4 (October-December 1989): 199–237, esp. 209–10.

CHAPTER 2

Recent Events in Perspective

The decrepitude of Mexico's current political system became manifest to the world in the presidential election of July 6, 1988. Carlos Salinas de Gortari was the first *priista* candidate in nearly fifty years whose victory was thrown into doubt hours after the nation's ballot boxes were closed.[1] The resulting confusion was compounded when headlines everywhere announced that Cuauhtémoc Cárdenas was winning in the crucial voting districts of Mexico City, according to unofficial counts. This surprising trend was headlined in the *panista* strongholds of Chihuahua as well.[2] The undefined situation encouraged the PAN candidate, Manuel J. Clouthier, to announce prematurely that the PRI had finally become the country's second party, and the PAN first.[3]

Contradicting Clouthier's claim, considerable evidence shows that Cárdenas and the Frente Democrático Nacional (FDN), the unwieldy alliance that supported him, gave the PRI and Salinas de Gortari, its standard-bearer, the most severe blow they had ever received. In what appears to be the best accounting of the election available at this time, Andrew Reding discloses that the official party lost popular support in 1988 in comparison to other election years, and it did so in shocking proportions.[4] Reding arrived at this conclusion by scrutinizing voting results in the electoral districts where "opposition vigilance drastically cut the use of phantom votes" and inhibited other forms of fraud. In districts where the balloting was least distorted, he found that Cárdenas won by sweeping 2-to-1 victories in Mexico City and in the surrounding states of Morelos and México and by a 3-to-1 landslide in Michoacán. The "modern heart" of the nation voted for Cárdenas, Reding asserts. Beyond the heartland he took into account the various instances in which pro-*cardenista* ballots were actually dumped into municipal trash piles or burned in remote areas instead of being counted, and he subtracted dummy ballots deposited on behalf of Salinas. Thus, he concluded, the PRI actually lost voters in astounding proportions.[5]

Applying a similar "corresponding adjustment" to the congressional races, Reding believes that the official party received "less than 51% of the total vote." He cites considerable evidence to show, however, that the government recognized ahead of time the legislative turmoil that would result, including the lower chamber's refusal to declare Salinas officially president-elect, which constitutionally it must do. Consequently, the government overruled all oppositional challenges, maintaining its hegemony by resorting to the illegal tactics that it had customarily applied in earlier elections.[6] This action prompted the opposition candidates, Clouthier, Cárdenas, and Rosario Ibarra de Piedra,[7] to issue a joint statement about the fraud that was being perpetrated even as they spoke to the public at dawn on July 7. Manuel Bartlett, former interior minister and president of the Comisión Federal Electoral (CFE),[8] responded by saying that appropriate guarantees had been given to the opposition parties, and that it was improper for them to charge irregularities without proof.[9] Opposition representatives on the CFE thereupon walked out in protest. On July 9, Cárdenas announced that inside information confirmed his own party's assessment that he actually had won the election.[10] Official electoral agencies nonetheless "validated" Salinas de Gortari's "victory." Thus began the Salinas administration. It may not be the last PRI government in modern Mexican history, but it may very well be a transitional one.

How could Cárdenas, an underdog who was ostracized by Mexico's powerful official party, attract so many votes? How could his electoral showing weaken Latin America's most stable party and thereby weaken the region's most durable political system, if not throw it into a period of prolonged crisis? More importantly, did the race of 1988 become a critical referendum on the system installed thirty or forty years earlier? Did the people clearly show their disfavor of

Salinas de Gortari in order to repudiate the economic burden government leaders had acquired in the 1970s, when an oil boom went bust and those same leaders were caught spending lavishly on themselves? The answers to these questions have yet to be given in full. In the meantime, the opposition leaders in this book assert that PRI heads should have known better than to run the nation into debt. The interviewees are dismayed also that the PRI stayed in power despite popular disapproval.

The trends summarized in the preceding chapter concerning the unique corporate political system that the Mexican leadership assembled during the 1930s and 1940s will play a vital role when these issues are finally explained. This chapter seeks to identify some significant developments that began about 1950, to give the reader a fuller background with which to interpret the interviews and thereby to grasp the consequential dimensions of the questions above.

Industrialization and the Control of Organized Labor

Reminiscent of governmental arrangements fashioned in the Iron Curtain countries during the same period, the Mexican political system was erected in order to move beyond a stratified agrarian phase and establish a competitive industrial society with a degree of social equity. As Finance Minister Eduardo Suárez said in 1941 in one of the earliest statements concerning the country's need to industrialize, "Mexico will manufacture a good portion of the articles which she now imports, in order to reduce, in time, her outlays abroad. It is proposed to produce [in Mexico] all the steel consumed . . . cellulose and derivatives, parafine and lubricants, vegetable oils, chemical products, and cement."[11]

To achieve these goals the political elite turned to the leaders of the nascent industrial unions and peasant leagues of the 1930s and ultimately created a "social pact." This so-called pact ostensibly recognized workers' social and economic rights arising from the revolution and inscribed in the constitution of 1917. It recognized these rights by offering labor and peasant leaders an assigned place in national politics so that the elite could negotiate successfully with them when needed, preserve political stability, and push forward the process of industrialization and the economic benefits it would bring, especially to themselves. In other words, the pact became the basis of an alliance between labor organized by the government and the men who made up the Mexican state. This alliance gave the nation an unusual degree of political stability and contributed to an exceptional economic growth rate registered into the early 1970s. Little social equity was gained, if any. Nonetheless, the pact acted as the sociopolitical cement in the "corporative" structure that Lázaro Cárdenas gave to the official party in 1938. An understanding of the original intent of the social pact may help the reader better appreciate how the old *cardenista* ideal became corrupted in the eyes of left-of-center critics, thus providing them with an incentive to vote for Cuauhtémoc Cárdenas in 1988 because he supported the pact's preservation. Such critics believe that Mexico's economic growth has been exhausted in its present form, and that the social pact has been jeopardized. This, they contend, has caused the weakening of the old political system.

In a recent study of the social pact, Jeffrey Bortz states that "the Labor sector [has been] arguably the strongest source of support for the party and the government."[12] He emphasizes two basic points: An ingrown relationship between handpicked labor leaders and the PRI has thrived since 1910, and its institutional dimensions may be demonstrated by the fact that official personnel of the national labor federations (CTM and CNC) are part and parcel of the labor wing of the PRI and the Labor Ministry. Contrary to the days of Lázaro Cárdenas, the practical effect is that the party and the government, in consultation with the co-opted labor leadership, are able to control 1) the registration of unions and peasant leagues, shutting out independent groups; 2) the occurrence of strikes (illegal ones are repressed); and 3) the demand for higher wages.[13] Bortz further argues that this powerful combination ultimately developed ancillary dimensions in business and government by encouraging the rewarding of workers in PRI-controlled unions with higher compensation packages than their peers, job security, and comfortable fringe benefits not available to others. The leaders in this book confirm these trends.

The development of a progovernment labor structure (*charro* unions and peasant associations) created a highly privileged labor bureaucracy aimed at benefiting national and international businessmen. In the postwar years, investors enjoyed protected markets and a labor climate controlled from the president's suite at all times. In what is referred to as the "Mexican Miracle," the economy grew by an average of 6 percent annually between 1940 and 1980,[14] thus fueling urban and industrial employment and swelling the ranks of PRI-controlled unions on the strength of wage contracts that the government permitted them to negotiate. Multinational corporations such as General Motors, Ford, Kodak, Sears, Anderson Clayton, and Dow Chemical streamed into the country in order to take advantage of the so-called Mexicanization legislation that was supposed to limit foreign investment to 51 percent but instead permitted many large multinationals to remain 100 percent foreign-owned while enjoying the guarantee of low wages.[15] Bureaucracies grew apace, as did the *priista* unions that managed their affairs.[16]

The symbiosis between the PRI and the government resulted in legendary levels of corruption and repression. The postwar decision to propel Mexico into the ranks of the industrial nations of the world encouraged government leaders and labor bosses to enter into corrupt relationships with each other due to the former's ability to attract foreign investment and the latter's willingness to control wage demands and meet the expectations of foreign investors. Men such as Fidel Velázquez, leader of the CTM, "tied themselves to state favors, class collaborationism, and upper-class aspirations and values."[17] If they did not receive government positions, they enjoyed hidden payments in exchange for their cooperation. When the average Mexican worker earned 200 pesos per month, the labor federation secretary-general received 30,000 per month plus allowances, and local union directors each received 10,000 per month in compensation for keeping a lid on labor demands.[18] Behind-the-scenes arrangements of this kind fuel the indignation of most of the opposition leaders interviewed for this book.

The Mexican Miracle aggravated the already skewed distribution of economic rewards in the 1950s and increased political discontent. Herein lies a parallel with the 1980s and an insight that may explain why tens of thousands of urban Mexicans became *cardenistas* in 1988–89: Economic pressures exerted on the average worker helped produce an undercurrent of antigovernment sentiment and activity. In the 1950s this situation led to several events that have acted as a legacy for the opposition. The devaluation of 1954 seems to have played a leading role.

Opposition Growth in the 1950s and 1960s

The 1954 devaluation, part of a long series, was announced during Holy Week on Saturday, April 17. On the 16th the peso had been exchangeable at 8.65 to the U.S. dollar, and on the 17th it rose to 12.50. The convertability of the peso thus dropped by 44.5 percent overnight, making this devaluation exceptionally severe. It immediately affected people in business or traveling abroad. Mexico City newspapers reported that foreign tourists using the city airport were hunted like prey by people demanding U.S. $8.65 to the peso in order to stave off their losses.[19] In line with earlier devaluations, the ostensible purpose was to correct the decline in the volume and prices of Mexican exports and the excessively rapid shrinking of the country's international reserves.

Theoretically, the devaluation would make Mexican products sold abroad more attractive because they would automatically cost less, and demand for them would rise. Walter J. Sedwitz, who analyzed the data in 1955, is not sure that the devaluations achieved this effect, although Mexico's economic position recorded a "spectacular advance." Nor did he ask himself how Mexican workers fared as a result; he merely observes that "rising prices" resulted as a domestic side effect.[20] After the devaluation, it took more pesos to buy foreign goods, and imports helped raise the prices of domestic goods. Many merchants, not waiting for the costlier imports to raise prices, changed them over the weekend. One observer reported that the price of chocolate for the traditional Mexican breakfast drink was priced at 4.25 on Saturday the 17th, but by the following Monday it had gone up to 8.00, or 78 percent. The workers were thus "pinned to the wall" in what the historian James D. Cockcroft calls "superexploitation (i.e., labor power is paid below its value while pressure to work increases)."[21]

The overnight halving of the nation's purchasing power stunned most labor leaders, who refrained from making public statements. Would the social pact withstand the blow of such a big devaluation? The answer came within days, when newspapers began to carry favorable advertisements placed by the various labor federations. Led by Velázquez of the CTM, nearly all of the nation's union leaders agreed, or so it appeared, that "the working class was willing to fight on behalf of national interests and uphold patriotic destinies once more."[22] Velázquez held a private meeting with President Adolfo Ruiz Cortines, and, upon emerging from the president's office, he issued a statement that the Mexican people have heard in countless versions ever since: "The link between the nation's workers and the government had been strengthened once more," as a result of their talk. This had "sealed the permanent friendship held with the nation's chief whom we [the workers] consider our leader and friend."[23]

Although many unionized railroad workers reportedly received a 10 percent raise in order to compensate for the devaluation, the first signs of trouble emerged from their ranks. The members of independent-minded chapters of the national railroad workers federation in Monterrey, Torreón (Guanajuato), Querétaro, and Guadalajara decided to defy their union bosses. They organized a slowdown in order to obtain a 30 percent raise plus benefits, but they were fired immediately. No dissidence was tolerated.[24] The social pact held a little longer.

The nation's teachers stepped into the breach left by the railroad workers. Beginning in 1956, a group of underpaid teachers became the first to reject their government-directed *charro* union, the Sindicato Nacional de Trabajadores de la Educación (SNTE).[25] At the start, low salaries acted as the primary stimulus for protesting; but when SNTE bosses acquiesced to Labor Ministry officials by rejecting a slate of independent leaders, some rank-and-file teachers bolted to form a new union, the Movimiento Revolucionario del Magisterio (MRM). Led by a Communist schoolteacher, Othón Salazar, the MRM filled the *zócalo* (main square) facing the president's office with tens of thousands of teachers, students, and other supporters. About forty thousand people marched on April 12, 1958, in one of the largest demonstrations reported in these years. As would happen time and

again, grenadier guards and auxiliary police forces
repressed the schoolteachers with force, but eventually the
government accepted all their economic demands except
one: the recognition of their independent union.[26] Union
workers in other key industries such as railroads, commu-
nications, petroleum, and electricity took note and began
organizing small independent chapters as well.

In 1958-59 railroad workers went on strike, and their
struggle became an important step in the gradual but difficult evolution of both independent labor unions and opposition political parties. The squelching of the 1954 slowdown
helped give rise in 1958 to the creation of an independent
blue-ribbon railroad workers' commission in the industrial
city of Torreón. Known as the Gran Comisión, it concluded
that rail workers' wages lagged behind inflation. Its package
of demands ultimately included the unharrassed existence
of independent rail workers unions, but managers rejected
its stipulations.

The workers retaliated. On the eve of a national presidential election, members of Section 13 of the Sindicato
Nacional de Trabajadores Ferrocarrileros Revolucionarios
de México (SNTFRM) organized chronologically ordered
work stoppages, and news of this plan spread rapidly to
other union chapters. Led by a Communist rail worker
named Demetrio Vallejo, thousands interrupted their jobs
at a designated moment on June 25; railroads across the
nation stopped with clockwork precision. A second strike on
the 27th lasted four hours, and, as with the first one, no
major violence took place.[27] Managers made an offer that was
not accepted by the strikers, at which point the nation's president asked to speak with the strike leaders. The meeting,
however, was not held immediately. A third strike, on
June 28, lasted six hours, and railroad cars became overly
congested in certain areas as a result. The 29th saw an eight-
hour strike that completely paralyzed the country, and on the
30th the time of the stoppage was extended to ten hours.

On this day, President Ruiz Cortines finally met with
the strike leaders, who accepted a significant wage increase
per month and an agreement to hold a plebiscite among the
workers to determine the proper union leadership. When
the election was held, fifty-nine thousand votes favored
Vallejo as the new leader of the SNTFRM, and nine favored
the progovernment candidate.[28] Popular discontent over

government-directed labor unions was thus underscored. The parties that supported the rail workers—the Partido Comunista Mexicano (PCM; the Mexican Communist Party), the Partido Popular Socialista (PPS; the Popular Socialist Party), and the Partido Obrero Campesino Mexicano (POCM; the Mexican Worker-Peasant Party)—expressed satisfaction because Vallejo's win validated their own independent status.[29]

After the national race, President-elect Adolfo López Mateos was sworn in on December 1, 1958, and Vallejo settled in as the new leader of his union. The battle lines were redrawn. Responding to fresh demands that included the right to press for the restructuring of the industry, railroad operators and the government decided that the limit had been reached. Criticism of Vallejo's links with the international Communist movement approached a new high in the media, which for the most part was antilabor at this time.[30] When the unions threatened with further strikes to press their demands, the military and selected police battalions stirred into action. Independent union leaders, the rank and file, and members of the left-of-center parties that had supported them were located, beaten savagely, and thrown into prison, including Vallejo. One writer observed that repression was unleashed throughout the country in a manner never seen before.

By the end of December the trains were running on schedule, due to armed guards on each one. The movement begun by schoolteachers in 1954 aimed at raising wages and reversing government-controlled labor unions had thus come to an end temporarily in 1958. It is noteworthy that, while certain sectors of society would rise against corruption and government interference in popular organizations once again, the workers as a body would not, and peasants least of all. The political opposition that had identified itself with labor was obligated to go underground in 1959. It is very likely that many of the militants who had struggled on behalf of the independent-minded railroad workers helped swell the *cardenista* ranks in 1988.

Popular discontent toward the PRI and the government welled up again in 1964. Medical interns working in state-owned facilities in Mexico City began protesting the low pay they were receiving and the bureaucratic mismanagement and corruption they faced in their daily tasks. They, too,

tried coalescing into several unions to defend their interests, insisting also on unions free of government control. In
the end, the government yielded only partially to their
demands at a key moment, but it was just enough to break
their militancy.[31] The interns did not receive public support
in the manner that the railroad workers had, perhaps
because the public saw them as initiates into high-paying
careers that excluded the average citizen. Their short-lived
struggle, however, is viewed as a prelude to an avalanche of
antigovernment protests and demonstrations that led,
among other things, to one of Mexico's greatest tragedies.

In the waning days of 1959 and the first ones of 1960, a
youthful guerrilla leader overthrew an aging and corrupt
dictator in one of the Caribbean Islands where political
tyranny had been a hallmark. This event, heralded daily in
newspapers everywhere, including Mexico City, helped fashion a sudden climate of change. In 1960 political vistas were
thrown open by the youthful revolutionaries who entered
Havana on New Year's Day. What was once considered politically impossible suddenly appeared within reach for the
price of a little effort. Stories about Fidel Castro's seemingly
single-handed ousting of U.S.-supported Fulgencio Batista,
decrees aimed at the nationalization of American properties
in Cuba, and the signing of commercial agreements with the
Soviet Union riveted young people throughout Mexico to the
latest news reports. Heberto Castillo and Cuauhtémoc
Cárdenas exemplify the thousands of young men who
already had been alerted in 1954 to the darker side of U.S.
practices in the region when the Central Intelligence Agency
(CIA) executed the downfall of the Jacobo Arbenz administration in Guatemala, which had been considered progressive by many Latin Americans. In 1965, triggered by this
knowledge and Castro's example, young Mexicans felt that
they at least had to protest "yankee aggression" in the
Dominican Republic, and they joined the militant Havana-
based Organización Latinoamericana de Solidaridad which
supported leftist insurgencies in the region. Their hope was
that such rebellions might somehow bring freedom from
oppression in Latin America and elsewhere.

As if in counterpoint, American military forces increased
their involvement in Vietnam, and heavy U.S. bombing of
what appeared to be disarmed peasants in Cambodia and
Laos was reported. Compounding matters, the United

States also appeared to be bleeding internally during these years as serious rioting spread from the black neighborhoods of Detroit to the Mexican-American barrios of East Los Angeles. And a similar malaise was spreading across the globe, having already provoked student rioting in Europe. Mexican papers supplied by international news services had reported the events well.[32] Paradoxically, the Mexican government had enthusiastically agreed to host the Olympic Games for that summer. Mexico City, especially, was engaged in the expensive process of construction and beautification in order to give foreign visitors the best possible impression.

Radicalism and discontent in Cuba, the United States, and France act as a background to the seemingly innocuous student skirmishes that developed in Mexico City in July and eventually led to the tragedy of October 2. The initiating conflict involved two groups of high-school students. One included many young people of blue-collar origin who identified with the local technical university, the Instituto Politécnico Nacional (IPN). The other attracted those hoping to enter the more exclusive UNAM. Perennial rivals, these two groups engaged in street clashes on July 22 that produced some property damage. On the 23d the police cordoned off a section of the downtown area in order to entrap the militants, without much success, until soldiers intervened. Several schools used by the youths as rebel headquarters were invaded by armed soldiers; in a widely publicized action, the door of one of the schools was blown open with a bazooka. The student groups were thus controlled temporarily.

The commemoration of the anniversary of the Cuban Revolution, on July 26, gathered large crowds that protested the tactics of the police and the soldiers. As confrontations with law enforcement officials continued, the rationale for protesting widened to include many of the old demands from the 1950s. Although most demonstrations were led by university students in an amorphous organization known as the Consejo Nacional de Huelga (CNH), many nonstudents joined together in the streets in unprecedented, growing numbers. Workers swelled the crowds, including schoolteachers involved in the 1954 conflict, railroad laborers from the bloody skirmishes of 1958, and others who had attempted to keep independent unions alive. However, few of the labor federations participated. A demonstration on August 27 reportedly attracted as many as three hundred thousand people to the heart of the city.[33] The reasons for their action were printed, painted, and scrawled on hundreds of placards and posters:

A MAN MUST NOT BE TAMED, HE MUST BE EDUCATED.

WORKER, DESTROY YOUR 'CHARRO' UNION.

PEOPLE UNITE, OPEN YOUR EYES.

THE REAL AGITATORS ARE IGNORANCE, HUNGER, AND MISERY.[34]

The climax was precipitated by a militant student decision, made at a rally on October 2 at the Plaza of Three Cultures (also known as the Plaza de Tlaltelolco), to march to the army-occupied IPN. To prevent this move, troops of the Olympia Battalion, already present to obviate disorder, opened fire on the crowd about 5 P.M. When the shooting stopped, scores of bodies lay on or near the pre-Hispanic ruins that take up a large part of the plaza. Human sacrifices had been made once more at the Aztec site, as Octavio Paz has written.[35] One student leader claims that he overheard a government official estimate that more than five hundred people were killed that evening.[36] The incident has never been examined officially.

It is remarkable that all but one of the few parties opposing the PRI and the government during Mexico's greatest political crisis since the 1910 revolution played an insignificant role. The PPS, for example, was quick to condemn the CIA for provoking the treacherous political climate in Mexico leading up to October 2, even though it did not present evidence, nor has any support for its allegation come to light. The PPS rendered little assistance to the student leaders and hardly criticized the PRI government at all. The PAN took a more honest position. It condemned the violence, proposed a negotiated solution to the student demands, and denounced "communist plotters," but it also recognized that Mexico's peculiar form of industrialization and development stood at the core of the nation's problems. However, to the credit of both opposition parties, their congressmen refused to vote in favor of a statement offered by members of the PRI and Partido Auténtico de la Revolución Mexicana (PARM) on October 4 in support of the government's firm hand on October 2.[37]

If any party bravely held up the standard of true opposition during these days it was the Mexican Communist Party. In the late 1980s, neo-*cardenistas* such as Pablo Gómez, secretary-general of the Partido Socialista Unificado Mexicano (PSUM), and Jorge Alcocer wistfully looked back to a time when the PCM valiantly took the high road in the drama of national politics. The Communists may be credited for unflinchingly recognizing the growing oppressiveness of the Mexican political system, especially when they resolved in their 15th National Congress, held in June 1967, "that the democratic transformations demanded by the nation's development were not going to come from the governing elite." They also concluded that the PRI, in conjunction with the country's bourgeoisie, had exhausted its reformist capabilities and that democratic change could come only from mass struggle. They were unable to define "mass struggle" to the satisfaction of everyone present at the congress, although they appear to have admitted, collectively, that its most probable form would be armed fighting. Officially, the concept remained undefined.[38] Perhaps this inability helped provoke the tragedy of October 2 because numerous desperate people aired their frustrations in endless meetings of the Juventud Comunista Mexicana (JCM). Many of them opted for the "most probable" option after October 2, although their older comrades held back. Valentín Campa, one of the most fiery leaders of the PCM in earlier times, remarked about this dilemma:

VC: We did not agree with the guerrillas because they lacked the proper perspective. This is what we told the boys in the JCM when they decided to go into the mountains.

Carlos B. Gil: They're the ones who organized the Partido Mexicano de los Pobres [PMP]?

VC: No. Well, Lucio Cabañas was the one who organized the PMP, and some of the boys went with him, but there were others who joined other guerrillas. There were many of them. In any case, that was our position.

CBG: During that period you folks—

VC: We helped Lucio Cabañas because we understood he was desperate. One time, for example, he was wounded, and we were the ones who rescued him, brought him and got him well again. It was his human right to survive so we cured him and took him back—

CBG: But strategically you were opposed.

VC: We had defined our position quite clearly: The kind of struggle they wanted was condemned to fail, as it did in the end.

CBG: The same happened with the others.

VC: We told the various guerrilla groups: "We are against this." They had been members of the JCM, where we said to them: "We are against your way of doing things, but we are willing to help you one way or another because your position regarding October 2d is a reasoned one." You'll recall that the repression against the people was brutal![39]

Indeed, a repression of the Left was unleashed. Cabañas, a schoolteacher turned revolutionary, has come to symbolize the fatal desperation that afflicted many young Mexicans in the late 1960s and early 1970s. Like the others to whom the aging Campa refers above, including Genaro Vásquez, also a schoolteacher,[40] Cabañas became rash and eventually paid with his life. Despite their small town, petit bourgeois origins, many such youths engaged in politico-military acts of protest. Others, tending toward the cosmopolitan haute bourgeoisie, resisted taking up arms but ultimately felt deeply disenchanted with the Mexican political system. Kenneth J. Middlebrook addresses this widespread phenomenon in his discussion of the political reforms that the PRI espoused in the 1970s.[41]

Political Reforms Introduced in the 1970s

The early 1970s witnessed a softening of the system, particularly toward members of the Left. Middlebrook cites three problems that impelled Presidents Luis Echeverría Alvarez (1970–1976) and José López Portillo (1976–1982) to engage in an *apertura*, or opening up, to incorporate marginal political groups, especially those on the Left. One cause was the presidents' recognition of the need to relegitimize themselves and their ruling regimes in the eyes of significant sectors of Mexico's urban middle classes. Middlebrook argues that the chief executives acknowledged that the 1968 massacre at Tlaltelolco had undermined the myth of the revolution and its attendant promises of progressive socioeconomic achievements and political justice. "Mexico's post-1940 development model" was exhausted, he writes, and democracy was still elusive. The second problem was that certain political groups had evolved since 1968 whose members were critical of the PRI system but, nonetheless, chose peaceful methods to make their views known. Third, the political arrangement that existed in the early 1970s was obviously failing to attract new blood. The PRI had experienced a decline in its ability to mobilize fresh adherents, and internal criticism was getting louder. Beyond the PRI and the PAN, a concerned citizen could only contemplate joining the PPS and the PARM, but by the 1960s it was common knowledge that these parties already had been co-opted by the PRI; their role as satellites of the ruling party was abhorred by many, young and old. The comments of most of the interviewees in this book concerning such *partidos paleros* are apt reflections of the biting views many politically minded Mexicans held. The kindest words come from Cárdenas and Muñoz Ledo, in part because they found it useful and necessary to work with the satellite parties.

Although the *apertura* of the political system had already been assayed in 1963 and 1972–73, presumably to counter the harsh repression of workers in 1958–59, it pulsed more vigorously in 1977, for the reasons noted above. Reform legislation passed on the last day of 1977 sought to give greater but measured political space to the opposition in four ways:

1) It reaffirmed a 1973 rule that permitted the official conditional recognition of opposition parties if they earned at least "1.5% of the total national vote in the election during which registry is sought" (parties that enrolled at least sixty-five thousand members were eligible for "definitive registry");[42]
2) it enlarged the lower house of congress to four hundred members, one quarter of whom could be elected by proportional representation "in party-list circumscriptions" in the manner described by Alcocer in chapter 8;

3) it offered a greater opportunity for opposition-party representatives to observe the methods in which electoral procedures were created and carried out and, for some, the chance to participate and otherwise be heard; and

4) it granted registered opposition parties specific access to television and radio and retained earlier franking privileges.

Succeeding elections reaffirmed the need for reform. Congressional races in 1979 demonstrated the existence of significant dissatisfaction in the body politic requiring legitimate vehicles of expression, because the new parties, all on the Left, soon obtained registry, and their number of supporters grew. These parties were the PCM, the Partido Socialista de los Trabajadores (PST), and the Partido Democrático Mexicano (PDM). Between 1976 and 1979 the opposition's share of the national vote increased from 15.1 percent to 26 percent, and opposition presence in the lower chamber increased from 17.4 percent to 26 percent. The need for more alternatives was evident in the presidential election of 1982, when four candidates theoretically competed for the office: Miguel de la Madrid (PRI), Pablo E. Madero (PAN), Valentín Campa (PSUM), and Rosario Ibarra de Piedra (PRT). While the PRI won easily, the election altogether gave it the lowest presidential vote it had received since 1929 (71.6 percent) and the opposition the highest (28 percent). Moreover, the 1982 election registered the highest electoral participation rate since 1946.[43]

As Alcocer enthusiastically recognizes in this volume, the *apertura* provided the PCM with an opportunity to project a constructive view of itself to the citizenry. The other fledgling parties enjoyed the same opportunity. Castillo, for example, the leader of the Partido Mexicano de los Trabajadores (PMT), in the interview included here, proudly recognizes that in 1986 his party may only have had six deputies in congress, but "we enjoy first place in attendance. . . . We are the third most important party on the basis of statements made before the entire chamber. In other words, with only six deputies, we participate almost on the same level as the PRI." The PCM also provided the PRI with considerable criticism, especially once it was reorganized into the PSUM and fashioned a *grupo de asesoría*, a support group to help the newly elected PCM deputies acquire knowledge needed for the successful analysis of bills. As Alcocer explains in this book, his handiwork, the *grupo,* helped neutralize the PRI's informational advantage and thereby affirmed the PCM's legislative role. Except for the PAN, the other opposition parties felt the same spirited challenge but never matched the organizational ability of the PCM turned PSUM.

The Middle Class as a Force of Opposition

A reanalysis of the *apertura* of the 1970s is helpful at this point in order to understand the Cárdenas phenomenon in the late 1980s. The reforms were aimed originally at young members of the Left who had become alienated by the repressive dimensions of the PRI and the government in the late 1960s and early 1970s. The development and official recognition of opposition parties in 1979 and 1982, including the PMT and the Partido Revolucionario de los Trabajadores (PRT), affirm this simple fact because all of them except one may be classified in the Center-Left.

The malaise that contributed to the national disenchantment was most audible and visible among members of the middle class, particularly those in the cities. The easily identifiable members of this alienated urban class were, more often than not, teachers, professors, students, bureaucrats, and office workers who were dissatisfied with their salaries and their government-controlled unions. Workers belonging to independent unions may be included here; peasant demands not expressed through official channels received little if any attention. According to Middlebrook, the traditional role of the PAN has been to act as the "vehicle for an urban middle class protest against corruption, growing national economic problems, and the government/PRI apparatus."[44] This feeling of alienation helps explain why the PAN netted its highest electoral scores in 1982 despite a "colorless and uninspiring campaign conducted by Pablo E. Madero." The party performed well mainly because it raised high the banner of government corruption for all to see. Corruption is probably the strongest common complaint among middle-class voters, since most of them work in the manufacturing, business, and service sectors (including bureaucracies) that are directly affected by government decisions.[45] Created in the early 1980s, the PDM, the PAN's short-lived competitor, failed to attract a sufficient number of conservative middle-class adherents probably because it was too closely identified with the old *sinarquista* peasant farmers interested mostly in agrarian issues.[46]

The trends noted above converge on a single, although highly diffuse, phenomenon that promises to play a crucial role in Mexican politics in the 1990s: the increasing middle-class dissatisfaction with the political system due mainly to governmental inefficiency and corruption. Soledad Loaeza defines this displeasure in terms of the middle class's need to "defend economic and political participation" in society and to safeguard politico-economic stability. Mexico's extended economic crisis in the 1980s may have spurred the people's insecurity and their need to protect what the state could not. However that may be, Mexico's urban middle classes appear to be responding to solutions that do not necessarily arise out of *panista* campaigns, and their role will be a preponderant one in the future.[47]

If the PAN is indeed unable to make the most of middle-class discontent, Madero and González Schmal may help explain why. They insist that the PRI's control of the media presents a distorted view of the PAN and that this prevents Mexican voters from fully appreciating *panista* ideology. For example, González Schmal's discussion of the Principle of Subsidiarity, which appears to nourish the party's political philosophy, is an idea that receives little or no attention in the national press. The parallels that he draws between the PAN and European Christian Democracy receive little or no public mention as well, because Christian Democracy suggests a political view, tinged with a spiritual orientation, that rubs against a PRI-sanctioned Mexican anticlericalism.

Middle-class Mexicans, including *panistas*, may have voted for Cárdenas in 1988 because the austerity of the 1980s was plainly linked to Mexico's foreign debt. Many of them probably concluded that assigning first priority to the faithful payment of the nation's mounting interest, owed primarily to American banks, as more Mexicans were brought to their knees economically, was a national policy deeply flawed by social irresponsibility. The argumentative vigor of both *panistas* in this book fades noticeably when they discuss U.S.-Mexican relations, including Mexico's debt to its neighbors. In discussing the economic crisis, they aim their sharpest barbs at the PRI and avoid direct criticism of the United States itself. Having noticed this inclination during the 1988 presidential campaign, many middle-class Mexicans may have considered it inappropriately uncritical on the part of *panista* leaders. In contrast, the Left took every opportunity to link the nation's economic problems to its foreign debt. Castillo, for example, employed the term "economic surrender" without equivocation during his campaign as a presidential candidate in 1988, and in doing so he may have expressed the feelings held by many Mexicans regardless of their political affiliation.

The Deepening Economic Crisis in the Late 1970s and the 1980s

The political reforms noted above gave the administration of President López Portillo a touch of hope at the start, but such optimism did not last long. Tensions were high when Echeverría removed the tricolored presidential sash from his shoulders and placed it on those of López Portillo, for he also handed his successor an economic crisis of monumental proportions. Fueled by high levels of public spending and an expansionary monetary policy that permitted state industries to mushroom during the Echeverría years, the economy was already becoming treacherous as early as 1974, when oil prices skyrocketed around the world and industrial economies started to decline.[48] Mexico was overextended, and the political mood of the country turned ugly even as the transfer of power was being prepared. In 1976 the peso was devalued from 12.50 to 20.00 to the dollar,[49] and reports of violent clashes taking place in the countryside between land-hungry peasants and owners of large holdings added to the gloom, along with rumors about the repositioning of army battalions. The private sector began to retrench, and monies were transferred out of the country. Economic growth fell to 2 percent, inflation rose to 27 percent, and the foreign debt grew to $22 billion.

The situation shifted dramatically, however. As Gabriel Székely stated to members of the U.S. Congress interested in knowing what was going on in Mexico in those days, nature appeared to come to López Portillo's aid. Oil was found within the nation's boundaries in quantities larger than previously estimated. Led by Jorge Díaz Serrano, Petróleos de México (PEMEX) engineers allegedly discovered the discrepancies only at this time. Consequently, "the national mood changed from moderation to euphoria." The regime was able to rid itself of an International Monetary Fund (IMF) stabilization program demanding strict spending guidelines, which it had accepted earlier, and Mexico began to receive a "great inflow of foreign investments and credits in subsequent years," Székely told Congress. Most of this capital was aimed at extracting oil more efficiently.[50]

Beginning in 1977, López Portillo's concern was to manage the nation's newfound resources and wealth, but he was not successful. Although Mexico's growth rates ascended to 8 percent between 1978 and 1981, when the economies of most countries were slowing down quickly, inflation doubled what it had been during the Echeverría years, reaching 17 percent in 1978 and 20 percent in 1979.[51] State spending in the form of subsidies and incentives to private capital increased rapidly, approaching as much as 40 percent of annual public investment.[52] State industries once again prevailed over the economy. Heavy investments poured into petrochemicals, making PEMEX the world's largest borrower after the Bank of China. It is estimated that the corporation alone borrowed about $16 million between 1977 and 1982.[53] Significant investments also went into steel and infrastructural upgrading. In Székely's words, "an expensive Mexican Food System (SAM)" was launched as well.[54]

In the early 1980s the situation slipped into reverse. Interest rates in the United States, where Mexico had incurred most of its $88-billion debt by 1982, jumped to at least 21 percent. This increase undermined Mexico's ability to pay what it owed, since an increasing proportion of the debt was tied to floating interest rates. Worst of all, the global economy declined into recession in late 1981, and the demand for petroleum dropped inexorably. Castillo, a politician who also manages a private engineering firm and probably knows more about statistics and mathematics than any other opposition leader, passionately discusses in his interview the implications of these economic shifts. After 1981, the country tumbled into a prolonged crisis whose political repercussions were going to be felt for a long time to come.[55]

Mexico's future was now gloomier than in 1976 when Echeverría stepped down. As Clark W. Reynolds explained it to members of the U.S. Congress:

> Mexico was vulnerable to the shock of higher interest rates because it had opted for a fast-track growth strategy in the late 1970s counting on increased oil revenue. Since the cash flow from oil lagged, due to the capital-intensive expansion of that industry, growth was increasingly financed by foreign borrowing against the promise of future oil rents. When higher interest rates came, and with them world recession, Mexico tried to insulate itself by resisting oil price cuts, failing to adjust the exchange rate, and resorting to further borrowing. As the real cost of the debt continued to rise, Mexico sank deeper into crisis.[56]

Dry words were never truer. Mexico planned as overabundantly as it spent, and almost all of the credit came from American banks. Reynolds employs the term "pathological interdependence" to refer to the extremely close economic relationship existing between the United States and Mexico since World War II. The negative dimensions of this interdependence brought the Mexican ruling elite its greatest headaches, and they have also created some difficult relations between the two countries.

The fear of total financial collapse increased in the last months of 1982. Mexicans with savings accounts in pesos searched frantically for ways to convert them into U.S. dollars or some other hard currency. Businessmen exported considerable amounts of capital in order to cut their losses. It is now estimated that "as much as $36 billion left Mexico from 1976–1982—a good portion of it in 1981 and 1982."[57] This situation led President López Portillo to make the most controversial decision in his career.

Well into his fourth hour in delivering his sixth and final state-of-the-nation address to a joint session of congress, President López Portillo shocked the listeners gathered before him or nervously following via radio and television. He announced the nationalization of Mexico's private banks. Even though the constitution requires the government to give private parties full prior notice whenever imminent public legal action may affect them, none was given, according to an apologist of the benumbed private sector.[58] The impassioned chief of state explained to his countrymen that

the reason why he nationalized the banks was to stem the
outflow of much-needed capital. While he did not single out
any culprits, it was clear that influential businessmen,
bankers especially, were to blame. In his speech, López
Portillo deplored their "weakness," their "lack of trust," and
their "ambition." In words not easily forgotten, he added:
"They make up a minority whose totality of actions dam-
aged the security of the nation and everyone in it."[59] Most
Mexicans were as astonished as they were perplexed. Many
members of the Left rejoiced, but not for long.

The opposition leaders interviewed below repeatedly
state that the people's "lack of confidence and trust" was
endemic at this time. According to government estimates,
the buying power of wage earners fell at least 36 percent
during these months, in part because jobs were being cut
across the board at the behest of the IMF. Independent union
federations insisted, however, that by 1984, 50 percent of
the economically active population, or 12 million people, had
no jobs at all. Considering the fact that 800,000 young men
and women entered the labor force in 1984 in search of jobs,
the federations reported that it was no surprise to see 100,000
people per month escaping across the border to the United
States in quest of employment.[60] In the manufacturing sector,
for example, the government reported that the number of
workers employed dropped from 605,000 to 525,000 between
August 1981 and August 1982 alone, causing a production
decline especially in truck and tractor manufacturing.[61]

The constrictions triggered by the economic crisis on the
average Mexico City worker, even if he belonged to
government-linked unions, began to surface with dramatic
force. As in most countries around the world, organized workers participate in labor day parades on May 1. Given the
social pact arrangements that have contributed to the nation's
massive corporate state, labor day parades in Mexico are
giant demonstrations rivaling similar events in the socialist
world. On that day the capital's enormous *zócalo* appears
dwarfed by the thousands of marchers that advance in battalion style below the balconies of the eighteenth-century
presidential palace, from which the president waves with
friendly formality to the marching throngs. In corporate
Mexico, May 1 is the occasion when the nation's labor leaders
render tribute to their president and show the orderly discipline each federation head commands by fielding thousands

of his loyal members in smooth cadence before the chief executive and other top government officials and their families.

The May 1, 1984, parade broke this mold. Instead of obediently displaying public support to the president, many independent workers stealthily prepared to display their repudiation of the austerity measures imposed by the government. At the last minute and contrary to orders, they unfolded giant cloth banners that communicated their grief. As the workers approached the president, the first banner criticized the actions of repressive labor leaders: GONZALO HERNANDEZ BETRAYS YOUR POLICY BY DIVIDING WORKERS AND PEASANTS IN ZACATEPEC, MORELOS! Other banners revealed deep discontent, as did well-rehearsed rhyming choruses chanted loudly in front of the president and calling for strikes or addressing the problem of low wages: PAIS PETROLERO Y EL PUEBLO SIN DINERO (We may have oil but we don't have money); HOY LOS POBRES MAS POBRES Y LOS RICOS MAS RICOS! (The rich still get richer and the poor get poorer). Even as President de la Madrid waved grimly at the marchers, a lighted Molotov cocktail was hurled from the parading ranks toward the officials but failed to reach its target. A second one followed and entered through one of the open windows. Hitting a wall, it exploded into flames and spilled on Alejandro Carrillo Castro, a health official, who was wrestled to the ground as he ran in terror through the ornate executive rooms; he was quickly bathed in a fire-extinguishing compound by alert security guards.[62] Five and one-half hours later, after 1.5 million workers had filed by, the tension between the marchers and the head of state began to ease temporarily. Everyone had been made aware, however, that May 1 parades were convenient moments to display worker discontent.

A meager salary is only one of the reasons why many Mexican laborers are willing to yell out their frustrations in front of the president and, in some cases, throw Molotov cocktails. A few months after the incident described above, *Proceso*, a widely read weekly, published an article that illustrated the iniquitous distribution of wealth for which Mexico is noted. The piece contained a list of 240 names of government officials in one of the largest state industries in the country, PEMEX, and the extra compensation that each received from the public coffers for the mere fact that he appeared on the "confidential list." In a declining and inflation-ridden economy where the average manufacturing worker earned 44,000 pesos per month, the lucky 240 managers, coordinators, and unit chiefs, who already received an average of 208,000 pesos per month, were able to take home supplements ranging from 23,500 to 118,500 pesos per month, depending on their importance.

Names of officials who had started to work for PEMEX only thirty days earlier also were on the list. *Proceso* suggests that these officials received the special supplements simply because they were friends of the director or perhaps had performed special jobs for the PRI. The special entitlements reportedly began only one month after Mario Ramón Beteta, a long-time PRI stalwart, was named director of PEMEX to succeed Díaz Serrano, who was forced to resign for extravagant corruption and was jailed soon thereafter.[63] PEMEX-like arrangements are believed to be widespread throughout the PRI governmental system, and they act as a wellspring of great discontent now that they are no longer contained quietly by the party.

The Earthquakes of 1985 and Their Mobilization of the People

Just as Mexican workers were seemingly willing to accept the economic crisis as a fait accompli, those living in Mexico City were hit by a devastating earthquake in the early morning of September 19, 1985. The waving and shaking tore the moorings of thousands of buildings, crumpled streets, and broke water, gas, and electrical connections. The terrible grinding of the gyrating buildings, combined with the wrenching of the ground, caused desolation and terror among a populace already worn to the bone. The temblor, ultimately measuring 8.1 on the Richter scale, flattened structures like pancakes. In one case, a large apartment building filled with panic-stricken residents separated from its foundation and simply rolled over on its side, carrying many of them to their deaths. Another quake, measuring 7.6, rocked the city the following day, and many weaker ones followed. Thirty thousand people were treated for injuries, and a minimum of six thousand lost their lives. Trauma struck the city. The destruction sank the economy of the country to agonizing levels as large government expenditures became obligatory overnight. Citing a UN study, a university professor concluded that 2,850 buildings were rendered uninhabitable, including at least 125 in which government offices functioned; 1,200 vehicles were destroyed, along with 300 buses; and the financial loss amounted to approximately 1.283 trillion pesos, or U.S. $4 billion.[64]

The quake produced in the Mexican heartland a wave of popular opposition to the government that grew just as the mountains of rubble and debris were being slowly cleared away. Suggestive of the kind of political ramifications that would begin to emerge in the days following the earthquake, one writer calculated that the interest that Mexico had paid on its foreign debt between 1983 and the day of the quake amounted to the cost of seven similar disasters occurring within three years of each other. He added: "Honoring the foreign debt is equal to suffering two great earthquakes per year."[65] Mexico City residents did not have to refer to the nation's foreign debt to realize that the emergency had uncovered many anomalies. It revealed, for instance, the collusion between building contractors and government officials by the simple fact that an unusual number of government office buildings collapsed or had to be condemned; shoddy work methods and materials were apparently used in order to maximize profits.[66] The earthquake also helped uncover "hidden" garment factories operating in the shadow of labor legislation and under corrupt union officials when a number of women were found crushed to death in unregistered sweatshops near the San Antonio de Abad subway station. The survivors told their plaintive story, and public indignation welled up quietly.[67] Borrowing the metaphor from Octavio Paz, a sociologist who survived the earthquake rendered the political dimensions of the experience as "a prodigious mirror" that spotlighted the contradictions of Mexican society and its political system. He added a list of grievances that coincide with those offered by the interviewees:

> The seismic phenomenon becomes a national political event that encourages observers to focus on: the failure of national austerity measures and budget reductions, growth of unemployment, decline of purchasing power, increase of capital flight, exposure of electoral fraud, attempts at our national sovereignty and, above all, the radical absence of hopeful alternatives in the short- and medium-term.[68]

The concept of a *sociedad civil,* or a society enjoying free-dom from government control, spread rapidly, especially among intellectuals, in the days following the earthquakes. The infirmities of the Mexican state in the late 1970s and early 1980s had already spurred some observers to speak in terms of a rising civil society that drew its strength from free individuals instead of the corporate, omnipresent state.[69]

Minutes after the earth stopped shaking the first time, ordinary people—mechanics, office clerks, high-school stu-dents—began to rescue friends or relatives pinned under the rubble. As one writer described it, "immediately after the earthquake, the city was taken [by civilians] who busied themselves with duties that the State traditionally under-takes."[70] As the days wore on, however, some government officials began to reassume their duties, mainly because they had to respond to the needs that volunteers and vic-tims began identifying and demanding. Housing, water, and food were scarce. Officials thus began working in their usu-ally unpalatable bureaucratic manner, but the people's tol-erance was limited.

Friction surfaced, and political demands began to take form. Preliminary organizing by civilian volunteers, for instance, produced the Red Metropolitana de Damnificados (RMD), or the Metropolitan Victim Network, which joined earthquake victims from nine of the *colonias* that were dam-aged the most.[71] Other groups united to press government agencies in a way not seen previously. An *Excelsior* reporter wrote that "never before had the State found itself obligated to make the relationship between governors and the gov-erned a permanent reality."[72] In one of the most damaged areas of the city, Tlaltelolco, a dynamic neighborhood orga-nization raised its voice time and again to criticize the inep-titude of government officials in responding to the people's needs. PRI propaganda was burned in protest there on at least one occasion.

Eventually, a city-wide Coordinadora Unida de Damnificados (CUD), or United Victim Network, was orga-nized and demanded that empty lots be expropriated for the benefit of quake victims, and the government stirred to respond.[73] Led by Cuauhtémoc Abarca, the group succeeded in obtaining government monies for rebuilding purposes and laid bare inefficiency and corruption in the very agencies obligated to aid the earthquake victims—Fondo Nacional para la Habitación Popular (FONHAPO), or the National Housing Fund, and Banco Nacional de Obras Públicas (BANOBRAS).[74] Several months later, the militancy of CUD members and their supporters led to a movement aimed at giving statehood to the federal district as a way of ensuring the greatest degree of political representation for its millions of residents. The federally appointed regent of the city, Ramón Aguirre Velázquez, received the brunt of the sharpened criticism from the budding *sociedad civil*. Typical of many officials, he was forced to admit one day that "the [people's] political maturity displayed during the earthquake emergency indicated the need to examine the statehood issue."[75] Public hearings were initiated. In city districts that were poorer than middle-class Tlaltelolco, self-help organizations at the neighborhood level also mushroomed and pressed the Consejo Consultivo, a group that advised federal officials concerning the needs of the people, to adopt democratic procedures in naming its director.[76]

Is there a link between the manifestations of a *sociedad civil* as discussed above and the neo-*cardenista* phenomenon of the late 1980s? University intellectuals such as Edmundo Jacobo, Luis Méndez, and Augusto Bolivar would not have thought so, several months after the earthquake. They concluded that Mexican society appeared like a "heterogenous mosaic" lacking "mediation mechanisms" between the state and society, and that, as long as structures of political opposition appeared as weak as they did in 1986, there was little hope of seeing concrete results.[77] If so, what might explain Cárdenas's electoral landslides in the Mexico City area in 1988?

The emerging understanding of Mexico's 1988 election results forces us to reexamine John J. Johnson's concept of emerging middle sectors[78] because evidence suggests that the people who rallied to Cárdenas may have come from those groups. Even though it was published more than thirty years ago, Johnson's *Emergence of the Middle Sectors* helps explain the rise of neo-*cardenismo*. The membership of such groups, he writes,

> ranges upward from the poorly paid white-collar employee in government, with a limited education and often a lack of helpful family connections, to the wealthy proprietors of commercial and industrial enterprises on the one hand and to the

educated professional men, teachers, and high-level government bureacrats, usually from old established families, on the
other.[77]

Johnson refuses to be more specific because the sectors "are
highly fluid and widely disparate."[79] His caution may also be
applied in any overview of neo-*cardenismo*. Nevertheless,
the groups he identifies above appear to be the ones that
supported the *cardenista* coalition of organizations, with one
exception. The people who favor Cárdenas seem to be concentrated on the lower end of Johnson's continuum, and
they appear to spill beyond its lower limits.[80] Included in
this latter category are families whose daily bread comes
from the earnings of both nonunion workers and government-
controlled union shops, along with tens of thousands of
street vendors and unskilled laborers, many of whom may
have recently moved into the big cities from the provinces
and live in wretched conditions. They all form part of an
urban proletariat voting for reform. It may be referred to as
a politicized proletariat, politicized by the very state against
which they have turned for reasons still requiring full appreciation. But, as Johnson suggests, solid members of the middle class are also present among Cárdenas's supporters.

Hard evidence confirming a linkage between the quake-
driven *sociedad civil* and the success of *cardenismo* is not
yet available. Part of the reason for this lack of evidence is
that *defeños*,[81] or federal district residents, do not enjoy the
right to vote for their political representatives. Thus, a
review of local elections since the crucial 1988 presidential
race to reveal voter discontent cannot be made. Other manifestations of dissatisfaction have to be identified, but first
let us look at trends outside the federal district in an effort
to identify postearthquake popular mobilization defying traditional political behavior in Mexico.

Growing dislike of the PRI administrations was registered outside the federal district after the earthquakes of
1985. It rose to the surface in twelve states that held elections for governor in 1986: Chihuahua, Durango, Michoacán,
Zacatecas, Oaxaca, Veracruz, Aguascalientes, Tlaxcala,
Sinaloa, Puebla, Guerrero, and Tamaulipas. The fierce oppositional struggle waged in these states suggests that
Mexicans in the provinces felt a grim determination similar
to that of the *defeños* at this time. In mid-1986 the first

electoral battle was joined in Chihuahua, where representatives of the federal government have long received a chilly reception. Local apprehension increased when electoral laws were modified by PRI officials, shortly before the 1986 balloting, to ensure that the outcome of the gubernatorial race would remain in the hands of the official party.[82] More importantly, the 1986 Chihuahua election also produced unusual alliances between political and social organizations of the Left as well as the Right. A byproduct of these alliances was the coordination of a campaign known as the Frente para la Defensa del Voto, or the Front to Defend the Vote, to safeguard the interests of independent-minded voters. The members of the front did everything possible on behalf of clean elections, but, despite their efforts, they gained only minor victories. A few weeks later, during the gubernatorial race in Durango, opposition forces again united across ideological lines and met a brick wall of *priista* defenses. Street battles resulted in at least one death, thirty-eight wounded, and an undisclosed amount of property damage. Similar clashes were later reported in Aguascalientes, Oaxaca, and Baja California. A political malaise may have been radiating across the country, but the opposition was gradually unshackling itself at the same time.

The new, postearthquake mood went beyond the creation of ideologically diverse alliances fighting for clean elections. Several instances are reported in which local parties actually set aside their differences in order to run common candidates in municipal elections in an attempt to beat the PRI machine. The best-known cases involved Juchitán (Oaxaca) and San Luis Potosí. Others are cited by Jorge Cadena Roa as having taken place in the states of Guerrero, Morelos, and Oaxaca, where several parties pooled their strength in a manner anticipating the political fusion that would give strength to the candidacy of Cuauhtémoc Cárdenas two years later.[83] One of the clearest examples of the postearthquake invigoration of the opposition, across ideological lines, may be seen in the Foro Nacional para el Sufragio Efectivo. It was organized in August 1986 by the most important opposition parties at the time (the PAN, PSUM, PRT, and PMT), in response to "the fraudulant elections in Chihuahua, Durango and Oaxaca." The forum issued a joint communiqué that called for the gathering of national forces in order

to make effective suffrage a reality as "promised the
Mexican people by Francisco I. Madero" in 1910. Two of the
goals for the nation were 1) replacing the PRI-controlled
electoral agency (the Comisión Federal Electoral) with one
that included opposition representatives and 2) reviving the
power of the legislature, which they felt had been weakened
by the office of the presidency. Two years later the *cardenistas* would make these and other reformist issues their
own, and their concerns would be validated by the people of
Mexico.

Antigovernment expression of a nonpartisan kind had
been developing earlier. Barry Carr has shown that popular
mobilization disconnected from electoral exercises was present during the early 1980s as a result of the tight economic
squeeze.[84] After studying leftist parties and independent
labor unions in Mexico, he concluded that these two organizational forms were on the defensive and suffered serious
defeats between 1982 and 1985. Carr claims, however, that
the frustrated Left spawned two radical and novel developments known as *coordinadoras* and *paros cívicos*. The former term refers to loose associations, such as the
Coordinadora Nacional de Movimientos Urbanos Populares
(CONAMUP), or the National Coordinator of Popular Urban
Movements. The CONAMUP coordinated "centers of resistance" against the government's antiworker and antipeas-
ant policies.[85] Condemning declining living standards, the
coordinadoras spearheaded leftist responses to the politics
of austerity, centering much of their activity on consumption needs defined geographically (that is, neighborhoods or
regions), especially by urban women. This approach is distinct from basing such activity on production, as in the case
of unions. *Paros cívicos* refers to an "innovative response to
the politics of austerity," including work stoppages, teach-
ins, marches, roadblocks, hunger strikes, and boycotts.[86]
According to Carr, the crest of these so-called innovative
activities is supposed to have occurred in 1983–84, when a
total of about two million people participated in two *paros
cívicos* that caused significant controversy. Thereafter mass
organizing and other special tactics entered a "defensive"
period.[87]

Did these activist organizations, made up mostly of the
wives and children of urban workers and having a partisan
identification that probably blurs across party lines, con-

tribute to the rise of neo-*cardenismo*? Evidence indicates
that they not only identified with it but also impelled it forward. Furthermore, they seem to act as interelectoral
reserves of popular momentum. The clearest example may
be seen in the Asamblea de Barrios, or the Assembly of
Neighborhoods, which was organized in 1987.

The Asamblea de Barrios was born as a result of the
earthquakes. It arose following the short-lived euphoria celebrating the government's expropriation of empty lots in
Mexico City for building housing for quake victims. Because
it soon became evident that the lots were going to be insufficient for the thousands of homeless, the victims organized
a new *coordinadora* made up of two groups: 1) the people
who lived in lean-tos on the rooftops of Tlaltelolco's massive
high-rise apartments (the Coordinadora de Cuartos de
Azotea de Tlaltelolco, or the Tlaltelolco Coordinator of
Rooftop Shanties) and 2) those who occupied the buildings
themselves (the Comité de Lucha Inquilinaria del Centro,
or the Renters' Plight Committee for the Central Area).
Spurred by their own needs and convinced that government
action would be insufficient, these two organizations decided
to take a housing census within their districts. They wanted
to know how many people were in need of housing, and both
the organizers and the subjects of the census gradually
became aware of the importance of their collaboration. A
chronicler of the movement writes that

> its members discovered, as did the thousands of Mexico City
> dwellers, that they all shared a problem and a vision; they
> had gone to the census taker not knowing what the whole
> thing was about and they stepped away with the understand-
> ing that, in order for them to have a roof over their heads,
> looking for individual solutions would not be enough. They
> learned they had to fight together; solidarity would guarantee
> what they wanted.[88]

This awareness led to the First General Assembly of the
Barrios of Mexico City, which gathered in an electrical workers' meeting hall on April 4, 1987. The assembly members
publicly announced in their First Declaration that five million Mexican families existed without homes; of these, two
million were located in Mexico City; and more homeless
were being created every day by virtue of laws favoring
landlords. The assembly insisted that this caused the daily

expulsion of scores of families from their living quarters. Considering their plight, especially after the terrible earthquakes, the group demanded of the authorities, among other things, that monies earmarked to pay the national debt be used for the construction of homes.[89] It was made known from the start that the Asamblea de Barrios, while focusing on very specific housing needs, was also looking at the government's dilemma in allocating scarce financial resources to satisfy social needs at the same time that American banks were demanding those resources as repayment of loans handed to Mexican officials years before the earthquake.

The Asamblea de Barrios also became linked with an urban folk hero who achieved a remarkable status in 1989–90. In fact, this outlandish figure may have contributed to the Cárdenas electoral landslide registered in 1988 in the Mexico City region. Ramón Tirado Jiménez, the chronicler of the assembly, has tried to envelop the origin of this personality, known as Superbarrio, with a gossamer of myth. He writes that, when postearthquake evictions of poor *defeño* tenants reached a peak one day in June 1987,

> a blinding red light appeared inside the tiny home of a Mexico City street vendor and a voice spoke to him saying "From now on you will be Superbarrio, the scourge of landlords" and thus it was that the vendor suddenly found himself dressed in red; shoes, trunks and cape in yellow; a red mask with yellow stripes; and on his breast the insignia SB.[90]

Dressed in a bizarre costume crudely reminiscent of comic book characters such as Superman and Captain Marvel, Superbarrio made his first public appearance on June 12 to the participants of a demonstration seeking remedies to housing shortages. He soon became "the symbol of an enormous popular movement that inexorably presses forward on behalf of worthy housing."[91] The modest, softspoken man behind the mask explained that

> Superbarrio recaptures certain cultural aspects from the wrestling world and places them within the framework of daily social struggle. He mocks the imported super heroes, the Supermans, and allows us to create our own collective figure. The mask I wear symbolizes the fact that our struggle is not limited to one person. It mirrors the struggle we all face as well as our victory. If Superbarrio is able to prevent someone

from being evicted it may not be because he was present but rather that everyone was, and this prevented the eviction.[92]

Superbarrio's observation reinforces this chapter's thesis, namely, that the spread of a collective awareness at the neighborhood level may explain the election results of 1988. A lone, David-like Cárdenas could not have staggered the Goliath of the PRI otherwise. This awareness was undoubtedly impelled as well by media predictions about inflation rates for 1987, which were supposed to exceed the 1986 rate of 105 percent,[93] and other reports about the aggravation of the nation's economic crisis, especially in connection with Mexico's foreign debt. A popular, neighborhood-level awareness of national problems and past struggles played an important role in the rise of neo-*cardenismo* in 1988, nevertheless. Heberto Castillo, who emulated his hero, Lázaro Cárdenas, by visiting the far-flung corners of Mexico during the 1988 electoral campaign, stated it most clearly when he enthusiastically laid down his own presidential candidacy in favor of Cuauhtémoc Cárdenas:

> Now [the Mexican people] can vote for Cárdenas and by doing so consolidate the party that gathered the great old fighters of the Mexican Left, [Valentín] Campa, [Miguel Angel] Velasco, and the rest of the champions who took part in the struggles of the railroad workers of 1958, the teachers of 1959, the doctors of 1965, and the students of 1968.[94]

Politicians Reflect the Popular Mobilization

The spreading consciousness among members of the Asamblea de Barrios and other ordinary folk regarding the government's decision to forsake dire social needs in favor of debt serving contributed to the formation of a dissident wing within the PRI in early 1987. Its members began voicing the need to open up the hermetic system and protect the common man from the ravages of the economic crisis at the same time. Cárdenas's tight-lipped personality has made it impossible to ascertain the moment when he decided to abandon his low profile and firmly stride onto the stage of national politics. Taking cues from his father's laconism, he has barely allowed in the interview in this volume that "it must have been between May and July of 1986" that he

began conferring with Muñoz Ledo regarding their drive
toward political reform in Mexico. Cárdenas insists that
they did not act before because "he was in one area, and I
was in another," even though they knew each other from
their student days.

Muñoz Ledo, who speaks easily, may indeed have mirrored the feelings of other Mexican leaders in and out of the
PRI, as he often claims he does, when he asserted, also in
the interview included here, that "the situation was already
clear when I left the government in December 1977."
Evidence suggests that he waited until he abandoned his
position as Mexico's ambassador to the United Nations to
spearhead the reform movement, and Cárdenas joined once
the movement lurched forward. By Muñoz Ledo's own
admission, critical steps had already been taken when the
PRI's 13th Congress convened in March of that year and,
among other things, repudiated the attempts of both him
and Cárdenas to democratize the ruling party. Once the two
men were rejected openly by their party, as both attest in
these pages, other disheartened leaders joined the growing
circle of reformers, including Cesar Buenrostro, Leonel
Durán, Ignacio Castillo Mena, Ifigenia Martínez, Armando
Labra, and Carlos Tello. Borrowing the term *corriente* from
Spanish politics, they became the leaders of the Corriente
Democrática, or Corriente Democratizadora, within the PRI.
Thus, they embodied the most important reformist faction
within the official party since its founding.

Cuauhtémoc Cárdenas Was Not the Lone Critic

The rise of neo-*cardenismo* may have blinded some observers
of the Mexican political scene into believing that Cuauhtémoc
Cárdenas has played a lonely battle against the PRI and
the state. Events since 1987 certainly suggest this unidi-
mensional role. However, even a cursory reading of the
interviews in this volume discloses that all of the opposition
leaders were engaged in efforts to democratize the political
system in one way or another long before 1987. A closer
analysis also shows that the *panistas* (Madero and González
Schmal) and the former *priistas* (Muñoz Ledo and Cárdenas)
have consistently stood for cleansing and reforming the
existing system, not overhauling it. Alcocer and Castillo, on

the other hand, not only have fought the state, including the PRI, tooth and nail for many years but also have insisted on fundamental changes in the political system. Castillo spent considerable time in jail and had to be nursed back to health after receiving severe beatings by government-appointed thugs. He and Alcocer are included in this volume because they played important roles in the Mexican Left from 1985 to 1990, and because their nonorthodoxy sheds light on the triumph of leftist moderates. Both men represent two significant groups within the pre-1988 liberal opposition, the PSUM and the PMT, which were pivotal in the reorganization of the Left as explained below.

Having rarely attracted more than 10 percent of the nation's voters, the Mexican Left underwent intensive soul-searching in the 1970s and 1980s. A fundamental issue, unresolved to this day, continues to be the extent to which liberal parties should advocate state intervention in the lives of ordinary citizens. The left-of-center leaders interviewed for this book address this question with some trepidation mainly because the PRI, their political enemy, has itself lost ground for practicing excessive statism. How Marxist dogma might be interpreted in light of this situation until recently has split and regrouped the Left several times. Enrique Semo, one of Mexico's leading Marxist historians, confirms the atomism of the Mexican Left which, like similar movements in the United States, West Germany, and Argentina, has been unable to act as a centralizing force.[95] This tendency may help the reader understand why Alcocer appears below as a member of the PSUM, which rose out of the union of various leftist political parties in 1981, and Castillo as the leader of the PMT, which acted as an independent organization in 1985–86; yet both parties were nonexistent by 1990. The PSUM and the PMT joined forces with other groups on the Left in mid-1987 primarily because the state was slowly but surely turning to the Right. This shift obligated many Mexican liberals to compromise on the issues dividing them.

Semo corroborates the statements made by all six leaders in these pages that a watershed of collective awareness was reached by many Mexicans, especially those on the Left, in the early 1980s. The booming "petrolization" of the economy in the late 1970s, followed by the grinding bust beginning in 1981, persuaded many activists to close their ranks.

More significant than any other factor was the combination
of President López Portillo's dramatic nationalization of the
banking establishment at the eleventh hour of his administration, on September 1, 1982,[96] and the attempt by Miguel
de la Madrid, his successor, to begin to reverse that decision. De la Madrid's action was accomplished, among other
measures, by compensating the bankers with shares in nonbanking enterprises and thereby safeguarding their capital
while further national economic transformations took place.
What was seen by many leftists as a hopeful breach between
government officials and capitalists opened by López Portillo
in September 1982 was disparaged by de la Madrid only a
few months later as a shameful courting of the Right.

The controversial decision to compensate the bankers
finally drove the Left toward unity.[97] Muñoz Ledo summarized the feelings of many disillusioned leaders in the 1980s:

> Conservativism is sweeping Mexico. The de la Madrid admin-
> istration is the farthest to the right. . . . López Portillo took
> actions that demonstrated a certain progressivism. His nation-
> alization of the banks and his inclusion of progressive officials
> within his administration demonstrates this.
>
> De la Madrid's conservativism partly reflects his own
> thinking. It also reflects the thinking of the team to which he
> belonged. . . . [The selection of the presidential successor indi-
> cates this.] Those of us who have been following the country's
> developments already knew that the finalist would not be a
> lawyer. It had to be one of the financial experts. And the one
> selected, Carlos Salinas de Gortari, was the one who best por-
> trayed the technocratic approach to government! His selection
> represents a kind of bloodless coup d'état.

The choice of Salinas to carry the PRI banner forward, via
rigged elections if necessary, was proof to the Left that capitalism would continue to make a comeback in Mexico in the
1980s, accompanied with various degrees of repression perhaps similar to those of the late 1940s. In Semo's words:

> Its symptoms include austerity programs, the technocratiza-
> tion of the state apparatus, the growth of a reactionary tone in
> the media, acts of violence such as the assassination of news-
> man Manuel Buendía[98] and assassination attempts against
> ex-guerrillas and peasant leaders, and increasing pressure
> against union organization.[99]

Despite the perception that conservativism was sweeping Mexico in the 1980s, the most successful attempts at unifying the Left finally came during the same period. The leftist least hampered by Marxist ideology in finally forging a movement from disparate elements was Castillo. In 1982 he led an attempt to unify five political organizations, including his own PMT and the PSUM, which embraced many former Communists. He failed in this early effort in part because he and his supporters resisted the adoption of the symbol of the hammer and sickle and other references to international communism. When it became crystal clear in mid-1987 that the PRI administration was determined to give the highest priority to paying Mexico's foreign debt rather than internally recapitalizing the economy and somehow easing the impact of a prolonged economic crisis on a populace already bloodied by inflation, Castillo again became instrumental in unifying the Left. Fighting an entrenched legacy of authoritarianism at the party level (he calls it *cacicazgos de partido*), he succeeded this time by helping form the Partido Mexicano Socialista (PMS), the broadest regrouping of the liberal opposition in recent times.

On September 6, 1987, testimony of his primary role in this marshaling of the Left, Castillo was democratically voted the PMS's presidential candidate for the 1988 elections in what was reported as Mexico's first primary race since the 1930s.[100] Castillo beat his competitors Eraclio Zepeda, a writer from the southeast, and Antonio Becerra Gaytán, a party stalwart and former teacher from the north, and thus initiated his *pemesista* presidential campaign. Plagued by insufficient funding, he shuttled from one corner of the country to another in a plebeian Volkswagen bus. Addressing mostly peasants, workers, and barrio residents, he carried a simple message, included in his interview, that is rooted in the semisocialist heritage of the Mexican Revolution: Mexico and all it contains must stay in the hands of the Mexican people, and its political and economic processes must remain faithful to its historical and cultural roots.[101] Moreover, Castillo believes that Lázaro Cárdenas, Cuauhtémoc's father, is still the chief executive who has best safeguarded the heritage of the revolution.

In late 1987, Castillo faced an excruciating dilemma. He had written reams and devoted thousands of hours preaching on behalf of a unified Left in Mexico, and yet, as the campaign for president intensified, the liberal opposition remained divided into two conspicuously large camps. One was the PMS, represented by Castillo, and the other was the Corriente Democrática working together with the FDN, led by Cuauhtémoc Cárdenas. Conscious of the role that a unified Left needed to play in the hazardous presidential elections of July 1988 and unwilling to dismiss the burgeoning popular response that Cárdenas began receiving in late 1987, Castillo and other PMS leaders caucused in midcampaign. They decided to tear down the fences that separated them from the neo-*cardenistas*.[102] Despite the fact that it is overlooked by most observers, Castillo's stepping down as PMS candidate to avoid splitting the leftist vote contributed heavily to Cárdenas's electoral showing.

The joining of the PMS to the neo-*cardenista* organizations helped create the most significant opposition group in modern Mexican history, but the collaboration did not occur easily. The Left was too heterogeneous to permit it. In the last months of 1987 the top neo-*cardenista* leaders were mostly renegade *priista* reformers who had nevertheless been well served by the PRI system. Instead of having been beaten, jailed, or otherwise harrassed and blocked from professional success, as most honest opposition leaders have been treated, they shared in the benefits generously given the members of the political upper crust in the form of top salaries and other special dispensations. Non-PRI opposition leaders reveal a hidden anguish in this book. Alcocer and Castillo clearly lived in danger, while Muñoz Ledo and Cárdenas were spared, at least until 1987, when they were forced out of the PRI. Muñoz Ledo probably spent many sleepless nights wondering whether his reformist posture was worth risking the political heights he had been able to scale. Cárdenas did not step down from the peak of Mexico's political pyramid as had Muñoz Ledo, although he undoubtedly suffered deep concern after 1987. The well-heeled appearance and the refined manner of many members of the Corriente Democrática may have offended leftist activists of proletarian bearing and in threadbare attire. These class differences did not separate them in the end, however. The politics of austerity brought them together.

When the PRI flatly refused to consider Cárdenas as its presidential candidate in the 1988 elections, he agreed to become the candidate of the PARM, a satellite party up to this moment. The way in which the PARM handed him the candidacy gave rise to a contentious problem within the Left, and Castillo played an important role here as well. His 1988 campaign speeches included many references to the belief, honed inside his jail cell in the 1970s, that *líderes naturales,* or natural leaders, rather than authoritarian caciques, needed to set a democratic example for the people, especially at the local level. Moreover, when Cárdenas announced to the nation that the PARM had consented to select him as its candidate, a wild stampede developed in left-of-center circles in his direction. Castillo, however, opposed the PMS's unquestioning embrace of Cárdenas. In a carefully worded article in *Proceso,* he accused Cárdenas of practicing unreformed PRI tactics when he accepted the PARM's designation because it was done without consulting that party's rank and file. "The people in the PARM are celebrating what they are condemning in the PRI," Castillo wrote sententiously a few days after Cárdenas entered the race.[103]

Nevertheless, after trading bitter swipes with the PARM candidate on the campaign trail, Castillo backed down in favor of Cárdenas four weeks before the election. Petitions for his withdrawal had also grown in number. Consequently, Castillo and other PMS leaders met with Cárdenas, and all signed an agreement on June 5 requiring Cárdenas to clearly renounce *presidencialismo* and *corporativismo.* PMS leaders also demanded that he agree to stay within the ranks of the opposition if he lost the elections and to continue fighting for proportional representation in the national legislature. Castillo thus demonstrated that the PMS did not simply jump on the Cárdenas bandwagon when it gathered speed and that his party remained faithful to its own democratizing impulse.[104]

Castillo met one of his lifelong goals on June 5, 1988: to unify the Left as never before. To make this possible, however, Mexico had to pass through one of the most prolonged and dire periods of austerity in its recent history, accentuated by a regime that gave priority to maintaining a satisfactory credit profile with foreign banks and subordinated emergency programs that might have helped the populace deal with the crisis. These conditions required the Left to modify its ideologies and make its modus operandi more pragmatic, changes that permitted the liberal opposition to compete vigorously with the official party for the support of the common people, especially peasants, workers, and members of popular organizations that had resisted being co-opted by the government payroll or system of benefits. This success would not have been possible if members of the Left had not rallied around Cuauhtémoc Cárdenas, the son of Mexico's most revolutionary president. He helped matters considerably by naturally and unassumingly expressing the no-nonsense populism free of Marxist rhetoric for which his father had become famous.[105] Bringing most left-of-center Mexicans together also required another leader who was unhindered by the radical ideologies of the early twentieth century. This need was satisfied in the person of Heberto Castillo, who admits that Leonardo da Vinci and Galileo Galilei are his intellectual guides, not Karl Marx or Lenin. A measure of this crucial unifying effort was the presidential election of July 6, 1988, which produced results of historic proportions.

Notes

1. The election of General Manuel Avila Camacho in 1940 nearly rivals both the watershed quality of the 1988 election and the deep-seated political differences present in the body politic. See Meyer and Aguilar Camín, *A la sombra*, 184–85; Luis Medina, "Domingo Siete," in Medina and Blanca Torres, eds., *Del cardenismo al avilacamachismo, 1940–1952*, vol. 18 of *Historia de la revolución mexicana* (Mexico City: Colegio de México, 1978), 117–31; and Albert L. Michaels, "The Mexican Election of 1940," Special Studies, no. 5 (Buffalo: Council on International Studies, State University of New York, 1971).

2. *Novedades de Chihuahua*, July 7, 1988.

3. Ibid.

4. Andrew Reding, "Mexico at a Crossroads: The 1988 Election and Beyond," *World Policy Journal* 5:4 (Fall 1988): 615–49. Similar views and data are offered in de Sheinbaum, "El estado mexicano," 199–200.

5. Reding, "Mexico at a Crossroads," 626.

6. Ibid.

7. Ibarra de Piedra ran for president on the ticket of the Partido Revolucionario de los Trabajadores (PRT), a Trotskyist party. She is not a Trotskyist; she achieved national attention as the leader of an organization seeking official responses to *desaparecidos* in the 1970s.

8. The CFE is the national agency responsible for electoral vigilance.

9. *El Universal*, July 7, 1988.

10. Reding, "Mexico at a Crossroads," 626.

11. Sanford Mosk, *Industrial Revolution in Mexico* (Berkeley: University of California Press, 1950), 61.

12. Jeffrey Bortz, "The Dilemma of Mexican Labor," *Current History: A World Affairs Journal* 86 (March 1987): 105–9, 129.

13. Ibid., 106.

14. Hansen, *Politics of Mexican Development*, chap. 3.

15. Cockcroft, *Mexico: Class Formation*, 158.

16. Bortz, "The Dilemma," 106.

17. Cockcroft, *Mexico: Class Formation*, 155.

18. Olga Pellicer de Brody and José Luis Reyna, *Período 1952-1960: El afianzamiento de la estabilidad política*, vol. 22 of *Historia de la revolución mexicana* (Mexico City: Colegio de México, 1978), 184–85; Nacional Financiera, S.A., *La economía en cifras* (Mexico City: Nacional Financiera, 1978), 414.

19. José Luis Reyna, "La negociación controlada con el movimiento obrero," in Pellicer de Brody and Reyna, *El afianzamiento*, 83.

20. Walter J. Sedwitz, "Mexico's 1954 Devaluation in Retrospect," *Inter-American Economic Affairs* 10:2 (Autumn 1956): 22–44.

21. Cockcroft, *Mexico: Class Formation*, 221.

22. Pellicer de Brody and Reyna, *El afianzamiento*, 86–87.

23. Ibid., 88.

24. Pellicer de Brody suggests that railroad workers were benefited by a 10 percent increase to help them compensate for the devaluation. They may have been the only workers to be thus compensated. (Pellicer de Brody and Reyna, *El afianzamiento*, 83.) The connections between the 1948 devaluation, which cut the peso's financial strength by 30 percent, and the notorious action to impose a progovernment federation leadership in the infamous *charrazo* of October 14, 1948, are suggestive as well. The devaluation took place in August, and the *charrazo* only two months later. Valentín Campa records in his memoirs that he and his coworkers were spurred by the devaluation to demonstrate. Soon thereafter the government placed Jesús Díaz de León, alias *el charro*, at the head of the federation, hence *el charrazo*. Díaz became the first of many *charro* leaders. See Campa, *Mi testimonio: Memorias de un comunista mexicano*, 3d ed. (Mexico City: Ediciones Cultura Popular, 1985), 200–202.

25. Pellicer de Brody and Reyna, *El afianzamiento*, 158–60.

26. Ibid., 131–49.

27. Valentín Campa, second in importance to Vallejo and also a member of the Communist Party, states that several people were killed by the police. See Campa, *Mi testimonio*, 243–45.

28. Ibid., 245.

29. Pellicer de Brody and Reyna, *El afianzamiento,* 173–82.

30. Ibid., 206–8.

31. Evelyn P. Stevens, *Protest and Response in Mexico: 1968–1980* (Cambridge: MIT Press, 1974), 104.

32. Carlos B. Gil, "Massacre at Tlaltelolco: Historical Perspectives and Bibliographic Notes" (unpublished manuscript, version A, 1986), 10.

33. Michael Soldatenko, "The Mexican Student Movement of 1968: Myth, Repression, and the Petty Bourgeois" (M.A. thesis, University of California at Los Angeles, 1977), 12–13; Carlos B. Gil, "Massacre at Tlaltelolco: Its Complexities and Its Literature" (unpublished manuscript, version B, 1986), 2.

34. Elena Poniatowska, *La noche de Tlaltelolco: Testimonios de historia oral* (Mexico City: Ediciones Era, 1978). See also the translation by Helen R. Lane in *Massacre in Mexico* (New York: Viking, 1971).

35. Octavio Paz, *The Other Mexico: Critique of the Pyramid,* trans. Lysander Kemp (New York: Grove, 1972), 71–112 passim.

36. *1968: El principio del poder* (Mexico City: Proceso, 1980), 153; Gil, "Massacre at Tlaltelolco" B, 5. Although some evidence points to provocateurs who infiltrated the student ranks and fired from on high at the commanding officer on the plaza, the issue of who shot first remains unresolved. Valentín Campa seemed to corroborate the argument that the general was struck down after the shooting began: "The events of October 2nd are connected to someone with a pistol. Feeling desperate upon seeing so many people killed, he shot the general. He was up on top and he shot from there. It had to be a desperate fellow!" Interview, Iztapalapa, Mexico City, February-March 1986.

37. Juan Luis Concheiro B., "En la lucha por la democracia y la unidad de la izquierda," in Arnoldo Martínez Verdugo, ed., *Historia del comunismo en México* (Mexico City: Editorial Grijalbo, 1985), 328.

38. Ibid., 325.

39. Valentín Campa, interview, Iztapalapa, Mexico City, February-March 1986.

40. Orlando Ortiz, comp., *Genaro Vásquez* (Mexico City: Editorial Diógenes, 1972).

41. Kenneth J. Middlebrook, "Political Reform and Political Change in Mexico," *Latin America and Caribbean Contemporary Record* 1 (1983):149–61.

42. See fuller details in Middlebrook, "Political Reform," 153.

43. Ibid. Lorenzo Meyer cautions the reader against full reliance on the data employed by Middlebrook here. On the margin of an early draft of this manuscript, he wrote: "Por lo ocurrido en 1988 sabemos que esas cifras fueron falsas."

44. Middlebrook, "Political Reform," 159.

45. The keen sense of competition, which can often develop into highly charged feelings of resentment between middle-class groups protected by government jobs and those who have to "go it alone" without the aid of government appointments, became very real to the editor in Chihuahua City, where in 1988, during the election, he visited *panistas* whose livelihood came from a small business. They lived next door to *priistas* whose bureaucratic appointments and governmental connections allowed them to enjoy a life-style equal to or better than that of the *panistas* without the stress that a small business brings, and neighborly relations were difficult.

46. Ignacio González Gollaz, interview, Mexico City, April 9, 1986.

47. Soledad Loaeza agrees with the editor's broad assertions regarding the middle class. She has found that the evolution of Mexico's political system is linked to that class's growth, in part because the system draws leaders from it. See Loaeza, "El estudio de las clases medias mexicanas después de 1940," *Estudios políticos* 3:2 (April-June 1984): 52–62.

48. Jaime Estévez, "Crisis mundial y proyecto nacional," in Pablo González Casanova and Hector Aguilar Camín, coords., *México ante la crisis: El contexto internacional y la crisis económica* (Mexico City: Siglo Veintiuno Editores, 1985), 1:45. See also Pablo González Casanova, "México ante la crisis mundial," in ibid., 1:13–28.

49. David Colmenares et al., *La devaluación de 1982* (Mexico City: Tierra Nova, 1982), 10.

50. Gabriel Székely, "The Mexican Economic and Political Situation," in House of Representatives, Committee on Foreign Affairs, 98th Cong., 2d sess., *The Mexican Economic Crisis: Policy Implications for the United States* (Washington, DC: Government Printing Office, 1984), 261.

51. George W. Grayson, *The Politics of Mexican Oil* (Pittsburgh: University of Pittsburgh Press, 1980), 131.

52. Judith Gentleman, *Mexican Oil and Dependent Development* (New York: P. Lang, 1984), 140.

53. Ibid., 90-92.

54. Székely, "The Mexican Economic and Political Situation," 262–63.

55. Norman Bailey and Richard Cohen. *The Mexican Time Bomb,* Twentieth Century Fund Paper (New York: Priority Press, 1987), 10–11.

56. Clark W. Reynolds, "Beyond the Mexican Crisis: Implications for Business and the U.S. Government," in Székely, *The Mexican Economic Crisis,* 10. The most thorough accounts of the crisis in the early 1980s are available in González Casanova

and Aguilar Camín, *México ante la crisis*, vol. 1, pt. 2. See also Carlos Tello, "La crísis en México, saldos y opciones," *Universidad de México: Revista de la Universidad Nacional Autónoma de México* 40:415 (August 1985): 3–10; and Bailey and Cohen, *The Mexican Time Bomb*.

57. Reynolds, "Beyond the Mexican Crisis," 13.

58. Cosme Haces, *Crisis! MMH ante la herencia de JLP. Crónica de un trimestre negro* (Mexico City: EdaMex, 1983), 52.

59. Luis Pazos, *La estatización de la banca: Hacia un capitalismo de estado?* (Mexico City: Editorial Diana, 1982), 24.

60. *Proceso* 391 (April 30, 1984): 8.

61. Alejandro Alvarez, "Crisis in Mexico: Impacts on the Working Class and the Labor Movement," in Barry Carr and Ricardo Anzaldúa Montoya, eds., *The Mexican Left, the Popular Movements, and the Politics of Austerity,* Monograph Series, no. 18 (San Diego: Center for U.S.-Mexican Studies, University of California at San Diego, 1986), 48.

62. *Proceso* 392 (May 7, 1984): 10-11.

63. Other PEMEX officials received direct payment for hospital care given to family members or friends, car rentals, and country club fees (*Proceso* 416 [October 22, 1984]: 8–9). For wage data see Table 1405, in James W. Wilkie, ed., *Latin American Statistical Abstract* (Los Angeles: Latin American Center, University of California at Los Angeles, 1989), 27:325.

64. Enrique Quintana López, "El terremoto: Efectos económicos y perspectivas de la reconstrucción," *El cotidiano: Revista de la realidad actual* 2:8 (November-December 1985): 88.

65. Ibid.

66. See Elena Poniatowska, "Los hospitales jamás deberían caerse," one of many timely and touching journalistic cameos in *La Jornada*, October and November 1985, concerning ordinary people responding to the calamitous human emergencies provoked by the earthquake.

67. See Jorge Cadena Roa, "Las demandas de la sociedad civil, los partidos políticos y las respuestas del sistema," in Pablo González Casanova and Jorge Cadena Roa, coords., *Primer informe sobre la democracia: Mexico 1988* (Mexico City: Siglo XXI, 1988): 306.

68. Luis Salazar C., "Sismo, política y gobierno," *El cotidiano: Revista de la realidad mexicana actual* 2:8 (November-December 1985): 19–20.

69. Samuel León and Ignacio Marván, "Movimientos sociales en México (1968–1983). Panorama general y perspectivas," *Estudios políticos* 3:2 (April-June 1984): 5.

70. Edmundo Jacobo M. and Luis Méndez, "Bueno . . . y después de todo, cual sociedad civil?" *El cotidiano: Revista de la realidad mexicana actual* 2:8 (November-December 1985): 23.

71. *El Financiero,* October 10, 1985.

72. "Necesario que el estado escuche las críticas y señalamientos del vecino," *Excelsior,* October 11, 1985.

73. *Unomasuno,* October 20, 1985.

74. Ibid., March 14, 1986.

75. *La Jornada,* January 6, 1986.

76. *Excelsior,* March 3, 1986.

77. Jacobo and Méndez, "Bueno . . . y después de todo," 26; Augusto Bolivar E., "La sociedad civil es burguesa," *El cotidiano: Revista de la realidad mexicana actual* 2:8 (November-December 1985): 27–30.

78. John J. Johnson, *The Emergence of the Middle Sectors* (Stanford, CA: Stanford University Press, 1958).

79. Johnson, *Middle Sectors,* ix.

80. A keen observer of the 1988 elections, Lorenzo Meyer believes that electoral results from the working-class barrios confirm these statements.

81. "D.F." is an acronym for *distrito federal,* or federal district (conceptually similar to District of Columbia), and is pronounced "de efe." Hence, district residents are known as *defeños* (in addition to the more pejorative *chilangos*).

82. This section is based on Cadena Roa, "Las demandas," 285–327.

83. Ibid., 314.

84. Barry Carr, "The Mexican Left, the Popular Movements, and the Politics of Austerity," in Carr and Anzaldúa Montoya, *The Mexican Left,* 1–18.

85. Ibid., 15.

86. Ibid., 17.

87. Cadena Roa, "Las demandas," 290.

88. Ramón Tirado Jiménez, *Asamblea de barrios: Nuestra batalla* (Mexico City: Editorial Nuestro Tiempo, 1990), 24–25.

89. *Asamblea de barrios de la ciudad. Tres años de lucha. Declaraciones* (n.p., n.d.), 4. See also *Asamblea de barrios de la ciudad. Cronología y documentos* (n.p., n.d.).

90. Tirado Jiménez, *Asamblea de barrios,* 26.

91. Ibid.

92. Superbarrio, interview, Seattle, May 8, 1990.

93. *Proceso* 560 (July 27, 1987): 7.

94. Ibid., 607 (June 20, 1988): 32.

95. Enrique Semo, "The Mexican Left and the Economic Crisis," in Carr and Andalzúa, *The Mexican Left,* 19–32.

96. Pazos, *La estatización,* 13–14.

97. Semo, "The Mexican Left," 26–27.

98. Manuel Buendía authored *La CIA en México* (Mexico City: Ediciones Oceano, 1983) and *La ultraderecha en México* (Mexico City: Ediciones Oceano, 1984).

99. Semo, "The Mexican Left," 27.

100. According to Lorenzo Meyer, primary elections were practiced in Mexico in the 1930s.

101. See a summary of Castillo's ideas in mid-1987 in *Proceso* 555 (June 22, 1987): 10–11. Regarding the modus operandi, see his comments in this volume and in most of his tracts in *Proceso, El Universal*, and other periodicals concerning *líderes naturales*, or those whose leadership is genuinely popular even though Western rules of selection were not necessarily observed.

102. A third and ideologically radical segment coalesced around Rosario Ibarra de Piedra. Most of its members belonged to the PRT, a small Trotskyist party, yet Ibarra de la Piedra declared she was not a Trotskyist.

103. *Proceso* 572 (October 19, 1987): 37.

104. Ibid., 607 (June 20, 1988): 34–35; *New York Times*, June 6, 1988.

105. Cuauhtémoc Cárdenas has given countless interviews. See, for example, Andrew Reding, "The Democratic Current: A New Era in Mexican Politics," *World Policy Journal* 5:2 (Spring 1988): 323–66, which includes interviews with Ifigenia Martínez and Porfirio Muñoz Ledo; and Cuauhtémoc Cárdenas, *Cuauhtémoc Cárdenas: Nuestra lucha apenas comienza* (Mexico City: Editorial Nuestro Tiempo, 1988), 9–36, which contains an interview plus twelve speeches given between November 29, 1987, and September 14, 1988.

CHAPTER 3

1994 and Beyond

Carlos Salinas de Gortari has been serving as president since 1988 with the lowest electoral margin ever given a Mexican chief executive. Technically speaking, both his legitimacy as the nation's highest official and the PRI's role as the majority party became questionable for this reason and will remain so until 1994, when his term comes to an end. Having a candidate gain access to a nation's top executive office by a slim electoral margin does not normally signify the beginning of a major crisis in an openly democratic nation. In Mexico, however, President Salinas's party has monopolized politics since 1929, and the slim margin obtained by him and his party in July 1988, if one was indeed gained, thus signals a critical moment, especially if fraud was employed.

In the late 1980s the Mexican political opposition became unshackled to an extent not previously seen, and it has gained inordinate strength. The opposition consists of two groups primarily: the members of the PAN, a conservative party that arose to counteract an early version of the PRI as early as 1939, and the followers of Cuauhtémoc Cárdenas, who came from various leftist parties and many community organizations in late 1987 to cast the highest opposition vote registered in Mexico in recent history. Neo-*cardenismo* influenced Mexican politics considerably more than *panismo* between 1985 and 1990. If it were not for the amorphous mass of supporters who organized and reorganized themselves in his support, Cárdenas would appear as the lone and practically defenseless David against the terrible Goliath of the PRI.

Will Cárdenas win in 1994? Will the PRI slip into a position where it merely competes as one of three important

parties in Mexico? If the *cardenistas* win in 1994, will it
mean that the old social pact between labor and the state,
as discussed in the preceding chapter, is finally dissolved? If
the PRI is able to gain lost ground and win again in 1994,
will it show that the party's model of economic development,
pursued for the last forty years, has finally been accepted by
the people? This book can only present these important
questions, in the hope that answers will be forthcoming.

Cárdenas's Chances in 1994

The possibility that Cárdenas might win the presidential
election of 1994 cannot be disputed. This could not be said of
any *panista* leader in 1990. Sobering as it may be, Cárdenas
holds a share of this singular and historic opportunity in
his hands. His role, however, is intimately connected to his
ability to control and direct a motley group of supporters
associated thus far with the troubled Left, whose fortunes
have inexorably declined since the 1960s.

Cárdenas's ability to exercise sufficient control over his
diverse organization, appears tied to at least two internal
factors. One is the semicharismatic moral authority that has
befallen him; he has not earned it completely. Evidence in
this volume strongly suggests that other members of the
Corriente Democrática moved with equal or greater vigor
than Cárdenas to jar the inner tranquility of the PRI in
1987 in an effort to install certain reforms. Nevertheless,
even though he may have been merely one of several
reformers within the ruling party, no one else could have
risen to the heights he reached. He inherited this moral
authority from the image created by his father, and it was
handed down to him in the established manner of most
father-son relationships. However, his father also
bequeathed a similar image, that of a no-nonsense leader
solicitous of the working poor, to an entire generation of
Mexicans and their children, who constituted the nation's
voters of the late 1980s. These legacies helped trigger
Cuauhtémoc Cárdenas into action; he discovered a way to
exercise them quite naturally and with convincing sincer-
ity. His use of the inherited images contributed greatly to
the popular support his candidacy attracted in 1988, not
only among reformist *priistas* but also among the citizenry,

especially urban workers and small-town farmers. This authority will reside in his persona indefinitely.

The second factor behind Cárdenas's leadership is linked to the strength of his backers and his ability to direct them effectively. The evolution of his support began with the Corriente Democrática and followed in the early phase of the 1988 presidential campaign with an alliance of divergent groups, the FDN. Prior to election day the FDN joined hands with the independent Left, gathered for the first time in a very long while. The two became the PMS, and together they formed the broadest left-of-center coalition seen to date. They were able to register the highest opposition vote in recent Mexican history. Following the 1988 election the neo-*cardenistas* found it necessary to regroup once more. Their latest political organization is known as the Partido de la Revolución Democrática (PRD), or the Party of the Democratic Revolution, the vehicle that is supposed to carry them on to 1994 and beyond.

Cárdenas's success in the 1994 election will depend particularly on the strength and efficacy of the PRD.[1] The cohesion of the party will be determined partly by the ability of its members to shed prior partisan loyalties, since almost all of them began their political lives in preexisting organizations, particularly the PCM, PSUM, and PMT. The top rungs of the neo-*cardenista* movement are filled with members of these now defunct parties, and loyalties in Mexico die slowly, as do ideologies. Reports of strife linked to former partisan associations were made in April and May 1990 in the states of Hidalgo, Nayarit, and Mexico.[2] If any significant foils appear for Cárdenas and the PRD before 1994, they will probably be connected to these loyalties, partisan *caciquismo,* and an allegiance to purist strategies founded on the class struggle.

The first significant reshuffling of PRD leadership was reported in early May 1990 in preparation for the party's first congress, scheduled for late 1990. Not surprisingly, Muñoz Ledo's role in the fashioning of the emerging party framework weakened as a result of the rearrangement. A divisive question led to the reworking: How much organizational structure should be agreed upon by the party heads before seeking ratification with the rank and file? The top PRD leaders could not agree; Cárdenas adopted one posture, and Muñoz Ledo, the second most important man in the party, another. The controversy reflected the sensitivity that leading *perredistas* shared in cementing a truly democratic organization. Open participation by party members, absent in the PRI, could not be dismissed easily. If democracy could not be practiced at the party level, how could the party practice it once in office?

PRD leaders were anxious to display the greatest amount of democracy within the new party and the least amount of *caciquismo*. In 1990 it may have been possible for the leadership to engage in open and fair decisionmaking regarding the party's future organization, but it remained entirely questionable whether middle- and lower-rank party members on the periphery could match and sustain the spirit of openness preoccupying those at the apex. One observer noted that fracture lines had emerged within the PRD leadership by mid-1990 between 1) "nationalist" and "Christian-inspired liberals," which included Cárdenas and Castillo, and 2) "socialists and social-democrats," who presumably included Muñoz Ledo and Alcocer.[3] It was too early to assess this ideological seam or any other at the time of this writing. Nonetheless, given Cárdenas's unique and unprecedented ability to garner the largest opposition vote against the PRI in modern history, PRD members appeared to have no choice but to continue to recognize his leadership and work with him for 1994 and beyond, regardless of partisan differences.

Cárdenas defines his party's platform in a straightforward manner that coincides fittingly with Muñoz Ledo's summary of the PRD's ideals. Absent from this platform is a willingness, articulated here by Alcocer, to "fight to bring an end to the exploitation of labor" or to "achieve the socialization of political power." The enthusiasm expressed in these pages by Alcocer is a clear dimension of the PSUM, to which he belonged in 1985 prior to its merging into the PMS and then later into the PRD. The former *pesumistas* now gathered around Cárdenas, Alcocer included, have found it necessary to temper their reconstructive vision.

Would the PRI sabotage Cárdenas, or any other opposition candidate, if he won in 1994? Events in Nicaragua may be instructive. Violeta Chamorro, who won that nation's presidential election in February 1990, was the candidate of an opposition coalition party formed shortly before, and her victory surprised almost all observers. Due in part to financing by U.S. intelligence agencies, Chamorro's hastily assembled coalition of fourteen miniparties obtained more votes than the Frente Sandinista de Liberación Nacional (FSLN), which, like the PRI, traces its origin to a successful revolution. Because of this background, the FSLN drew its strength partly from the people and partly from the many symbiotic relationships it developed with the government of Nicaragua during its ten years in power. Like the PRI, the FSLN became indistinguishable from the government. Moreover, Chamorro's supporters appeared to be as socially and politically diverse as Cárdenas's faction, and very few had enjoyed recent national administrative duties. González Schmal, former PAN secretary of international affairs, candidly condemns the PRI government's attempts in the early 1980s to assist the Sandinistas in fashioning a political system akin to Mexico's.

Most instructive was the FSLN's ability to undermine the Chamorro administration in early 1990 by using labor unions it dominated as foils against her programs. A few months after the elections, for example, as many as one hundred thousand civil servants belonging to FSLN unions went on strike until their demands were obtained for a 200 percent pay raise and laws that would safeguard their employment against future cuts in the bureaucracy. The demands later included a governmental agreement to protect the status quo of state-owned companies and of land expropriated by the Sandinista government from privatization. The strike, which paralyzed the country by mid-1990, was interpreted as a "test of political wills" and a demonstration by the FSLN to "rule from below." The party enjoyed this advantage thanks to its ten-year links to popular organizations, including labor unions.[4] Similar developments took place in the educational field, where the Asociación Nacional de Educadores Nicaragüenses (ANDEN), a Sandinista teachers union strengthened by government subsidies and forced deductions from public employees' salaries, also blocked Chamorro's programs. If a non-PRI candidate is elected in Mexico in 1994, will there be a way to counter the party's grip on popular organizations and its ability to employ them as battering rams against the first opposition president?

Humberto Belli, Chamorro's educational vice minister, provides a partial answer. He foresaw that the FSLN's grip

over popular groups would eventually loosen as the public
subsidies they received and the dues forced upon their members were removed. This weakening would provide opportunities for the Chamorro administration to pursue its own
goals untrammeled.[5] Even though the FSLN "is rich in
property and installations," Belli writes, and they "owned
two newspapers, radio stations and countless buildings,
businesses, cars, trucks, giant loudspeaker systems" and so
on, they would eventually be separated from these assets
because they depended on government subsidies. "When
their loudspeaker system needs a part, no longer can they
charge the expense to the Ministry of Culture nor can they
exempt themselves from import taxes."[6] Just how long labor
unions and other community organizations that once thrived
on state support would continue to function without it in
Nicaragua, and in Mexico if an opposition candidate were to
win, is difficult to predict. The parallelism is sobering in any
case.

The Role of Corruption

The results of Mexico's 1994 presidential election depend
mostly on President Salinas de Gortari. Fate seems to have
destined him to ride a tiger as the century draws to a close.
Indeed, he seems to have been cast properly for his role as
the head of one of the most pivotal administrations in modern Mexican history. His decisive actions in the first two
years of his administration appear to have boosted him out
of the shadow cast by the disputed elections that brought
him to office.

In the area of political corruption, where Salinas draws
heavy criticism from opposition leaders in this volume, he
has cast an initially favorable impression. Seeking to register with the Mexican people his determination to reduce corruption, especially in strategic niches of government, the
president toppled a hitherto untouchable labor leader,
Joaquín Hernández Galicia ("La Quina"), from the helm of
the national oil workers union, one of the nation's most powerful. With a dramatic flourish that served to punctuate the
president's decisiveness, the front door of the union boss's
home was blown off with a bazooka, and a cache of arms
was allegedly found in the house. Salinas canceled La

Quina's untouchability overnight, and the nation cheered. He also removed the equally powerful Carlos Jonguitud Barrios from the leadership of the national teachers union. Both labor bosses had displayed the most negative aspects of Mexico's corporatist apparatus by converting their respective unions into personal fiefdoms based on corruption, fraud, and repression. Employing machine guns and hired thugs, Jonguitud, for example, took over the teachers federation in a veritable coup d'état on September 22, 1972, and supervised the giant federation in a manner reminiscent of the American Mafia, with total impunity as long as he overtly supported the nation's president.[7] These two caciques symbolized governmental practices that had greatly disillusioned the general citizenry and most probably contributed to the PRI's weak electoral results in 1988. Salinas's surgical excision of these two political cancers, however, may not have been enough to counterweigh the growing discontent.

Political corruption in Mexico of the kind associated with the unions controlled by La Quina and Jonguitud Barrios is not new, nor is it yet fully understood. Common sense advises us to identify, at this point, at least two types of political corruption, personal and institutional. The former applies to individuals in public office who trade political favors for economic rewards when almost everyone else refrains from such activity. This situation may be said to reflect individual idiosyncracies, and psychology may be the best tool for its analysis. Institutional corruption, however, refers to collective behavior molded by routinized procedures and values that are ingrained in a significant way and encourage individuals to trade political favors for economic rewards.

Resisting ingrained procedures and values is difficult; hence, a person with good instincts may become corrupt easily. Roger D. Hansen, who examined the economy of Mexico at the end of the 1960s, quotes a respected observer of the country who noted, in 1944, that "politics is the easiest and most profitable profession in Mexico."[8] Hansen offers English-language readers a brief but now outdated discussion of the functional role that political corruption plays in the body politic.[9] Gabriel Zaid, a leading essayist in the late 1980s, wrenchingly asserts that corruption remains a part of modern life in Mexico, and that attempts to be honest have become tragicomical at best. "A Mexican who tries to be transparent in what he does, especially in public life, risks appearing as ridiculous," he writes.[10] Politically connected corruption still needs to be studied seriously; one observer, at least, believes that it became more widespread and complex during the administrations of Luis Echeverría and José López Portillo than ever before, partly as a result of the growth of the state and its resources.[11] President López Portillo became, in fact, one of the most vilified national executives, once he stepped down from office, for this reason.[12] Political corruption may be said to exist in all nations; it takes on obvious manifestations in some countries and subtle ones in others. Political scientists working with organizational specialists and cultural historians may someday explain it best, as far as Mexico is concerned.[13] The interviews clearly suggest that corruption helped the opposition achieve its historic gains in 1988 and may do so again in 1994.

A third form of corruption, however, began infecting Mexico in the last years of the Miguel de la Madrid administration and continued unabated in the first two years of Salinas de Gortari's term of office. It is linked to the production and transportation of illicit drugs, mostly marijuana and cocaine. When questioned about drug-connected corruption, the interviewees said little, relatively speaking, probably because it was just emerging as a national problem. Although it appears to be encouraged by the second type of political corruption, which was reported as endemic in the 1970s, the drug-based variety is more threatening because it has generated quantities of cash on a scale never seen before. Whereas corruption of the 1970s may have given to a PRI favorite, for example, double or triple government salaries, as reported by Kenneth F. Johnson, or opportunities for embezzlement in connection with government contracts, the amounts of actual cash made available by drug traffickers for the purpose of suborning individuals in and out of public office appears to dwarf earlier forms of reward.[14]

The implications of drug-based corruption are diverse, and high-level officials associated with the de la Madrid and Salinas administrations may one day attest to its complexities. Richard B. Craig has begun to delve into the implications as they apply to selected South American countries.

He has outlined the social, economic, and political ramifications of drug trafficking in Bolivia, Colombia, and Peru, and, in doing so, he has identified violence perpetrated on persons, property, and institutions as one of the social outcomes.[15] Economic implications include inflation, altered interest rates, exacerbated black marketeering and smuggling, inflated wages, and unregulated agricultural production. Bolivian peasants, for example, organized themselves for the purpose of defending their production of coca leaves from which cocaine is extracted.

The political implications involve the co-optation of people entrusted with governmental authority, their consequent dismissal of public service as a worthwhile value, and the deterioration of loyalty among the citizenry to the nation's ideals. Law enforcement personnel tend to become involved with corruption at the outset because their organizations play a frontline role in attempting to curb drug trafficking. Craig reports that the army eventually acted as a protective cover for drug traffickers in Bolivia. This situation undermined the relations between the president and the nation's security forces and thus corroded the political legitimacy of the president's office. Craig studied these South American countries because institutional corruption by drug money appeared at an advanced stage there in the late 1980s.

Available evidence cited in these pages tells us that Craig's discussion applies to Mexico as well. Events in the 1980s clearly indicate that public cynicism toward venal government officials had reached new levels with the availability of great sums of drug money. One of the country's most frustrating criminal cases in recent years appears to be connected to drug-motivated corruption. It involves the distinguished journalist Manuel Buendía, who was assassinated in 1984. In an eighteen-year period (1970–1988) that reportedly saw at least fifty-five journalists slain, the Buendía case received considerable publicity, beginning with President de la Madrid's denunciation of the crime soon after it took place and his personal order that a thorough investigation be conducted.[16] For five years, however, police and other officials reported to an inquisitive press that they had not yet found any reliable suspects or probable causes. Police officials produced alleged suspects several times and later discarded them. One reporter summarized the Buendía

case in June 1989 as being plagued by "irregularities, negli-
gence, cover-ups including false witnesses, conspiracies,
false clues, loose ends, intrigue and deceit."[17]

The case took a dramatic turn when secret U.S. documents were released in the Enrique Camarena trial in Los
Angeles, as discussed below. Using these documents, the
noted American columnist, Jack Anderson, was one of the
first to report in September 1990 that Buendía had probably
been killed because he discovered information linking high-
level Mexican officials, U.S. intelligence agents, and drug
traffickers. Anderson writes that drug traffickers established airstrips in Veracruz which CIA agents used to facili-
tate the transporting of arms to the Nicaraguan rebels
known as contras. The federal documents also indicate that,
in return for this assistance, the drug smugglers were
allowed to ship to the United States and refuel on the CIA
airstrips while highly placed Mexican officials looked the
other way. Buendía was killed by Mexican federal agents
because he had begun gathering the names of top officials in
the de la Madrid administration who condoned the operation and received illicit compensation.[18] José Antonio
Zorrilla, head of the Directorio Federal de Seguridad, or the
Mexican equivalent of the U.S. Federal Bureau of Investigation, was found guilty in 1989 by Mexican judicial authorities. The formerly secret documents confirm the suspicions
held by Anderson and his assistants that other highly
placed accomplices may have been involved, including at
least one individual who has been a member of presidential
cabinets since 1982.[19]

Another publicized case involving drug-related corruption is linked to the 1985 slaying of Enrique Camarena. As
an officer in the U.S. Drug Enforcement Administration
(DEA), he met his violent death while working in Guadalajara to help Mexican authorities control the production
and transportation of illicit drugs.[20] Five years elapsed, once
again, before anyone connected to his assassination was
identified and brought to trial, and it appears that a considerable amount of U.S. pressure was needed to initiate the
process on the Mexican side.

The prosecution did not begin, however, before diplomatic relations between the United States and Mexico
reached their lowest point in many years, as a result of
what Elaine Shannon has called the Mexican government's

attempt to "cover up" evidence leading to Camarena's torturers and assassins and a fire storm of public protest that raged over what was portrayed as U.S. interference in Mexican affairs.[21] Mexican police officers belonging to various organizations became involved in protecting men whom Shannon calls "drug lords" in exchange for large quantities of money. Some of them served as personal bodyguards for the drug traffickers. When Camarena, a Mexican-American, began following the trail of a $20-million drug operation connected with Ramón Caro Quintero, a Guadalajara drug lord, a plan was organized to get rid of the investigators and many Mexican police officers participated. One of the first officials to be charged in the slaying was Armando Pavón Reyes, a *primer comandante,* or head commander, of the Policía Judicial Federal. By the time the first convictions were announced five years later, twenty-two persons had been indicted in a Los Angeles courtroom, including former President Echeverría's son-in-law, Rubén Zuno Arce, scion of one of the most prominent families in the state of Jalisco. The jury concluded that he acted "as a link between the highest levels of the Mexican government and a multibillion dollar drug cartel based in Colombia."[22] The jury also decided that he and others had conspired in the capture of Camarena, and that their actions led to his torture and death.[23]

Corruption in the body politic is only one of the major challenges that President Salinas faces as he prepares for the crucial election of 1994. While the political *apertura* of the late 1970s, discussed in Chapter 2, may have been accompanied by an apparent decrease in repression, considerable evidence points to a reemergence of politically motivated repression in Mexico in the 1990s.

The Continuance of Repression

On the eve of the strongly contested presidential elections of 1988, Amnesty International, a human rights organization, reported the existence of a very troubled situation in Mexico. Apart from at least fifty-two *desaparecidos* (persons whose whereabouts are unknown) who had been missing since 1972, Amnesty International found that twenty-three "prisoners of conscience or possible prisoners of conscience" remained incarcerated in 1988, including seven peasant leaders arrested in Chiapas in 1986. The organization also reported dozens of killings in rural areas in 1988–89, many of which were perpetrated by "armed civilian bands acting with the acquiescence of local authorities."[24]

As election day approached, politically motivated violence appeared to increase. Four young *cardenista* campaign aides were dragged from their vehicle, which had been forced to stop, by unidentified gunmen who shot them dead at point-blank range.[25] Two days before the balloting began, the assassination in broad daylight of two of Cárdenas's campaign aides (Javier Obando and Román Gil) set the tone for the Salinas administration in the human rights arena. About one and one-half years later, Alcocer and other members of the PRD filed a complaint with the government about political repression. They alleged that sixty politically motivated assassinations took place between October 1989 and March 1990 alone. Some of these crimes were related to what was reported as a virtual military occupation of the state of Michoacán in early 1990, where the PRI had suffered electoral losses, and where members of at least twenty-two *alcaldías* (city councils) were physically removed from their offices because of contested local elections.[26] Stories circulated that, in Michoacán, young people in automobiles were stopped by soldiers and forced to answer questions while guns were pointed at their heads.[27] In northern Puebla, a paramilitary organization known as Antorcha Campesina, said to be affiliated with the CNC, was reportedly engaged in suppressing rural unrest. Its leadership was linked to President Salinas's brother, Raul, and a former PRI senator and head of the CNC named Mario Hernández Posada.[28]

Politically motivated repression became so apparent after Salinas de Gortari's election that the Society of Jesus in Mexico also felt obligated to raise its voice against the PRI government. The Jesuit Center for Human Rights named for Miguel Agustín Pro, a cleric executed by a government firing squad in 1926, issued a report in February 1990 in which it concluded that the level of "repression increased during the course of Carlos Salinas de Gortari's first year in office" and that any "democratic advances that might have been established [during this period] did not go beyond the representative democracy controlled by the PRI and the government."[29] America's Watch, an organization based in Washington, DC, published a scathing report in June 1990 concerning the violation of human rights under Salinas. Noting an increase in domestic and international attention to conditions in Mexico, America's Watch acknowledged patterns of human rights abuses as being "prevalent for years," but it recognized election-related violence as a new phenomenon.[30]

It may be helpful to recall Enrique Semo's prediction, cited in Chapter 2, of a rise in political repression due to the restrengthening of capitalism in Mexico, along with Muñoz Ledo's warning that "conservativism [was] sweeping" the land in the 1980s. This trend has led some analysts to assert that President Salinas chose to open up Mexico's economy to the international marketplace but to keep its political system hermetically sealed and under control at the same time.

President Salinas had two important opportunities to give substance to his repeated assertions that he and his party sought to loosen the shackles of the opposition and thus usher in full democracy during his administration. The first came when PRI leaders advised him, soon after the July 6 election, that the new congress contained more opposition members than anyone had expected. Because the lower chamber ratifies the outcomes of popular elections, Salinas's victory remained in jeopardy, as did that of any other disputed winner and any *priista* legislative proposal, for that matter. Instead of demolishing existing legislative barriers constructed against the opposition forces, the *priista* leaders crafted a package of reforms known as the Código Federal de Instituciones y Procedimientos Electorales (COFIPE), which did the opposite.

The approval of this code was bitter and prolonged. The most controversial portion of the reforms, and the least publicized in official documents, reaffirmed an existing electoral clause that guaranteed the PRI its majority rule in the chamber even if congressional elections gave it less than 51 percent of the chamber's membership at any one time (although not when it had less than 35 percent). As a result, before the 1988 election the PRI was already guaranteed 251 of the 500 deputies who make up the entire lower house, whether or not the nation's voters had elected fewer than these. The amendments added in 1989 gave the PRI a wider margin of control by allowing it 2 additional deputies for every 1 percent the PRI obtained between 35 percent and 60 percent. The less controversial portions of the code, and the most publicized officially, created new electoral procedures and agencies, substituting existing ones with the intention of minimizing vote fraud and maximizing electoral satisfaction during the balloting period.[31]

The second opportunity that Salinas had to show his faith in democracy in Mexico came up at the PRI's 14th Congress assembled September 1–3, 1990. It gathered amid agitation and controversy started three years before by the demands for reform made by members of the Corriente Democrática at the 13th Congress. Adding to the party's sense of crisis were its abysmal showing in the 1988 presidential campaign, its loss to the PAN in the gubernatorial elections in Baja California in 1989, and the creation of a new reformist wing within the party, the Corriente Crítica, to succeed the much-maligned Corriente Democrática. Not surprisingly, President Salinas obtained mixed results here, too.

Procedures for the much-heralded democratization of the PRI were handed down from the pinnacle of the party to the delegates of the congress in a classically authoritarian fashion, thus demonstrating that in 1990 the PRI could talk about democratization but was not yet capable of it. Observers reported that, despite the need to demonstrate openly a reformed and democratic PRI, new aspirants to the party's presidency were foiled when Luis Donaldo Colosio, outgoing president of the PRI, ensured his reelection by the clever manipulation of the power of his office.[32]

The middle-of-the-road *Excelsior* reported a considerable amount of enthusiasm among the tumultuous ten thousand delegates gathered in several cities, but they offered little criticism. Few important questions were raised, and the relationship between the party and the government, problematic in any true democratization of the PRI, was never discussed. A PRD observer remarked that the proposals handed down to the delegates "were approved in such a unanimous fashion that it makes it difficult to believe them; they weren't even submitted to a complete vote; in fact, no one even had the chance to abstain [had they wanted to do so]."[33] Rodolfo González Guevara, leader of the Corriente Crítica and a long-respected *priista* whose resignation from the party a few days after the 14th Congress made national news, complained that everything was prearranged for the PRI meeting despite the prolonged criticism of the intolerance for democratic procedures. "Even the distortion of the public address systems prevented listeners from hearing what speakers were saying and in this way a delegate could not tell what was approved. What was not heard nor understood was approved. However, the sound system worked perfectly well when Salinas and Colosio gave their speeches."[34] Presaging González Guevara's decision to abandon the party, the over two hundred members of the Corriente Crítica had decided to boycott the 14th Congress because they believed that it would produce few reforms, if any.

Nevertheless, several notable measures were adopted, including: 1) the right to secret balloting; 2) the right to "free and individual" party membership, instead of membership through sectors only; 3) the establishment of clear and open guidelines for anyone seeking to run as a party candidate for designated offices; 4) openness in the party's financial affairs; and 5) denial of "administrative" or government jobs for members already on the party payroll. Depending on how these measures are applied, their ultimate effect may indeed contribute to the democratization of the PRI in the years to come. Observers have noted, however, that as long as the PRI depends on the government and its inner structure relies on sectorial representation, it will change little.

Opening the Economy

One final issue not only will greatly affect the 1994 election but also will bear heavily on the fate of the PRI and the future of the Mexican people, especially in their relations with their northern neighbor. This matter is the opening of the Mexican economy to the world, particularly to the industrial powers. Muñoz Ledo reveals in these pages his belief that Salinas de Gortari, the chief technocrat, was chosen to serve as president in order to open the economy beyond the point to which his predecessor, de la Madrid, had gone. Led by de la Madrid in the mid-1980s and counseled by the nation's top technocrats, who had studied abroad, the most important members of the "revolutionary family" presumably gathered many times in different ways and places and decided that the country had no choice but to liberalize and otherwise restructure its economy. In other words, Mexico's most influential *priistas* concluded that the state had to reduce its tariffs and other import restrictions, accept greater quantities of foreign capital and know-how, and force the people to work harder and smarter in order to reduce the debt and sell their goods and services abroad in a way that would exceed anything they had done in the past, perhaps even in the age of Porfirio Díaz. The political cost in 1994 of this decision and the manner in which it has been handled remains to be calculated.

In all fairness, it may be said that, in its decision to liberalize the economy, Mexico's "revolutionary family" was merely looking into the future and acting decisively, albeit in its usual patriarchical manner, because events of the late 1980s have confirmed its call for major changes. A usually caustic observer of the Mexican scene notes that four worldwide trends have given the country's leaders practically no choice but to face some important developments in the 1990s: 1) a global economic restructuring resulting from a new international division of labor, 2) the dismantling of the welfare state and the altered relationship between the state and its workers that will come with it, 3) the emergence of regionally integrated economies, and 4) the crises of single-party states.[35]

The liberalization of the Mexican economy, begun in 1986 with President de la Madrid's unilateral decision to make Mexico part of the GATT and furthered by President Salinas's move in 1990 to seek a free-trade agreement with the United States, constitutes the biggest gamble PRI leaders have ever taken. That they have pursued it without real popular consultation will merely add to the multiple repercussions that will flow from the crucial decision itself.[36] The stakes are the highest in modern Mexican history, and the reverberations are difficult to predict.

The mainsprings of the decision to reorient the Mexican economy are reflected in the interviews contained in this volume. All of the opposition leaders agree that the economy was in dire jeopardy in the 1980s because it had been gravely mismanaged. Alcocer and Castillo, who are farther to the left than any of the others, also argue that the Mexican economy required basic restructuring in addition to good management. Nevertheless, the PRI government petitioned the United States on September 7, 1990, to begin negotiations on a free-trade agreement as soon as possible, and this overture had the ultimate effect of confounding the political debate in which the PRI was engaging the newly strengthened opposition.

Outwardly, President Salinas and his team of neoliberals view a free-trade agreement with the United States in glowing terms. Beyond embracing a new chapter in cooperation, free trade between the two countries is seen as an opportunity to bring prosperity to the people of both nations, especially Mexico. As Salinas declared to the press during his June 1990 visit to Washington, DC, to press for the trade agreement:

> The most important concern underlying our economic policy is to make sure we receive enough investments to generate the jobs which the Mexican people require, especially those that were denied them by the economic crisis. We also wish to create the conditions that will bring about growth and price stability at the same time. A by product of our policies so far has been the return of capital which began with certain intensity last year and continues stronger this year.[37]

The dramatic intensity that President Salinas gave to his economic liberalization project, redefined in terms of a free-trade agreement with the United States, stymied many of his critics and gave him an advantage he lacked at the beginning of his administration. When he also called for a North American free-trade pact that would include Canada as well, he appeared to have increased his edge significantly. Seeking to press his advantage further and capitalize on the trend toward global regionalization demonstrated by Western Europe and certain Asian countries, he boldly proclaimed the idea of a Latin American free-trade zone. His initiative to tour South America in October 1990 and announce his readiness to sign agreements with Brazil, Argentina, and Chile gave him a secure lock on political and economic initiatives in the eyes of the Mexican electorate.[38]

Independent experts in favor of a U.S.-Mexico free-trade agreement underscore the advantages that closer ties between the two countries would bring, along with the realism involved in a closer relationship. They point at the extent to which economic integration is already occurring across the Rio Grande, including: 1) capital flows, mostly U.S. investments in Mexico; 2) interdependent manufacturing processes whereby vehicle parts, for example, are manufactured in Mexico and assembled in the United States; 3) the distribution of labor, legal and illegal, to industrial centers requiring it on both sides of the border; and 4) the interchange of material culture and daily life in the border regions and beyond them.[39] Some of these experts may have eliminated the fear, expressed by Salinas at one point, that most U.S. venture capital in the early 1990s would be seeded on the postsocialist ruins of Eastern Europe. Capitalists who were planning such moves were advised in the *Harvard Business Review* to change their minds. Two business professors asserted: "They are looking in the wrong direction. . . . Mexico is North America's regional opportunity. [It] has recently begun to emerge from decades of state intervention, antagonism toward its neighbors, and resistance to foreign investment. The revolution going on there is not as visible as in Eastern Europe, but it is almost as profound."[40] Preliminary analyses of Europe's industrial giant seemed to confirm this view. On the eve of the reunification of the two Germanies, reports filtered out from East Germany outlining the sheer magnitude of its economic woes in 1991–92 including predictions of alarming unemployment rates coupled with an estimate that only one fourth of its businesses might survive the impact of a free-market arrangement with West Germany.[41]

Experts who do not favor a free-trade treaty between the United States and Mexico believe that the much-ballyhooed monies may never materialize as predicted. Jorge Castañeda, Salinas's strongest critic, writes that the president gambled on the free-trade project in order to neutralize the political flak his administration began receiving when foreign debt renegotiations revealed meager advantages for Mexico. Castañeda calculates that the long and arduous parleys with American bankers and U.S. officials produced such modest financial support, including a 35 percent reduction of principal and interest, that Mexico's foreign debt would probably grow larger.[42] The six interviewees attack both de la Madrid and Salinas because the PRI's commitment to honor its foreign debt was taken at a time when the Mexican economy was driven into the ground, along with workers' purchasing power. The 1988 election results most probably reflected the repudiation of these policies. Even if the PRI government is strong enough to carry its reforms "to the bitter end," Castañeda asserts, Mexico may not receive the projected capital inflows because it "will be competing against other nations for what will be, in relative terms, a shrinking amount of U.S. investment abroad."[43]

A more controversial assertion about the negative consequences of a free-trade agreement involves Mexican businesses. For example, newspaper headlines in 1990 began to confirm Castillo's predictions in this volume that opening of the economy would devastate private Mexican enterprises. A controversial case, even among capitalists, involved Empresas Gamesa, the parent group of one of the nation's leading cookie makers. Due to PRI-sponsored legislation that made it possible for foreign firms to buy majority stock in Mexican enterprises, Empresas Gamesa was acquired by Pepsico of Purchase, New York, considered the twenty-second biggest firm in the United States. Alberto Santos de Hoyos, former PRI congressman and president of Empresas Gamesa, explained bitterly to the press that he had no choice. The liberalizing policies of the Salinas administration had weakened his firm and left him no option but "to enter the ring against the giant foreigners in a weakened condition and fall to the mat right away." Mexican businesses, he added, "have become decapitalized by controls on prices, salaries, interest rates, and exchange rates," and this trend places them on the cutting block. His Mexican stockholders earned nothing in eight years, as a consequence; "these [foreign] firms, however, have the luxury of losing money for ten years and nothing will happen to them."[44]

The pros and cons regarding a free-trade agreement may not be settled until after 1994. However, even though such a treaty had not been signed as this book went to press, a significant opening of the Mexican economy under GATT-inspired rules was long under way, as the discussion above suggests. The reduction of tariffs by 90 percent had already permitted a plethora of foreign-made consumer goods to enter the Mexican market. Imported foodstuffs, for example, were reported as being not only more widely available, and more expensive, but also preferred by Mexican consumers over the national products.[45] Furthermore, stories in late 1990 indicated that 20 percent of the nation's dressmakers had closed down because of foreign competition,

leaving approximately twenty-five thousand textile workers
out of a job as a result. The producers of rice, soybeans, cotton, fruits, and vegetables were reportedly being squeezed in
a similar manner. A CNC official in charge of marketing the
agricultural produce of *ejidatarios* may have been speaking
for thousands of small Mexican farmers when he complained that "we are not used to negotiating with countries
that have open economies."[46] Foreign competition was said
to be causing the bloating of warehouses in various parts of
the country with growing quantities of potatoes, sorghum,
rice, and copra that could not be sold in the marketplace.
Trying to guess Mexico's future by examining Canada's
experience as a result of its own free-trade agreement with
the United States in 1988 is not possible because of the
recency of its agreement at the time of this writing. In addition, the Canadian economy differs drastically from
Mexico's, in part because the latter is labor-intensive while
the former is not.[47]

Salinas's gamble, to force Mexico into a free-trade agreement in order to cover up the shortcomings of debt renegotiations with the United States, may be a shrewd move,
because it puts the political opposition into the arena of foreign affairs, where it can only contemplate and judge.
However, the plan may backfire as well. Beyond the economic imponderables concerning wages and prices that
economic liberalization brings, as suggested above, the president has committed himself and his party to a political
objective that may ultimately act as the Achilles' heel of the
PRI in 1994 and beyond.

Opening Mexican resources to the highest bidders, as a
free-trade agreement would require, forces the president
and his party to weaken, if not cancel, some of the country's
most cherished legacies. In the 1990s it is worth observing
that some of these legacies grew out of Mexico's bitter history as a neighbor to the world's most powerful country. The
semisocialist, nationalist orientation of the Mexican constitution of 1917 may have to be altered in the 1990s with the
consent of the majority of the people because its fundamental purpose all along has been to protect the citizenry from
predatory capitalism. One of the most hotly debated articles
during the 1917 constitutional convention in Querétaro, for
example, was Article 27, which sought to guarantee Mexican
control of the nation's resources, underground and above-

ground, in opposition to the virtual vise grip that foreign companies enjoyed at the time. This and other articles in this remarkable charter gave the Mexican republic a certain prestige internationally in the twentieth century. As Castillo caustically reminded President Salinas after the nation's banks were reprivatized in mid-1990, "[Article 27] reflects the genius of the writers of our constitution; they made of private property not an original or divine right, as nineteenth century liberalism had established, but rather a right that was delegated and subordinated to the nation itself. [Article 27] does not allow privatization."[48]

The Mexican people, of course, have a right to change the letter and spirit of their constitution or to retain the charter unchanged in whatever way they may choose. They may privatize their banks or socialize them. The PRI, however, has taken these consequential steps without the genuine consultation of the people. If the U.S. government chooses to block Mexico's intention to become more socialist than in the past, as it did in Chile in 1973, the violent repercussions would probably spill over onto American soil.

In some ways, 1994 may not bode well for democracy in Mexico because global markets and international capital are pressing the body politic for profit and market opportunities. The presence of large amounts of foreign capital aimed primarily at expanding exports may affect countries with older industrial structures differently from Third World countries whose industrial fabric is new or nonexistent. Economic experts, let alone politicians, cannot yet predict the impact that the entry of greater numbers of powerful multinational corporations will bring to Mexico. These global pressures may hamper not only an opportunity to improve the lives of the people but also their right to choose which economic or political system may be best for them.

As we have seen, a significant portion of Mexico's working people supported Cárdenas in 1988 mostly because they were rejecting the inappropriate management of the nation by an antiquated and corrupt party. If he runs for president in 1994, will the majority of voters prefer him over a *priista* candidate, even if Cárdenas does not strongly embrace economic liberalization and his party's platform continues to uphold the original spirit and letter of Article 27 as bequeathed by the Mexican Revolution? Perhaps voters will prefer a PRI candidate, once President Salinas has demonstrated tangible benefits from his liberalization project, although this program may mean that Mexican-made goods will be severely reduced in number at the marketplace, foreign-owned job sites where Mexican citizens would find a job will increase in number, and foreign ownership of the nation's resources will spread even more than at present.

The choice that the Mexican people will make in 1994 is one of the most important events waiting to transpire in the history of the Americas. It is certainly important for the United States. We wait earnestly and hope that events will unfold peacefully and democratically.

Notes

1. Lorenzo Meyer's contention that Cárdenas is the leader of a movement instead of a party is more than a wise observation, but it does not necessarily negate the need for party organization to win in 1994. Meyer's interpretation, nonetheless, would become crucial if Cárdenas ceased to be the leader of the PRD for whatever reason.

2. *Proceso* 705 (May 7, 1990): 32.

3. Ibid., 31.

4. *New York Times*, May 16, July 10, 1990.

5. *Wall Street Journal*, June 22, 1990.

6. Ibid.

7. *Proceso* 639 (January 30, 1989): 6–7, 16–17. See also a thumbnail history of Mexican teachers unions in *Proceso* 651 (April 24, 1989): 12–13.

8. Jesús Silva Herzog, Sr., quoted in Hansen, *Politics of Mexican Development*, 125.

9. Ibid., 124–27.

10. Gabriel Zaid, "La propiedad privada de las funciones públicas," *Vuelta* 120 (November 1986): 26.

11. John J. Bailey, *Governing Mexico: The Statecraft of Crisis Management* (New York: St. Martin's, 1988), 35.

12. The fictional works of Luis Spota place a spotlight on corruption during the Echeverría years. See his trilogy, *La costumbre del poder*, which includes *El retrato hablado* (Mexico City: Editorial Grijalbo, 1975); *Palabras mayores* (Mexico City: Editorial Grijalbo, 1976); and *Sobre la marcha* (Mexico City: Editorial Grijalbo, 1976). Many popular books were written at the conclusion of President López Portillo's administration that censured him for allowing and participating in high levels of corruption. See Forrest D. Colburn, "Mexico's Financial Crisis," *Latin American Research Review* 19:2 (1984): 220–24, for a review of

three of these, including Ignacio Burgoa Orihuela, *Acusamos! Que no queden impunes los culpables de la crísis!* (Mexico City: Edamex, 1983). One of the most controversial publications of this genre, inspired by López Portillo, is José González G., *Lo negro del negro Durazo* (Mexico City: Editorial Posada, 1983).

13. See George W. Grayson, "An Overdose of Corruption: The Domestic Politics of Mexican Oil." *Caribbean Review* 13:3 (Summer 1984): 23–24; and Patricio E. Marcos, "Paradojas de la corrupción," *Revista mexicana de ciencias políticas y sociales* 28:110 (October-December 1982): 123–38.

14. See a hypothetical example of double or triple salaries and a discussion of "The Great Pemex Scandal" in Kenneth F. Johnson, *Mexican Democracy: A Critical View* (New York: Praeger, 1984), 165, 185–96, respectively.

15. Richard B. Craig, "Illicit Drug Traffic: Implications for South American Source Countries," *Journal of Inter-American Studies and World Affairs* 29:2 (Summer 1987): 1–34.

16. America's Watch, "Human Rights in Mexico: A Policy of Impunity," (n.p., June 13, 1990), typewritten manuscript, 94.

17. *Proceso* 660 (June 26, 1990): 6–10.

18. *La Opinión*, September 18, 1990; telephone interview with Jack Anderson's reporter, Dean Boyd, who did most of the investigation for the article, October 10, 1990.

19. The documents originated in the U.S. Drug Enforcement Administration and were presented as appendixes to United States v. Rafael Caro Quintero et al., "Memorandum in Support of Further Cross Examination of Witness Harrison; Memorandum of Points and Authorities; Declaration; Exhibits," CR 87-422-ER, U.S. District Court, Central District of California, vol. 47, July 5, 1990, to July 9, 1990.

20. Elaine Shannon, *Desperados: Latin Drug Lords, U.S. Lawmen, and the War America Can't Win* (New York: Viking Penguin, 1988).

21. Ibid., 231–57, passim.

22. *Los Angeles Times*, August 1, 1990. Zuno's defense lawyers appealed the decision on the basis of jury tampering; John L. Carlton, interview, Los Angeles, October 22, 1990.

23. *Proceso* 708 (May 28, 1990): 6–28; *New York Times*, July 17, 1990; *Los Angeles Times*, July 31, August 1, 1990.

24. *Amnesty International Report 1988* (London: Amnesty International Publications, 1988), 124.

25. *Amnesty International Report 1990* (London: Amnesty International Publications, 1990), 138.

26. Telephone interview with Jorge Alcocer, May 31, 1990.

27. Interview with the mother of one of the young women treated in this manner, Jacqueline Rosebrook, Seattle, May 31, 1990. In April 1990, Guerrero PRD officials sought to obtain the

release of Eloy Cisneros Guillén, a longtime activist who had gained a reputation by decrying government control of teachers unions; he had been jailed at least four times before and reportedly tortured as many times. PRD officials were also engaged in obtaining the release of at least thirty-two other members of their party who were imprisoned for political activity, and they sought to defend thirty-seven additional PRD members against whom arrest warrants had been issued. See *Proceso* 703 (April 23, 1990): 24.

28. *Proceso* 645 (February 26, 1990): 10–11; telephone interview with Jorge Alcocer, May 31, 1990; Lorenzo Meyer's editorial notations.

29. *Proceso* 699 (March 26, 1990): 14.

30. America's Watch, "Human Rights in Mexico."

31. "Electoral Reform" (fourteen pages of faxed materials provided by the Mexican embassy in Washington, DC, on October 13, 1990); *Proceso* 711 (June 18, 1990): 14; preliminary draft of an article by Juan Molinar and Jeff Weldon, "Elecciones de 1988 en México," being prepared at the Center for U.S.-Mexican Studies, University of California at San Diego.

32. *Proceso* 722 (September 3, 1990): 6–7.

33. The remarks are attributed to Ramón Sosamontes Herreramoro, *Excelsior,* September 4, 1990.

34. *Proceso* 724 (September 17, 1990): 8.

35. Adolfo Gilly, "The Mexican Regime in Its Dilemma," *Journal of International Affairs* 43 (1990): 273–90. This issue, which contains other excellent articles, is dedicated exclusively to Mexican contemporary affairs.

36. Note Castillo's affirmation that President de la Madrid never consulted with the Mexican legislature about the country's entry into the GATT. Reports indicate that the PRI-controlled senate only nominally consulted with the citizenry concerning a free-trade agreement with the United States. See *Proceso* 725 (September 24, 1990): 6–9.

37. *Excelsior,* July 13, 1990.

38. *La Opinion,* October 2, 1990.

39. Gilly, "The Mexican Regime," 286.

40. Susan Walsh Sanderson and Robert H. Hayes, "Mexico—Opening ahead of Eastern Europe," *Harvard Business Review* 68:5 (September-October 1990): 32–42.

41. *New York Times,* September 20, 1990.

42. Jorge Castañeda, "Salinas's International Relations Gamble," *Journal of International Affairs* 43:2 (Winter 1990): 415–16.

43. Ibid., 419.

44. *New York Times,* October 4, 1990; *Proceso* 728 (October 15, 1990): 12–13.

45. *New York Times*, September 14, 1990.

46. *Proceso* 728 (October 15, 1990): 6–7.

47. See a review of seven studies about the Canadian-U.S. free-trade agreement in Kenneth Woodside, "The Canadian-United States Free Trade Agreement," *Canadian Journal of Political Science* 22:1 (March 1989): 155–70.

48. *Proceso* 705 (May 7, 1990): 36.

The Right

CHAPTER 4

Jesús González Schmal

The son of a Chihuahua rancher, Jesús González Schmal claimed the nation's attention in the late 1980s as a possible successor to Pablo Emilio Madero as president of the PAN. Of Spanish-German-Mexican origin, he wore the robes of leadership with ease.

González Schmal attended private schools in Mexico City and later obtained a degree in industrial relations from the Universidad Iberoamericana. At the UNAM he earned a master's degree in sociology, and upon graduating he entered private business with family members.

In his interview,[1] he easily dispels the stereotype that *panistas* are ultraconservative, proclerical radicals. Although he reveals his inclination for Christian Democracy, he nonetheless discusses PAN ideology in a lucid and intelligent manner. As secretary of the PAN's International Relations Section, he offers a sweeping critique of Mexican foreign policy.

CBG: Please share some biographical information with us so that we can begin to know something about you.

JGS: My name is Jesús González Schmal. I am the PAN's congressional coordinator in the Chamber of Deputies at this time. I am also a member of the PAN's National Executive Committee and the secretary of the PAN's International Relations Section. I am a native of Delicias, Chihuahua. I was born on November 6, 1942. My ancestors founded the community of Delicias fifty-five years ago, and I therefore feel as a son of pioneers, of people who worked hard. My grandparents on my father's side were Spaniards and on my mother's side Germans. My German grandfather arrived in the United States in the early 1900s. Initially, he lived in El Paso, where half of my relatives live today. On my mother's side, my grandfather was German and my grandmother Mexican, and I, like my parents, was born in Mexico.

CBG: So you come from a family of landowners, of cattle people?

JGS: No, quite to the contrary. They were merely average farmers. They opened land to cultivation from nothing.

CBG: How about your education? Where did you go to school?

JGS: I went to school in Delicias at the start. Later, when my maternal uncle moved to Mexico City, my parents concluded that it would be a good thing for me to attend school here. My brothers and I moved to Mexico City, as a result, and we attended primary school at a German school known as Alexander Von Humboldt. After my uncle died, my father moved here, and we switched to a school that was no longer German. It was a regular Mexican school known as the Colegio Franco Español, where I studied through high school. Later, I enrolled at the Universidad Iberoamericana, where I earned a bachelor's degree in industrial relations. I enrolled at the UNAM afterward, where I earned a law degree and a graduate degree in sociology after that.

I worked as a lawyer in the private sector, in banking and industry, specializing in labor relations, human resources, and personnel development. I did this for about twenty years until the demands imposed by my political activities pressed me into working on my own. Today, my brothers and I run a firm of our own where we offer consulting services to firms and private individuals. (I have also taught sociology. It is something I like to do a lot but I have no time for it now.) This arrangement lets me spend time on my political activities associated with my position as a congressional deputy. I can't devote myself exclusively to this position because in two more years I'll be unemployed. At that point, I expect to return to my private activities.

CBG: Why wouldn't you continue with politics full time?

JGS: I can't because deputies in Mexico cannot be reelected. This makes it impossible for a citizen who opposes the government to hold public office for more than three years. The prohibition acts as a controlling mechanism for PRI deputies too; at the end of three years, they too vacate their office. At that point they turn to the system, which places them elsewhere in the government.

CBG: They have that advantage, but you folks don't?

JGS: We do not have that advantage.

CBG: They continue to go up the ladder, but you can't?

JGS: We go out the door, that's right.

CBG: So it becomes like a structure?

JGS: A premeditated one, yes.

CBG: It guarantees a career to them but not to you?

JGS: That is so. Our career is interrupted completely. We have to go out for three years in order to be able to come back in. If it is true that a PRI deputy can continue his career in another area of the administration, it is also true that this arrangement allows the system to control that deputy. He can't make a career out of the legislature; he has to interrupt it and ask for another position, and this makes him dependent on the people who make those decisions. Citizens are thus denied getting to know a deputy who can be reelected and act independently or one who enjoys a political career free of partisan pressures. In two years, for example, I have to return to my private business.

CBG: How did your political interest begin? Why?

JGS: When I was a political science student at the national university, in 1962–63, I attended a series of lectures given by various political party leaders who discussed their political beliefs. On the Left, I had the opportunity to listen to [Vicente] Lombardo Toledano; on the part of the Communist Party, I heard Valentín Campa; and, from the Social Christians, I heard Padre Velásquez. I also had the great opportunity of listening to Manuel Gómez Morín, the founder of the PAN. The truth is that I quickly leaned toward the PAN, and I soon showed up at their party offices. I joined the party's youth organization and from then on I was "swamped." As my political science teacher José González Torres, who ran for president on the PAN ticket, used to say: "The PAN is like a swamp." The more you want to get out of it, in order to free yourself from the work involved, the more you sink into it because the more convinced you are of the importance of citizen participation in politics.

One of the reasons why Gómez Morín persuaded me that day is because he saw the human person as the pillar of society. This gave political activity a special meaning. He spoke of democracy in its widest sense by recognizing the equality and the dignity of the human being. He spoke of democracy as a logical derivation of this. Democracy needed to be grafted onto the political structure. I understood this link between the value-laden origin of man and man's political manifestations as the most complete proposition I had ever heard.

In those years I had become familiar with Marxist-Leninist ideas. I had studied Marxist philosophy, naturally, and I had always found it to be limited. It didn't address the origin and the purpose of politics, which I found in the humanist ideas presented by Gómez Morín.

CBG: I am very interested in this because it appears to be one of the distinguishing features separating the PAN from the rest of the parties. I have read that Gómez Morín speaks about a type of "political humanism," a larger purpose of society (beyond the merely political and economic) which may even be classified as a "spiritual" one. Does this ideology still exist within the PAN, or does it belong to the past?

JGS: It persists to this day, of course. Look, I believe I entered the PAN for intellectual reasons. As a young man, I was searching for answers to still my anxiety, and the PAN offered me something which I perceived as transcendental. It offered a structured doctrine and a hierarchy of human values, it addressed the purpose of the human person, it explained what society was all about, and, finally, it drew its conclusions from principles and values.

I was also captivated by Gómez Morín's own personal history. As a university student, I had learned he had taken part in [Francisco I.] Madero's revolution and that he had rescued university autonomy in 1933 when he served as rector of the national university. I learned that, as an intellectual, he founded Mexican institutions like the Banco de México, coauthored its legal structure, and wrote the original legislation for the agricultural credit agencies and the nation's monetary organization of the time. The PAN attracted me all the way from its doctrines to the way its founders had legitimized them in moral terms.

CBG: The PAN allows a politically minded person to join his economic, political, and spiritual values all at once. Yes or no? In other words, this viewpoint gives room to the Catholic church in Mexico, right?

JGS: Well, I don't think these are religious matters, in the church sense of the word. These are issues for a layman.

In other words, I obviously understand that the primary question that man asks himself is: "Where do I come from and where am I going?" Everybody's response is to recognize God in one form or another, so it makes sense that the PAN gathers people who are trying to translate the meaning of life into something that is compromising, personally, socially, and politically too. We naturally need to recognize that the PAN also attracts many people who fought for religious freedom. Don't forget, the religious conflict took place in this country in 1926. As a result, the church was persecuted even though a great majority of the people considered itself Catholic. The issue of religious freedom indeed represented a major issue when the PAN got started.

Those of us who came later did not take part in these activities. Even so, we do recognize that the PAN acts on behalf of what is right. We take part in it because we want to give something to it, not because we want to get something out of it personally or otherwise. This gives the PAN a certain consistency; it makes it different from the other parties. Whenever we compare the PAN with the official party, we better appreciate the fact that the PAN represents an organization based on doctrinal values, whereas the official party is largely pragmatic. The PRI acts in order to maintain itself in power. It doesn't try to achieve the realization of valuable principles and values. It simply jockeys to stay in power, instead.

CBG: This is the philosophy of the party, according to you?

JGS: Yes. Now, addressing the issue of the church more specifically, there exists a widespread belief that the PAN is linked with the church, in one way or another. The truth is that, in my twenty years in the PAN, I have never seen anything of this sort. Quite to the contrary, from my point of view; the PAN has anticipated the church in seeking political compromise. As a consequence of the religious conflict of the 1920s, the church slumped into an extended lethargy which sapped its ability to make moral demands, even though some of these might have had social and political dimensions. By contrast, the PAN, as an organization separate from the church and very much on its own, did, in fact, present relevant proposals and alternatives by actively participating in politics. The essence of *panista* ideals is founded on Christian values in the end.

CBG: You're now referring to the Principle of Subsi—
JGS: Subsidiarity.
CBG: Tell us what the Principle of Subsidiarity is.

JGS: Subsidiarity teaches that, whatever a lower society, entity, or organization can do, the upper one ought not duplicate it. Subsidiarity permits middle-level entities like the family, a school, a union, or an organization of any kind to act on their own. It expects them to find solutions to their own problems; it lets them live out their own dynamic. Subsidiarity opposes the takeover of middle-level organizations by the state, which can only condition them and control them. In other words, Acción Nacional's philosophy says that, if a healthy middle-level organization like a company, a union, a club, a school, or a church functions in accordance to its internal purposes, the state's function ought to confine itself to higher functions. The state should never seek to integrate nor supplant lower-level entities.

CBG: This leads me to a related question. I am reminded that one of my students[2] has written that the PAN is very close to Christian Democracy. Yes or no?

JGS: I believe that it shares its philosophical background. Christian Democracy begins with Christian values. I do believe there is an affinity between the PAN and Christian Democracy. Christian Democracy has enjoyed a very different kind of experience. In Europe it was one thing, and in Latin America another. Christian Democracy has experienced some hard times too. I believe, however, that the rechanneling and redefinition it has undergone in recent years is giving it greater affinity with us, and, vice versa, the PAN is enjoying greater affinity with Christian Democracy.

CBG: Please say it in another way.

JGS: Christian Democracy, founded after World War II, took one form under Konrad Adenauer in West Germany, another with Alcide de Gasperi in Italy, another in Venezuela, another in Chile, another in Guatemala, and so on. I would also say that Latin American Christian Democracy leaned toward the Left, while European Christian Democracy remained in the Center. I would say that Venezuela's Christian Democracy, which kept close ties to Europe, represents the mainstream of this current in Latin America. I would also say that Christian Democracy is being rescued and redeemed in Latin

America, it is emerging from its troubled years. In comparison to the 1950s and 1960s, today it represents a clear and central position.

CBG: And you believe that a Christian Democratic party did not develop here, first because the PAN already existed and second because of the ultranegative viewpoint held toward the Catholic church arising out of the Mexican Revolution.

JGS: Of course. First, Venezuela's COPEI [Comité de Organización Política Electoral Independiente], Christian Democracy's most important party in Latin America, was organized after Acción Nacional was organized. Its founders, Dr. Rafael Caldera among them, were present when the PAN held its first constituent meeting on September 15, 1939. He admits that he benefited a lot from the ideas in which Acción Nacional believed, at that time. It is possible to say that Acción Nacional stood ahead of several humanist propositions which later gave rise to Latin America's Christian Democratic parties. Second, Acción Nacional's own sense that it ought to remain a domestic party, a party enclosed within the Mexican republic, played a major role in limiting Christian Democracy in Mexico. And, as you point out, the term "Christian" became a factor too. In Mexico, the term immediately links up to a specific religious sect. The truth is that Christian Democracy needs to be understood as a cultural-philosophical current not connected with a given church but rather with values rooted in what the world knows as the Christian West. This is the way I can explain the absence of Christian Democracy in Mexico.

For all these reasons the PAN decided not to consider itself a Christian Democratic party, even though many of its principles are akin to one. Finally, I need to mention a legal factor. In Mexico, religious names cannot be applied to parties. This is something that lies connected with our historical atavism that confounds social realities and thereby prejudges the church and so forth and so on.

Some links between the PAN and Christian Democracy have taken place. Some of our young *panistas* attended some seminars in Venezuela in the past. The Venezuelans visited us, and we visited them, but this kind of relationship was interrupted for about two decades. In the 1980s, however, we've begun to reinitiate fraternal contacts with some of the Christian Democratic parties again.

CBG: Let's get on to another subject. Please discuss the PAN in terms of its political force today. Where is it strongest? Why is it strongest in the north?

JGS: In order to answer that question, I have to go back to the origins of the PAN. I believe the PAN arose as a response to what was already becoming a one-party system. There are ten years between 1929, when the PNR (now the PRI) was born, and 1939, when the PAN was organized. The first person who foresaw what the one-party system was going to be like was José Vasconcelos, who decided to oppose the official party candidate in the election of 1929. As you know, a fraud took place, he went into exile, and his movement came to an end. Nonetheless, Gómez Morín, who had participated in the Vasconcelos campaign, took up the cause on behalf of political change in Mexico free of a single dominating force.

The struggle of the people against the state evolved at the university level from 1929 to 1939. This is why I mentioned the fight for university autonomy earlier as a very important historical event. The [Lázaro] Cárdenas regime followed, augmenting and consolidating the one-party design. Acción Nacional arose in 1939 in response to all of this, and it did so despite the barriers placed upon it by newspapers, radio, and other media. What was achieved was really the result of a personal effort on the part of Acción Nacional's first members, who fashioned a political option for the nation. We have to take into account the fact that the political monopoly had been in place for ten years in 1939 and that it satisfied many Mexican citizens. The country had achieved a certain amount of progress and development. People had been channeled, and they accepted the official model unconsciously.

The willingness of people to do work on behalf of the PAN was weak at the beginning. This is why many decades went by and a lot of enthusiasm and insistence was expended in order to reveal clearly that the official model contained the seeds of its own destruction and the ruin of the official party. Many people did not understand the PAN's early spokesmen. Somebody could have said: "What do you need democracy for if you have progress and development, if you have a certain amount of tolerance?" Note that it is "tolerance," not "liberty." Several decades had to go by for the PAN to grow.

Today the rise of the PAN cannot be restricted to any one region in the republic. It took hold in Yucatán, Oaxaca, Puebla, Chihuahua, Jalisco, and Baja California in the 1950s and 1960s. It did so in an irregular fashion. It arose in Baja California, for instance, with a popular candidate whose campaign inevitably caused a riot; the troops had to be called in. This also happened in Puebla, Yucatán, et cetera. There was no coordination between these events either.

Only since the 1980s has a coincidence of events begun to take place throughout the republic. This may have resulted from the government's efforts to weaken the PAN by helping create new parties and giving leftist parties official status. If so, the effect was contrary to the desired result. Like seeds cast on fertile ground, what the PAN had already sown began to sprout. It took four decades for the people to begin to understand what the PAN represented.

This is why the PAN is the only party that has grown constantly since 1979 when the electoral laws were reformed, even though other parties have grown too. The PAN has been shown to grow even when you use official balloting data. By contrast, the new leftist parties registered an increase in their membership only in the year they joined the political fight, 1979. We believe the government actually inflated their numbers. The new leftist parties didn't do well in their second electoral joust in 1982.

What all this means is that the people's alienation from the PRI and the government was being channeled into the PAN. While you may enjoy seven political options in 1986, it is only the PAN that grows stronger each day. The rise of sympathy for the PAN parallels the rise of antipathy for the PRI. This is why I believe that one cannot confine the strength of our party to any one region. Even so, it does appear to be evident that our party has gained in the northern states of Chihuahua, Sonora, Baja California, Coahuila, Tamaulipas, and so on.

CBG: Why in these states?

JGS: To begin with, the founder of our party was a northerner. Gómez Morín was from Chihuahua, and this is a factor, indeed. Second, the impact of the United States is more obvious in these states. Many citizens in the north have directly or indirectly experienced the United States. They may have relatives on the American side, or they may have worked there or visited as tourists. The infrastructure which is visible for anyone who merely looks across the border is obviously impressive. You don't have to be college educated to see that a different form of reasoning takes place in the United States. My fellow northerners often ask me: "Why do the Americans have the roads, the hospitals, the different kinds of services they do, and we don't?" One conclusion naturally comes to mind: The public resources are handled more honestly on the other side than on this side. This knowledge fuels a feeling of opposition. It also helps people realize that political participation may mean a better life.

Panismo became strong in the north for yet another reason which is hard to explain. Don't forget that the Mexican Revolution of 1910 flourishes in the northern states. Less intermixing with the native people takes place in these areas. A man dedicates himself to the land in this region, he perseveres against harsh physical conditions. A greater sense of independence from the center develops in the north too. The center is less able to control things in the north. All of this helps explain why the PAN has become more evident in the north in recent years when compared with the south generally.

CBG: Licensiado, please tell us now how you would characterize Mexico's political system.

JGS: I said earlier that the constitution of the one-party system contained the seeds of its own destruction. Certain historians claim that Mexico needed to unify the atomized revolutionary forces of the 1920s and that a one-party system showed the way to reduce the impact of caudillismo and thereby the fragmentation of the political currents. They claim that, within its larger purposes, an official party was needed for the development of a national hegemony and a sense of unity. They also claim that the existing political forces needed streamlining in order to generate democracy, all within the framework of such a party.

CBG: And achieve unity?

JGS: Yes. Well, this has gone on long enough. Instead of evolving toward democracy, we are now going backward toward authoritarianism, centralism, and intolerance. This discussion reminds me that an idea of mine is quite valid. I've laid down a "law" that says that, for every inch of popularity that the government and its party loses, its control grows by a foot. I mean economic "controls," and, of course, they are expensive.

CBG: So this is the González Schmal law. Why don't you explain it a little bit more?

JGS: In the 1970s the government discovered deep popular distress; it found that the people really wanted change. An important sign was the 1968 student movement, which was unable to define itself clearly, but it revealed widespread disillusionment nonetheless. Latin America inched toward political participation as a result of an outside influence, the John F. Kennedy period in the United States and the Alliance for Progress program. I believe that his proposals regarding fiscal, educational, and political reform somehow had to do with the people's demand for more participation in 1970.

CBG: Don't you think the Cuban Revolution had anything to do with all that, in addition to the Kennedy image?

JGS: Of course. Kennedy's proposition was meant as an answer to the Cuban Revolution. Nevertheless, in 1970 the Mexican government asked itself: "My hegemony and the permanence of the system are at risk; what is the solution?" The answer was economic participation. The government began breaking up the old model that sought to balance the participation in the economy of both government and society. The government's share began to grow. Don't forget that the government already enjoyed control in the countryside via the *ejido* system that leaves the use of the land to the peasant as long as the government remains titleholder. This represents the best form of control.

The government controls the press because it supplies newsprint. It controls radio and television via official concessions made at the discretion of government officials (which may be canceled at any time). It controls education by allowing private parties to furnish education, but only if they are licensed to do so. It controls labor unions through the national federations, whose leaders are offered public positions in exchange for control over the workers. Things are fine as long as the government tolerates it. The influence of the government had already grown in many of these areas, but it didn't yet control a segment of society still unaffected: private enterprise. Here I mean independent professionals and self-employed workers. You may include the university too, which it had already been pressing. The government demanded participation.

The government hit upon a change of strategy as a result of all this. It called for government intervention in areas of the economy it had no business entering. Thus, during the six years that Luis Echeverría was president, 1970–1976, the government bought up factories, restaurants, bars—it bought what it could. It bought up shares belonging to many foreign firms too, American ones especially, since it didn't trust foreign investment. This undermined the system. The *priistas* brought us chronic budget deficits. They made it necessary to increase our foreign debt because their policies coincided with certain changes that were taking place in the industrial countries. So, instead of increasing direct investment, these countries began extending more credit than ever before, with "strings" at the beginning, then later without them.

The state grew by leaps and bounds. In the last days of the Echeverría administration, the bureaucracy was bloated to include more than two and a half million employees in the central sector and the state enterprises alone. This is not counting employees working for state and municipal governments.

This tendency of wanting to control popular organizations and intervening in economic activities went one step further. When the Echeverría administration ended in 1976, new oil deposits were discovered, and these began to be pumped. The government then hit upon yet another excellent method of control. It no longer needed the people, taxpayers, or private enterprise. It could now live on oil alone. It was as if the government had become drunk with power. It kept growing, indebting itself, and choking private enterprise out of the economy. It came to the point it should have foreseen. It failed to obtain the benefits other oil countries obtained when prices climbed to their highest point. Far from becoming a creditor nation like the Arab countries, Mexico went further into debt. This I consider a grave error.

Not only did it not take advantage of the circumstances, it also congested internal credit. It was unable to avoid this. The government's budget kept growing, more employees were hired, and its activity kept on going. This put the government into the noose it is in now. It can't get people off the payroll, because doing so will aggravate the crisis. It can't pay on its debt either, because it'll choke itself financially. This condition affects workers who are not employed by the government. For example, no one in Mexico can explain why salaries are kept as low as they are when the inflation rates are so high. The explanation is that the government is the biggest employer in our country, and it doesn't have enough money to adequately pay its own people. It can't fire them either, because doing so will cause conflict.

Consequently, the government faces atrophy born of its own growth spiral. It can't borrow internally, because it already expropriated the national banking system. It has taken advantage of all of the available resources (from abroad, from production, from taxes), and it has reduced economic activity in the private sector. This is why a state of crisis exists today. It is a tendency that began in the 1970s, reaching a choke point in 1986, and now the government does not enjoy any resources, because national savings are exhausted. It can't borrow abroad, because the growth of its banks is limited, and it can't rely on oil revenue, because the price of oil is at an all-time low.

The government does not have a consistent plan that will stimulate the economic activity of the private and social sectors. I say this because, in its decisions, the government requires total power; monopoly must be maintained. This has encouraged it to put economic and political interests into conflict. Sometimes it yields in the political area, sometimes in the economic. At one point, it expropriated the banks, and later it lavishly compensated the bankers to console them. The situation got more confused, in the meanwhile, when the government began absorbing bank funds. The result was that private sector credit became unattainable. This is why I say that the government's actions are contradictory. The government itself (its size, operation, composition) is a contradiction.

CBG: Your answer dealt both with the political and economic aspects of the problem, on a general plane. Can you give us some details? In other words, how is political control exerted? How are people appointed? It all seems like a confused web to me.

JGS: In purely political terms, the government is both a web and an enigma. Many theories exist about a group of "notables," or influential men who sit behind the president and are connected somehow with his decisions concerning appointments to the government and the party and the way national politics are handled. This way of doing things may

have been true in the past. The ex-presidents and the most
influential members of the system may have stood as direct
advisers to the incumbent president.

Things have changed, however. The president now
responds to pressures put upon him by the sectors that
make up a political power core. By this, I mean the peasants
represented by the CNC, the workers in the CTM, and the
general citizenry in the CNOP [Confederación Nacional de
Organizaciones Populares]. The president is also pressed by
private enterprise groups, foreign interests, actions taken
by the various states in the republic, and so on. Many influences impinge upon the president. If you try to find out how
key government appointments are made, I would say that
they stem from negotiations between the sectors I mentioned above and the Secretaría de Gobernación [Office of
the Government Secretary], which represents the president
of the republic.

In the Secretaría de Gobernación, for example, lists are
made up of those who will become congressmen, depending
on previously used sector formulas. The "fine-tuning" is done
there. Officials of the Secretaría de Gobernación probably
say: "Two more are needed for this sector, three for that
one"; or, "John is fine here, but Jack is inappropriate there."
This is the way I really think it works. The same is done
with state governors. There are governorships that belong to
the central institutions linked with the administration from
the start. For example, it is well known that the CTM is
entitled to three or four governorships. The CNOP enjoys
the executive suites in other states, the CNC still others.
Some belong to the president of the republic. All of this
reveals a process of negotiation by the various sectors or
corporate entities; they are part of the powerful central
institutions, and the government finds itself obligated to
this arrangement.

CBG: So what you're describing is an intraparty consensus, formed only at the highest official level, which enjoys
the president's tacit approval because the needs of his office
are involved as well?

JGS: Correct. But you can't really speak in terms of an
intraparty consensus because our party does not consider
the PRI a party in the rigorous sense of the word. *Priistas*
do not participate freely within it. They do not express their
opinions freely. My description above refers to agreements

made at the leadership level by sector heads in combination with the president of the republic.

CBG: You direct the party's Foreign Relations Committee. What is its position regarding Central America?

JGS: With regard to Central America, we have sustained the principle to which the PAN subscribes in its basic documents: self-determination and nonintervention in the affairs of other peoples and their governments. We have censured the foreign policy of the Mexican government in recent years because it has trampled the Mexican tradition of nonintervention, in effect, by intervening in the affairs of Nicaragua and El Salvador.

In the case of El Salvador, we censured an agreement, signed in France, that recognized the Salvadoran rebel groups. We considered this agreement interventionist. The Mexican government reaffirmed a petition before the United Nations Commission on Human Rights, to give the belligerent forces in El Salvador juridical recognition. This is more evidence yet of our interventionism. With regard to Nicaragua, we've been able to ascertain the frank intervention of the Mexican government there for the purpose of transplanting the Mexican political system. Let me be a little bit more specific on this.

When the Organization of American States [OAS] was addressing the Nicaraguan issue, and it voted to expel Anastasio Somoza, the Mexican government stepped ahead of everyone else and disavowed the Somoza regime, knowing full well that the OAS was going to do it anyway. Later, Mexico took up the Nicaraguan issue again by sending former PRI Secretary-General Augusto Gómez Villanueva as ambassador. He took a team of political advisers in order to help him create a model of the Mexican official party in Nicaragua. This effort supposedly included direct economic aid too. These advisers traveled to Nicaragua to help with the elections, which evolved there in true Mexican style. The candidate was an official candidate (Commander Daniel Ortega); the party was an official one; state resources were employed in the campaign, including labor unions; and public opinion was controlled, as were the media. These resources were marshaled in the Mexican manner; the control of the electoral process was identical to Mexico's. The Electoral Council, for example, was made up of representatives of the government and the opposition parties. The latter, however, played such a clear minority role that they withdrew from the elections.

Why did Mexico do this? I believe our government officials feel they need to export our Mexican system in order to bring support to it from the outside. People frequently say that, if Mexico is attractive to many governments in Central and South America, it is due to the fact that it offers the appearance of democracy and liberty. In practice, however, it is a party dictatorship that blocks opposition movements from power. It imposes itself by controlling media, labor unions, peasants, and everything else it can.

CBG: Did this take place during the Echeverría administration?

JGS: Yes. That is, in fact, when it took place.

CBG: Was this intervention commented on in the press?

JGS: No, for one simple reason. The press was closed to the PAN.

CBG: Don't you have evidence to back this up?

JGS: Absolutely. We have documented it in our position papers, it's been part of our platform. It has been part of our debates here, in congress, and its proceedings. It's been part of the posture we've taken. Moreover, as PAN congressmen, we were invited to observe the elections in El Salvador and Nicaragua, and we made our views public based on what we saw. The press printed some of our statements about El Salvador.

The administration refused to send observers to the elections in El Salvador even though it was invited to do so. It refused precisely because it didn't want to be obligated later to invite foreign observers to its own elections. Just recently, in fact, there was another instance in which the Mexican government insisted once again before the United Nations Commission on Human Rights on giving some kind of legal recognition to the Salvadoran rebels. This is further proof of Mexican interventionism from our point of view. We believe, however, that the countries involved in the Contadora process, like Colombia, Venezuela, and Panama, have been acting in good faith. Our view regarding the Mexican government, however, is that it sought an opening in order to intervene and to influence the political situation in Nicaragua.

CBG: What you're doing is criticizing.

JGS: Indeed, we're criticizing it!

CBG: The fact that the Mexican government is acting contrary to Benito Juárez's admonition—

JGS: —to never interfere abroad. As he used to say, "Respect for the rights of another is the way to guarantee peace." This has become known as the Estrada Doctrine of nonintervention and self-determination.

CBG: What is the party's position on the contras and the role the U.S. government has played, as the whole world knows, in supporting them and even inciting them into armed attacks against Nicaragua?

JGS: One central fact rises above all the others: They are Nicaraguans. Many of them took part in the Sandinista Revolution against dictator Anastasio Somoza, and they deserted it later because the governing junta turned toward Marxism and totalitarianism. From this viewpoint, therefore, we believe these Nicaraguans have the right to be considered in the governing of the nation itself. Secondly, there was no impartial electoral procedure guaranteeing the rights of all citizens to participate in the elections, and this made the existence of the contras justifiable.

Nonetheless, the PAN has censured intervention in the region not only by the United States but also by Cuba and by the Soviet Union. We desire to see both the United States and the Soviet Union stop intervening in Nicaragua. The United States says that it is intervening because of Cuban-Soviet involvement there. We are persuaded of this not only because U.S. officials tell us this but because we hear about it from Nicaraguans who reside here, in Mexico, and elsewhere in Latin America. We know of the existence of Cuban personnel in Managua from personal experience because they are easy to identify at the good cafés and restaurants there. We also know that the State Department has pinpointed Cuban-Soviet bases and armaments there. The bottom line is that we understand the U.S. intervention in Nicaragua, but we do not condone it.

CBG: Regarding Cuba, do you folks have a position that criticizes the administration?

JGS: Yes. We have always criticized the Cuban government because it is not approved by the people in a legitimate way. If we wished to understand the revolutionary process and justify its origin, I'd say it's fine and good that a revolutionary movement led the way to a provisional government. However, that the same revolutionary government has existed for thirty years is something we do not understand. We believe in democracy as something based on the consultation of the people. So, if there is no consultation of the people in Cuba, on the basis of free elections and political freedom, then we can't rightly believe in the Cuban government.

This is why we have criticized the Mexican government's support of the Cuban regime. Given the respect we hold for nonintervention, it wouldn't be so bad to have fraternal relations with it. This is something that falls to us as Latin Americans anyway, but not with the frankly pro-Cuban posture that the Mexican government has shown. I believe that, for reasons of neighborliness, we ought to show respect for the Cuban people by having a relationship with its government, but we can't justify a government that is not legitimized by public vote.

CBG: Would you favor breaking relations with the Soviet Union?

JGS: Definitely not. We believe we ought to have relations with all of the countries in the world as long as they respect Mexican national sovereignty. Diplomatic ties with us, however, do not justify intervention in our affairs, nor do they justify excessive diplomatic activity nor having an unusually large diplomatic representation in our country.

CBG: With respect to U.S.-Mexico relations, do you accept what the Mexican government has done, and, if not, how would you change it?

JGS: We have taken a critical stand in this area too because the United States represents the most important country in the world. It is our neighbor, yet things are not right between us. Historically speaking, there have been bad moments in our relations. We shoulder a very difficult burden with the United States. I can cite the Mexican-American War right away.[3] Evidence that American ambassadors intervened in our affairs is available too.[4] All of this is history now, however.

We believe we have to keep our feet on the ground by reminding ourselves that our neighbor represents a world power, that many Mexicans travel there, and, most importantly, that our interdependent relations are fundamental to both sides. This is why we have demanded priority from our chancellery in its work with the United States. In reality, we believe that our chancellery has mismanaged our relations with the United States, because it has sought instead to export our governmental model to Nicaragua and seek influence in South America. For example, we think it would have been opportune and convenient to have held intense diplomatic talks with the United States regarding both the problem of our undocumented citizens who live there and this whole process connected with the Simpson-Mazolli Law. We're not so disingenuous to believe that the United States does not enjoy the right to decide who can enter the country or not. Nevertheless, we believe that Mexico could have taken an important role in the formulation of the measures contemplated in that law. We also censure the Mexican government because, not only do you have people going there who can't get jobs here, but you also have criminal trafficking connected to it as well.

Police authorities in the northern states make it easy for crossing agents (we call them *polleros*) to take people into the United States illegally. These agents don't do it out of necessity, they do it simply to earn extra money by commission—they make money off our brothers who have to emigrate! We know that certain people visit towns in Zacatecas or Jalisco, for example, looking for people wanting to cross into the United States illegally, and they charge them a given amount for the service. I believe that if the Mexican government has not done much to discourage this practice, the U.S. government has the right to complain about it.

Nonetheless, we believe that, given the natural flow of Mexicans to the United States on account of the grave economic situation we face in this country, Mexican diplomatic activity about it ought to be intense. The same can be said about commercial relations, the foreign debt, et cetera. The bottom line is that we believe both the interest and priority that ought to have been given to Mexico's foreign policy toward the United States are lacking.

CBG: Does your party have anything to say about the Mexican people who reside in the United States?

JGS: Yes. We believe it is possible to enter into an accord with the United States to permit Mexicans to work temporarily as long as their rights are respected. The United States would thus be guaranteed the number of workers it needs. This would also eliminate the trafficking of human beings, which is bringing somebody a lot of money.

CBG: I mean, does the PAN have any relations with the Mexican communities in the United States? Does it have branches there? Do you do any political work there?

JGS: No, we haven't done that kind of work there, even though many of the Mexicans write to us constantly. Those who know about us or have had some experience with us go to the length of sending us donations, but the PAN does not actively work over there, nor do I see the possibility either.

CBG: I mentioned to one of your colleagues that I believe the majority of Mexicans living in the United States is probably quite critical of the Mexican government and the official party.

JGS: Naturally. It is very evident. Those who have had to emigrate due to Mexico's poverty feel resentment, and those who notice our mishandling of relations with the United States must feel hurt too. Those who see their home country falling into corruption and know about the official system of monopoly naturally have to be against the government. In this light, I do see Mexicans in the United States as our potential supporters, but our party can only do so much.

CBG: The idea of the absentee ballot doesn't exist in Mexico, right? Wouldn't it be a good idea?

JGS: To have Mexican residents in the United States cast their absentee ballots in our consulates and embassies someday is an excellent idea. I know that, when elections take place in the United States, American residents in Mexico vote here. You have to keep in mind that our embassies are controlled by the PRI administrations, and they would block this kind of activity. This is why we're not very optimistic about it. However, I agree that this is something we could look into with great interest in the future.

CBG: Something else, *licenciado*. You're aware that Mexican-Americans like me, born in the United States, have a strong interest in what goes on in Mexico. Have you folks ever tried making institutional connections with Chicano or Mexican-American organizations in the United States? With people interested in knowing how the United States government conducts its relations with Mexico?

JGS: No, we've been passive from that perspective. Again, I point to our limitations. We're a party that owes its existence to the effort of volunteers. Our economic strength is very limited. But we're inching in that direction; we're gathering our strength.

Notes

1. The interview was held February 27, 1986, in the congressional office building known as the Palacio Legislativo del Congreso de la Unión, near San Lázaro, Mexico City.

2. Jeff Weldon.

3. Recent scholarship confirms what Mexicans have always suspected, that is, the United States took unfair advantage of Mexico in 1848 when it had to give up Texas, Arizona, New Mexico, and California. See Glen W. Price, *Origins of the War with Mexico: The Polk-Stockton Intrigue* (Austin: University of Texas Press, 1967).

4. See Howard F. Cline, *The United States and Mexico* (New York: Atheneum, 1963), 130–33, for the infamous incident in which Henry Lane Wilson, the American ambassador, successfully plotted against Mexican President Francisco I. Madero in 1913. See also Price, *Origins of the War,* concerning numerous examples of plainly shameful intrigue on the part of U.S. ambassadors in the early 1800s; and Charles C. Cumberland, *Mexican Revolution: Genesis under Madero* (Austin: University of Texas Press, 1952), 255.

CHAPTER 5

Pablo Emilio Madero Belden

The Madero surname is a hallowed one in Mexico. Not without irony, Pablo Emilio Madero Belden is the nephew of Francisco I. Madero, who initiated the much-proclaimed revolution of 1910, out of which the PRI emerged. In some ways, Pablo Emilio has enhanced the glow of the family name because he stood up nobly while *priistas* vilified him and his party, the PAN, as it has been customary to do over the years.

Like most other members of his distinguished clan, he was born a *norteño*. His father was forced into exile in the United States when Pablo Emilio was a child, and this affected his intellectual formation. He speaks English fluently and has a strong admiration for the United States.

He attended the national university during Lázaro Cárdenas's heyday, where he earned a degree in chemistry. His famous uncle's experiences, as well as those of his own father, led him into politics on the conservative side at an early age. Madero's ascension to power was not automatic; he worked hard to scale to the very pinnacle of his party. He served the PAN in Nuevo León in the middle 1970s and sat on the National Executive Committee from 1975 to 1985. He became a *panista* congressman in the late 1970s and early 1980s and was selected as the PAN's candidate for president in 1982.

CBG: Tell us your name, your occupation.[1]

PEMB: My name is Pablo Emilio Madero. I am the president of the PAN's National Executive Committee.

CBG: Please tell us where you were born, the date of birth, and provide us with an outline of your family, your

youth, education. What brought you to this point in your
life?

PEMB: I was born on August 3, 1921, in San Pedro de
las Colonias, Coahuila, a small town near the city of Torreón
in northern Coahuila. My father, Emilio Madero, a farmer,
was also a division general and brother to Francisco I.
Madero, the man who unleashed the Mexican Revolution of
1910. My father took part in the revolution; but, when I was
born, he had already taken up farming in an area called the
Laguna district of Coahuila. In 1926, when I was five, I
remember we had to go into exile for political reasons. We
thus spent a year in California, two in Texas, and then
returned to Mexico in 1929.

I joined the PAN when I was a chemistry student at the
national university here in Mexico City, not at the exact
moment it was founded, but pretty close to it. The PAN was
founded as a political party in September 1939, and I gained
admittance three months later, in December 1939. I joined
as a young student because I wanted to take part in the
nation's politics. I was not happy with Mexico's political
future. This took place on the eve of the [Juan Andreu]
Almazán campaign of 1940 in the last days of General
[Lázaro] Cárdenas's administration. The campaign itself
became quite tempestuous. My father served as president
of the Partido Revolucionario de Unificación Nacional
[PRUN], which supported Almazán and consequently
brought together a lot of folks who wanted to see some
changes made in this country.

This episode is well known already. Scandalous frauds
were committed in the election following the campaign, and
the victory was handed over to General Manuel Avila
Camacho, the candidate who had in fact lost the election.
In any case, my political interest was born in the heat of a
hard battle in which my father led the Almazán party, and it
grew afterward. My father became very disillusioned with
Almazán's inconsistency; he had abandoned the fight and
those who had supported him throughout the campaign.
These people faced a lot of problems as a result.

The leaders of the emerging PAN knew better than to
support a candidate at that particular moment. Having been
organized in 1939, if they had gone ahead and backed
Almazán, they would have given the impression they were
formed merely to support him, which was not the case. The

PAN was born precisely at that moment in time because it wanted to fight a host of ideas, not to support a caudillo. This is the PAN's contribution to the political life of this country.

I have taken part in the PAN since that time. I have been a candidate for the mayor's office of the city of Monterrey, for a seat in congress, and in another election I was actually elected a member of the 51st Congress, where I served from 1979 to 1982. In 1982, I ran against Miguel de la Madrid as the PAN's presidential candidate. This is my story in a nutshell.

CBG: Why would you like every Mexican citizen seriously to consider joining your party?

PEMB: Because it offers a different way of thinking. In other words, we base our political action on a special philosophy that provides us with a unique viewpoint concerning Mexico's labor unions, its international relations, farm problems, educational freedom, agrarian reform, politics, urban issues, the definition of the state, how government is defined, and so on. As a token of our commitment to the people at a given moment, we offer them a platform each time we kick off a campaign. We invite the people to join us in our struggle not on behalf of a caudillo but rather on behalf of a set of ideas.

Our philosophy is based on the concept of freedom. We believe that the fundamental rights of man—the right to life, truth, justice, and freedom—ought to be respected. When we talk about freedom, we mean freedom of conscience, expression, speech, and association. We mean freedom for any candidate to take part in the political activity of the nation by writing, speaking publicly, and traveling. We believe in liberty. The Mexican people understand us very well.

While other parties may propose collectivist solutions, we believe that solidarity will help us find the solutions to our problems. In other words, we believe in the dignity of the human person, but we also believe that a person has the obligation to lend support or solidarity to society. The progress our party has enjoyed over the last forty-six years demonstrates that our message has cast a deep impact on the Mexican people. The people believe our message and the programs we propose.

CBG: One of the PRI's secretaries of political training, Arturo Núñez Jiménez, stated one day that "bi-partyism in

Mexico is not possible because there is a basic lack of consensus for it."[2] Would you comment on this?

PEMB: I have to say that his statement misinforms, because a two-party system doesn't depend on his will nor on mine. It depends, instead, on how the people vote. If the will of the people is respected, they are the ones who will have to decide if our country is going to have two, three, or four parties. It shouldn't be a party decision. I recognize that the government party would like to exist by itself. Its members would like to see just one party; they would enjoy monopartyism. However, we simply say: Respect the will of the people.

CBG: No doubt you believe there is a tendency toward bipartisan politics, given recent voting patterns?

PEMB: Based on official data already skewed against us, the reality is that, as a political party of opposition, we already receive more votes than the rest of the opposition parties put together. Official figures indicate we receive 52 to 53 percent of the total opposition vote. I say we shouldn't accept these figures because they're flawed; they come from vote counts in which ballot boxes have been stolen, where make-believe voters are included—electoral fraud. We think these figures have a lot of "bugs," yet our strength is greater.

CBG: Would you briefly describe Mexico's political system?

PEMB: In Mexico we have limited liberty. For example, we can wage a political campaign and travel around the country trying to get our message across. This is important. You can't do this in other countries like Russia or Cuba. Whoever tries to deliver a message to established authorities in Russia ends up in Siberia or in a mental ward. [This situation began to change radically for the better by 1989.] In Mexico we enjoy the right to organize such a campaign; as a party, we can create candidates. You and I are sitting in the offices of the PAN, and we have the liberty to act here.

What we need in Mexico is an electoral process that allows the real political opinion of the Mexican people to be recognized. Let me explain what I mean. The lists of voters need to be credible and not manipulated as they have been in the past. In June 1985, for example, we discovered the existence of a computer system that had been set up to alter national voting lists. When some of our people learned how to break into it, we found out that the system was operating everywhere. A cybernetic fraud had been attempted. This is why I say we need voting lists that are trustworthy.

We also need honest and impartial officials on electoral commissions. These are entrusted to maintain a clean electoral process, to be honest and impartial. These commissions should not be made up of people from one party only, as we have at present. We need to have the electorate (workers, peasants, office employees, et al.) to be free to vote. They should not be forced to vote for the official party under the threat of losing their job or their government-given plot of land. We need to know that the vote cast will be counted honestly, that the overall results show clearly who won, and that the power thus earned be handed over to the victors. This is what is needed in Mexico.

CBG: Explain the manner in which the government and the official party work together. Much is said about presidentialism when referring to the existing governmental system. How does it show up in the parties? Tell us something about subsidies to the parties. Do you think they're a form of control?

PEMB: In Mexico the official party and the government become confused because they're one and the same thing. In fact, the official party works much like a government office; you could almost say a government department. This is because the party head is named by the president of the republic, who also holds the power to dismiss him. This is why there's confusion and why the government encourages that confusion. They do not want us, the people in general, to distinguish between a government administration and the country. They want us to mix nation, party, and state altogether.

When we wage an opposition campaign, they attack us as "traitors to Mexico." This, of course, isn't true. As a political party, we are obligated to take part in the political life of the country. We have to fight to take our people to congress, to the governorship of a state, or to the presidency. They intentionally confuse the people by saying that whoever opposes the president also opposes Mexico. *Priistas* go to the length of using the national colors (green, white, and red) on their party logo. This encourages the voter, who may not have much schooling, to vote for the official party because he may think he's voting for his country; confusion is thus created.

CBG: You believe that government officials have manipulated images and used propaganda?

PEMB: The government confuses the people because the PRI [is the only party that] uses the colors of our national flag on its logo [which also appears on the ballot itself]. If the people aren't careful, they help the government achieve its goal by becoming confused. Presidentialism is a dimension of this system. The president of Mexico cannot reelect himself, but he enjoys absolute power during his six years in office. A change occurs at the end of six years when a new president begins with full power and the outgoing one is displaced. In fact, he falls from prestige. In other words, total power is enjoyed for six years only; the occupant cannot go on. The only one who ever tried it was assassinated.[3]

Presidentialism is manifest in many areas. Social, political, and economic decisions are made, as López Portillo used to say, "in the solemn air of my office." Without consultation, he alone makes the decisions that affect the entire country. In my opinion, this is not good.

CBG: Don't you think these decisions may reflect an interplay of interests within the party itself, since the party stretches itself widely? Some of you don't even consider the PRI a party, right?

PEMB: We maintain that the PRI is not a party; we consider it to be a placement agency that does outreach work at election time. It is not a party, because a party gambles its fortune at election time, so to speak. The PRI does not do this, because it uses government monies; it doesn't jeopardize its own funds. This is why it is not a party but a mere government agency. When we compete with them in a given election, we don't compete against another party, we compete against the government. The government is supported by the police, the army; it has plenty of money; it enjoys the support of the media, the legal system; and it relies on repression. It would be an easy thing for us to compete against another political party. Instead, we are obligated to compete against the government and its pressure to distort election results. This is a very serious matter.

CBG: How does presidentialism control the party system? Give us some examples.

PEMB: There is a subsidy for political parties. We in the PAN do not accept it, because it is not a budgetary outlay distributed by mathematical formula. Political parties in the United States enjoy access to a subsidy, but this subsidy is not based on the whim of the president or the secretary of state. The same thing occurs in Spain, where subsidies are given to political parties based on the most recent election results. This means that an arithmetical mechanism is used to determine how much is to be given to each party without having to negotiate with the government all of the time. A political party account does not exist openly in Mexico. The fund is kept secret, and the amounts allotted are negotiated between the government and the political parties.

We in the PAN do not wish to take part in this kind of game, nor do we wish to negotiate with the government on this. We do not wish to receive anything from the government, because we don't want conditions placed on our behavior nor on the tone of what we say nor on the posture we take with the government.

CBG: Is there another party that does the same?

PEMB: There is no other party that takes our position. All of them accept the subsidy. We wish total independence so we can depend solely on the Mexican people and on no one else.

CBG: You ran for the office of the president, and it is entirely possible your party may someday win. Would you folks not use the subsidy system?

PEMB: If we did, it would have to be an open procedure. We would do things the way the Germans, the Spaniards, the Canadians, or the Americans do, where the subsidies are part of the budget and are based on a mathematical formula. It certainly would never be based on the whim of the government secretary, especially when he is already negotiating with the political parties. We believe that the subsidy concept is a good one, because [in it] importance is not restricted to the party enjoying the greatest resources. The subsidy guarantees that all parties receive official support in proportion to their electoral weight. However, allocation of this sort must be free of political pressures from those in power.

CBG: Isn't it possible to argue that the situation may really be an attempt at encouraging democracy? Otherwise, how would the PST or the PRT keep going?

PEMB: If these resources are given proportionally according to [the parties'] strength, then fine! On the other hand, if they're given disproportionately, then what you have is a negotiation, and this is what happens today. Right now tiny parties exist that don't earn many votes;

sometimes those votes are inflated just to keep them going. They don't win anything, yet they receive positions in the Chamber of Deputies. I'm talking about the PST, the PARM, and the PPS. They've haven't won anything at all, yet they're given positions in congress to continue. This is how you create satellite parties that vote with the government, at critical times especially. The government can in this way claim that it enjoys "the support of opposition parties," which are really not in opposition.

Presidentialism is also felt when candidates are designated. The president decides who becomes a candidate. Fifteen days before a convention gathers to elect official party candidates, people know who the triumphant ones are going to be. This cannot lead to an election. This represents centralized decision making.

CBG: Does this not reflect the rank and file of the party, somehow?

PEMB: The party base is not consulted. It is not a democratic process; it is an autocratic one. There is no monitoring; in other words, no balloting. Instead, the president simply says: "I've taken everybody into account." He might have but then again might not have. No one knows what the procedure is for sure.

CBG: You're familiar with the civil service system in the United States where a bureaucrat enters public service and works without the fear—

PEMB: —of losing his job, if he doesn't belong to the president's party.

CBG: Is there something like this in Mexico?

PEMB: Everything to the contrary.

CBG: Does your party support something of the sort?

PEMB: We believe that the right of the public servant to his job should be independent of his political affiliation. We believe that, when a public servant is threatened with job loss because he belongs to a party that is not the official party, his constitutional right to liberty is under assault. His human rights as a public servant are being violated. We have said this many times; our position on this is part of the public record.

CBG: What is your opinion of the role of the Left in Mexico [prior to the 1988 election]?

PEMB: First of all, the Left is represented by various parties. Some of them, like the PSUM, the PMT, and the

PRT, are authentic leftists. Others, like the PPS and the PST, are not.

I believe that the role of leftist parties in the life of a nation enjoys a certain purpose. It gives people who believe that Marxism is a serious option the opportunity to speak and vote on its behalf. I've always told them that, God forbid, the day the country "went Marxist," the first thing they would do is to eliminate all political parties, because there isn't a single country governed by Marxists where political parties are allowed. Dissent is snuffed out, and I, of course, don't wish this on my country. I do believe, however, that they ought to campaign and express their viewpoint and let the people decide. The people's response to Marxist parties, to this day, has been minimal. The Marxists have not been able to persuade the people of Mexico because the people aspire toward liberty. We are fighting an oligarchical dictatorship, and we don't want to fall into the dictatorship of a system practiced in other countries.

CBG: The Mexican Left is very atomized.

PEMB: That's right.

CBG: Can you offer an explanation?

PEMB: The Left is atomized because its supporters see it in many ways. Some of them are Maoists, others are Trotskyites, others Marxists, still others Castroites, and so on. Each person lends it his or her own slant. Moreover, it is in the government's interest that many of these parties exist because it can merely point to the existence of nine parties in Mexico and boast to the world that democracy thrives here. The atomization of parties makes sense this way. When a critical moment comes up, say in a meeting of the Federal Election Committee, the parties we refer to as "satellite parties" cast their vote in the manner they are instructed, and atomization thus makes a lot of sense to the PRI members of that committee.

CBG: Can you identify the satellite parties of the Left?

PEMB: The PPS and the PST, not mentioning the PARM, which is not of the Left.

CBG: Isn't the PMT a Marxist party?

PEMB: They say they're not, but certain statements in their platform belong to a collectivist-totalitarian genre. For example, on the subject of education, they say the government enjoys the right to impose its own educational principles. This is a Marxist way of doing things, even though

they don't say it outright. PMT leaders speak about the need
of the state to intervene in the economy. This is not liberty,
because they give a lot of strength to the government. We
believe the government should serve society instead of society serving the government. Their belief is based on
Marxism in many ways.

CBG: Speaking about Marxist parties, I noticed that the
PRT recently expressed its support to give priests the right
to vote. I've also heard this from former Communist Party
members. Your party is criticized as a "confessional party."
How does it view the idea of giving a priest the right to
vote?

PEMB: We believe that a priest, and the church in
broader terms, should not participate in political campaigning. At the same time, however, we consider that a priest, as
a person and as a Mexican, enjoys the rights of a citizen
and should not be denied these rights simply because he is a
priest. We believe this is a contradiction and a human rights
violation, too, because we should all be free to choose whatever activity we see fit as long as it is licit. Our constitution
says so. Why is it, then, that, when a young man decides to
study for a licit activity like the priesthood, he ceases to be a
citizen? A contradiction exists, and we propose that it be
corrected. Let the priest vote, let him talk politics as long as
he doesn't do it from the pulpit, because the church must
serve everyone. It would be incorrect to employ the church
and its pulpit to campaign for the benefit of a party, no matter which party.

CBG: You know perhaps better than anyone else in
Mexico that the PAN is accused of acting as a front for the
interests of the clergy. Please comment on this and tell us
something too about the Opus Dei, because I've heard people
talk about its influence within the party.

PEMB: Broadly speaking, we respect the church. The
church, however, does not have anything to do with the
PAN. We represent a political party, and the way we make
decisions does not involve consultation with any religious
organization. As party leaders, we know that a majority of
the PAN members are Catholic, and I don't doubt it, because
the majority of Mexicans also happens to be Catholic too. If
we consider ourselves as representing a cross section of the
Mexican people, then it's logical that a majority of our members will be Catholics, because the majority of the Mexicans

are Catholics. Our membership applications do not have fill-in blanks about religious affiliation. We do not ask anybody what religion they belong to. We feel it's their right not to mention it.

Regarding the participation of the Opus Dei in our affairs, I will say the following. The Opus Dei is a church organization that enjoys influence in governmental affairs, according to many newspaper commentaries. These commentaries also suggest that important government officials belong to the Opus Dei. I do not know who these officials might be, and I cannot confirm these commentaries, nor can I deny them, because I just do not know enough about it.

CBG: So the Opus Dei does not enjoy any interference in your party?

PEMB: Absolutely none. Of this I'm certain. We do not depend on any religious organization; we do not receive orders from them, nor do we give them orders of any kind. We respect them because everybody has the right to worship God in accordance to their conscience. We do not mix religion with politics.

CBG: I'd like to go on to economic matters. Mexico suffers from high inflation rates. What is the PAN's policy on inflation?

PEMB: One of the biggest problems that we have in Mexico right now is inflation. It has become a tax which is paid by the poor, who already suffer from misery and starvation. We believe that a frontal assault ought to be waged against inflation. However, to attack the root of this problem, you have to take care of something which is elementary: the lack of trust or confidence. In Mexico the root cause of inflation is the lack of trust. The people do not trust the government. This is why we say that the first step to take is to win back the people's confidence and trust. In other words, begin by affirming the need to respect the people's vote. I can't ask for the people's confidence if I assault their will. I've told President de la Madrid that more important than the foreign debt is the fact that the people do not trust what the government does; inflation cannot be resolved as long as this situation continues.

CBG: This means that business does not invest?

PEMB: If there is no trust, there is no investment. If there is no investment, jobs are not created, taxes are not paid, and there is no production of goods and services. If there is no trust, there are no savings; and, if you have no savings, you don't have the necessary elements to make the economy develop. This is why we say that we need a climate of trust, so that the person who has money and is looking ahead may invest it rather than spend it; the person who has an idea about producing something new may invest into it in order to create a good or a service. Right now we lack hope and trust.

CBG: Anyone who visits Mexico, however, will agree that, despite what you say, production still goes on. There is a capitalist class in Mexico that collaborates with the government. The members of CANACINTRA [Cámara Nacional de la Industria de Transformación] recently elected an "official" candidate who is also a member of an industrial clan, and he and many others are willing to work with the government. Put the two ideas together.

PEMB: It is true that, despite what I have just said, we can look around and find a functioning industrial sector. The investments have already been made, and production is going on; employees are working; debts are held; markets exist; buying and selling goes on right now. Anyone can see this by looking out their window.

I'm talking about new investments. The investments that already exist do not increase the number of employees, and so the problems of the country continue. Don't forget that we have a million young people who reach working age each year, and they need jobs. A million jobs have to be created, and we don't want unemployment to go up. This is what I'm referring to. There are people in industry and business who support the government, of course. We don't believe we enjoy a monopoly on the people's support.

CBG: Does the PAN receive support from a majority of Mexican businesspeople?

PEMB: I don't believe we have majority support from the business sector. I believe that a large proportion of the business class, especially big-business people, find themselves tied to the government.

CBG: What do you mean by "big"?

PEMB: By big I mean PROTEXA, Galletera Mexicana, S.A., or Gamesa, Alfa, Visa, Conductores de Monterrey—all of those groups who sell to the government mostly. They depend on the credit the government makes available to them through the nationalized, or what I call governmentized, banking system. Credit is government controlled. Demand is controlled by the government—decentralized or state-owned firms alone represent 70 percent of the market. This is why I say that the government wields a club with which it keeps big-business people in control. By conviction or by convenience, they are tied to the government.

CBG: What type of businessperson supports your party?

PEMB: The small- and medium-sized-business person. Of course, we also get support from the small farmer, the worker, the housewife, the teacher, the self-employed professional, the manager.

CBG: Generally speaking, however, big-business people do not support the party?

PEMB: They're very vulnerable. They can't express themselves openly, because they can be threatened. And the threats can be carried out too.

CBG: About three months ago, I read a commentary about a member of the Garza Sada family. Do you remember the incident?

PEMB: One of the Sada clan[4] was pressured this way. He belonged to the Vitro group, whose employees were threatened against participating in politics. This kind of situation really constitutes a very serious matter because whoever does it is violating an individual's human rights. The United Nations Charter of Human Rights states that we all have the right to participate in the political life of the country. So, if the most powerful person in an enterprise says: "No one can do such and such a thing, and, if someone does it, I'll fire him," certain rights are being violated.

CBG: Why do you think the young businessperson in question suddenly decided to act more cautiously?

PEMB: If the government threatens you, and you become scared, you would become cautious too. I believe that freedom begins when a person begins to lose his fear. Where fear exists, there can be no freedom.

CBG: How would your party handle the economic crisis which is now hitting Mexico so hard if it were—

PEMB: In power? In the first place, we would not have fallen into the enormous trap of mortgaging the country by accepting credit the way those who were managing public affairs did. Let me refresh your mind about certain statistics. In January 1970 our foreign debt stood at $3.2 billion. President Echeverría multiplied our debt to $21 billion by

1976, and López Portillo to U.S. $85 billion by 1982. We asked for too much credit; that's where the problem lies. A portion of the loans went for corrupt purposes, another portion to unbridled expenses, and another into investments that were no good and ended up in failure. *Paraestatales* [state-owned industries] were multiplied too. We believe government penetration in the economy of this kind is negative. The government ought to take part in strategic areas that are vital to the country, but not in everything!

CBG: As *panistas,* then, you accept the existence of *paraestatales* as necessary?

PEMB: Only some. In other countries, oil is in the control of private hands. We believe that, because of the condition Mexico is in right now, the nation itself ought to be the owner of its oil reserves. It would be a mistake to hand them to other countries. This, then, ought to continue unchanged. In secondary petrochemical industries, however, there is no reason why the government ought to enjoy a monopoly. It should control the primary source but not the secondary. Industries based on petroleum ought to be open to those who can do something with them.

CBG: Isn't that a socialist notion and therefore contradictory to party principles?

PEMB: No, because socialism says that all industries ought to be in the hands of the state, along with all other goods and services. We say that a majority ought to be in private hands, and only a minimum ought to be in the hands of the state. The strategic ones should go to the state.

CBG: I think the requirements of the 1917 constitution have a lot to do with what you're saying—it demands this type of control.

PEMB: Don't forget that the constitution has been amended 330 times. It's like a patched balloon. To refer to the one written in 1917 is very different from referring to the one we have now. We believe that more amendments are necessary in the field of education, for example. The bottom line is that we believe there ought to be full freedom.

CBG: You would maintain *paraestatales* in strategic areas?

PEMB: Our policy is to maintain only what is strategic and vital. In other areas we would offer freedom of enterprise, and we would help stimulate investment.

CBG: The government also uses the word "strategic" when justifying its *paraestatal* policy, but it's gone beyond.

PEMB: If you study the matter, you'll learn that thousands of these industries exist, of which maybe a dozen may be defined as strategic. The rest have no reason to be labeled as such.

CBG: Carlos Tello, a well-known Mexican economist, recently stated that "the main problem with *paraestatales* is that they are not run as integrated industries. For this reason, the state ought to intervene in order to run them as 'harmonic' units so that they can thus support each other."[5]

PEMB: The idea you attribute to him agrees with other economic perspectives of his. Both his manner of speaking and his actions are not easy to understand. When the banking system was nationalized or, as I term it, governmentalized in 1982, Carlos Tello enjoyed a very important role in the process. He instituted the exchange controls that led to the nationalization of the banks. It turned out to be a national disaster. What stood for an exchange rate of 27 pesos to a dollar in February 1982 ought to have been 35 in order to prevent the peso from being overvalued. The actions of López Portillo, with Mr. Tello at his side, precipitated so much distrust that the exchange rate is now 500 pesos to the dollar. That's what Mr. Tello's theories produce. He's a convinced socialist. He believes in socialism. This is why he advocates efficiency for state enterprises. He wants an efficient socialism. State-owned industries can't be efficient, because they lack incentive.

CBG: [Tello] accepts that a profit rationale cannot function in state-owned enterprises?

PEMB: Yes, and then he proceeds to look for some other incentive mode so that his theory might work: management groups that may be better supervised by the government somehow. No, no; it won't work, because the capital at risk doesn't belong to the officials in charge; it belongs to the government! So, if you go into the red, all you do is ask the government to subsidize you. That's where the problem lies. There's no incentive. Moreover, if the officials of these parastate enterprises proceed as they normally do, by hiring only people who are recommended to them by influential people or by hiring their own friends, then what you've done is create a cult to mediocrity.

The situation is not a healthy one. State-owned industries have not succeeded anywhere in the world. This is why we believe that a large part of these enterprises ought to be

sold, giving preference, if so wished, to workers, who could
have the option to buy them. If not, then sell them to somebody else. Part of our platform advocates worker coowner-
ship. It's a good idea. This has been tried in the United
States, for example. Eastern Airlines employees (pilots and
stewardesses) control 25 percent of the company; they'll take
care of their enterprise. But not the government! This is
what we believe.

CBG: I suppose you folks do not favor a moratorium on
Mexico's foreign debt?

PEMB: Define what you mean.

CBG: I believe it was defined, to an extent, in President
de la Madrid's speech of February 21, 1986.[6]

PEMB: We do not favor a moratorium where you don't
pay what you owe. In contrast, the Left says: "Don't pay."
We say: "Debts entered into must be paid." To do otherwise
would destroy our national credibility. Mexico must continue
to promote progress; it has to keep on buying and selling.
This is why we can't think about a moratorium with
impunity, believing that no consequences will follow. The
Left's position on this is that nothing will happen as a result
of a moratorium, and we believe this is wishful thinking.
We agree, however, that things are pretty bad right now
with oil prices down.

In order to earn foreign exchange to pay what we owe,
and while oil prices recuperate, we need some time to reactivate the products we sell abroad, along with our industries and services. Given the oil reserve situation around
the world, we believe oil prices will go up in about two years
or so. This will give us some breathing space at that time,
but we should not depend exclusively on oil to pay our foreign debt. We should export other goods and services.
However, this can't be done overnight. We need time to
develop our capacity to export so that we can pay what we
owe. We believe that what we owe we ought to pay. If
responsibility rests on the international bankers, who
offered credit to Mexican officials in the absurd way they
did, all we ask for is the lowest interest rates possible. I
insist that the lenders share responsibility in this too.

CBG: I suppose debtors are at fault too, because the
president stated on February 25 that the economic crisis in
Mexico was not created by "revolutionary institutions" but
rather by mere excesses committed?

PEMB: This is a mere play on words, because the nation's institutions are directed by the same people who are governing Mexico right now, and that's where the responsibility lies. They've enjoyed absolute power for more than half a century. They can't share their responsibility with anybody else. Those who govern this country are completely responsible for the crisis we face right now. They can't share the responsibility when they've enjoyed all of the power.

CBG: With regard to the General Agreement on Tariffs and Trade [GATT], what kind of economic development does your party pursue and what kind of industrial policy?

PEMB: Our policy is to promote private investment as much as possible and help finance it in the most agile way. If you examine the matter, you'll learn that, in order to finance [the] deficit, all banking capital is controlled by the government, and this cuts off all possibilities for private development. This is an error. We believe that public expenditures ought to be reduced in order to save resources that can be placed in the hands of the people so that they can invest them in the creation of enterprises. This way, development occurs thanks to people's enterprise, not government enterprise.

CBG: Heberto Castillo, PMT president, has stated that foreign investments are going to convert Mexico into one giant *maquiladora* [foreign-owned assembly plant], where salaries will be the only way to earn anything along with some taxes. All profits will flow out of the country, and all that will remain in Mexico will be "second-class technology, junk," he says. This leads us to ask you about industrial policy. Is this what you want, a giant *maquiladora*?

PEMB: The premise is that all investment that comes to Mexico will be aimed at creating a giant *maquiladora,* and we don't agree with this. Remember that *maquiladora* is defined as the temporary importation of capital aimed at exporting finished goods. This is what you find in Ciudad Juárez on the border. But there's a purpose for this. Taiwan had *maquiladoras,* as did Korea. Now they have a solid industry with exporting capability, no longer a mere assembly system. This is why we believe the *maquiladora* policy has a purpose.

It can bring about the well-being that you find along the border, for example. Unemployment is unknown in Ciudad

Juárez. Why? Because a lot of *maquiladoras* offer jobs. We believe they offer a sense of justice too, because the salaries they pay out are important for society's well-being. Critics say that the only thing these businesses offer is salaries plus "a few taxes." We'd love to see the millions of undocumented Mexicans who live in the United States working here in Mexico just to earn their salaries. They go to the United States because they can't find work here.

We believe we must face the challenge of creating jobs for Mexico. Jobs will be created if Mexicans save their money by investing it here. Jobs will also be created by inviting foreigners with savings to invest here. This kind of arrangement doesn't only yield salaries, which in itself is a lot. It doesn't only yield jobs and positions which are valuable in themselves. It also leaves us technology and experience. If an electrical industry is developed, it leaves behind experience and technology. The ideal is that foreign investment will bring technology we don't already have, and that it will give us products for export, if possible. That's the ideal. If we're able to attract investment for export purposes, that's good for Mexico, in our eyes.

Japan, for example, has the opposite problem. It has a $50 billion surplus in trade with the United States. And they've achieved this through hard work and much struggle. The Americans are looking for ways to invest in Japan; but the problem is that the Japanese are now investing in the United States, and the Americans are becoming worried about this because it represents competition. But this process creates jobs, introduces technology, and pays taxes. We live in an interdependent world.

CBG: So the fact that *maquiladoras* are increasing in numbers is not a harmful situation? It has positive results.

PEMB: It isn't harmful. We ought to ask *maquiladora* workers what they think about this. They're the ones who are benefiting, and they contribute to the economy too. What would happen in Ciudad Juárez if all the *maquiladoras* were to be shut down? Or in Piedras Negras or Agua Prieta? It'd be a problem because the jobs and services would be lost; they represent something important.

CBG: I get the impression that President Miguel de la Madrid wants to amend legislation that places a 49 percent limit on the foreign ownership of Mexican firms. This has been discussed in congress recently. What is your view?

PEMB: The fact is that there are foreign investments that total 100 percent of a firm's capital. In other words, firms that are 100 percent foreign owned exist in Mexico. The Ford Motor Company, for example, is not limited to 49 percent.

CBG: So any amendment increasing the foreign proportion would not amount to much?

PEMB: The tendency ought to be toward joint ventures. They're a good thing because they enable Mexicans to invest their savings too, thereby producing a cooperative process that includes foreign capital and technology.

CBG: But if you take away the 49 percent limit, then the notion of joint ventures becomes more of a dead letter than ever.

PEMB: What I'm saying is that there are firms that are 100 percent foreign owned even with these regulations in effect. The whole thing has been specious in many ways, honored in the breach rather than in the observance. The tendency is always in that direction. Nonetheless, joint ventures are a good thing for a foreigner because an association with national investors provides insights into the home market and into our national reality. We believe that joint ventures will increase, because even foreign capital benefits from them too.

The Left talks about nationalizing or governmentalizing all of the industries: pharmaceuticals, the hotel industry, construction, et cetera. That's a Marxist point of view. We believe that the contrary is the best. The government ought to focus on strategic industries and not get involved in areas they have no expertise in. To do so otherwise is to invite disaster. That the Left considers the production of medicines a strategic area is not unusual either. Following that line of argument, then, the tortilla industry ought to be considered strategic too, because we can't live without tortillas. You can go to the extreme by including auto repair shops, because they're essential, as well as auto factories (what can you do without a car?). Everything is essential, because of the civilization we belong to. Shoe factories—what would we do without shoes! Wear huaraches? We believe that the government must use its budget to govern. To govern does not mean compete with the citizen. Rather, it means to look for the common good, but not to own the economy.

CBG: At the closing ceremonies of the 11th National Meeting of Local Legislators, held in Tijuana on February 15, 1986, President de la Madrid reportedly stated that "the sovereignty of the Mexican people cannot admit foreign intervention in our electoral processes as legitimate, not even as a mere tactic to win an election." Commentators like Francisco Cárdenas Cruz of *El Universal* wrote that the president's words were aimed at your party and the United States. What is your opinion?

PEMB: The Mexican government had been able to keep the world ignorant of what was happening here in Mexico for a long time. It had been able to monopolize information on this. You may recall that last year, Mr. [Manuel] Alonso, the president's information secretary, distributed an array of PRI documents written in English. This shows that they are vitally interested in what is said abroad about Mexico. Mexican government officials enjoyed a monopoly because the world depended on what the government said about Mexico. The world believed that democracy existed in Mexico, that human rights were respected, that the official party won all the time because it was very popular. It didn't know that repression existed here, along with the violation of the ballot box, riding roughshod over people, and so on.

In the PAN we don't depend on anyone. We don't seek support anywhere. We have simply taken the position that there will be no monopoly of information. This is why I'm talking to you who come from the United States right now. I answer your questions because you manifest an interest in what is happening in Mexico, and I give you my version about it. I don't do it because I seek the help of the United States. I do it because I consider it an honorable thing for the American people to become familiar with *panista* points of view. We have been the object of distortions and caricatures far too long. This is what we always do when we speak to reporters.

CBG: Is that what you think the president was referring to?

PEMB: I suppose so. I've always told him to speak clearly. If he is referring to us, he ought to call us by name. If there is something concrete he is accusing us of, he ought to state it clearly. I can't defend phantoms; I can't answer statements that are said in between the lines.

CBG: Along the same lines, Adolfo Lugo Verduzco, PRI president, stated March 6, 1986, that "the opposition in Mexico is reactionary. It takes advantage of the economic crisis in the country in order to break the law of the land, it tries to destabilize the country and it threatens democracy by raising the banner of democracy at the same time that it burns down city halls, it blocks vital highways" and so on.

PEMB: Yes, that's the image the official party tries to portray of us: burners of city halls. The fact is that they burn them and then place the blame on us. We believe in democracy, and we ask the leaders of the official party and the government to put it into practice. We ask them to count votes honestly. We ask for impartial courts. We ask them to remove the political monopoly they've established, that there be equal access to the media. It's easy to attack when you have the media at your fingertips. I also believe it's fine for Mr. Lugo Verduzco to say whatever he wants, but give us the opportunity to reply through the media. This is what we affirm.

Let me respond to two statements by the president of the National Placement Agency (that's my view of the official party). He speaks of reaction. Indeed, there is a reaction to their national misgovernance. To accept this misgovernance would be tantamount to utter conformity. To fight against it and the governmental system they've put together is to fight on behalf of the country.

They say they're worried about the economic crisis and that we are taking advantage of it. They should not think they're not going to pay when they've led the nation to disaster, when they've let the peso go from 25 to 500 for every dollar in four years, and when they've presided over a precipitous drop in the citizen's purchasing power. How can they avoid paying for what they've done? The government that shows its inability to govern must pay at the ballot box. This does not mean that opposition parties are taking advantage of the economic crisis. It means that those who misgovern must pay for their ineptitude on election day. This happens in France, the United States, England, Costa Rica, and anywhere else you have democratic elections. What the PRI president wants obviously is to go scot-free! He doesn't want the people to demand payment of a bill that is overdue. The *priistas* brought the country to ruin, and the people know this.

CBG: I see it as a bizarre identification of a party for a nation.

PEMB: The official party? Yes, they try to identify themselves with the nation. They'd like to say: "We are the nation, and whoever attacks us attacks Mexico!" This is a

false posture. We love Mexico! We fight for Mexico! Mexico is
our country! They are not our country! They are a party
made up of inept and corrupt individuals, and we are fighting to remove them from government office!

CBG: Drug trafficking has become a major problem in the
relations between the United States and Mexico. You also
know, as everybody else does here in Mexico, that some ugly
scenes, including assassination, have taken place in the city of
Culiacán and other cities too in connection with this trafficking. How do you think the Mexican government is responding
to this problem, and what is the PAN's policy on it?

PEMB: Drug trafficking is a grave problem. We think it
is a cancer for the nation. People say that all kinds of
narcotics are sold in the United States, beginning with marijuana and so on. History reveals that a country that produces drugs ends up consuming them. Even if we didn't face
the specter of drug consumption at home, the idea that we're
exporting drugs abroad and thereby undermining family
life—in the United States, for example—is hard to accept. It
becomes a heavy responsibility for us. We concur that a concerted effort needs to be made to end drug production of the
type that eventually winds up in the United States.

We are conscious too, however, that the supply is merely
meeting the demand. In other words, the problem is not only
Mexico's; it is also the United States'. It has to be attacked
from both ends. A close cooperation should exist between
the two countries to stop drug production and trade. We
think this problem should be resolved because violence is
beginning to appear in our Pacific coast communities where
production takes place.

We do not think the current effort to stop drugs is
enough, even though there is much talk about it. Evidence
suggests drug trafficking has received a certain amount of
political protection because there is a lot of money to be had
in connection with drugs. We need to provide alternate crops
to those who grow the drugs. You can't simply prohibit production and let the producers die of hunger! We have an
educational problem on our hands, but it is also a social
problem, as well as one of communication and trust. All of it
has to be resolved together. It's not just a matter of destroy-
ing plants; you have to get to the bottom of the problem.

CBG: Do you think that drug trafficking is undermining
political institutions at the local and state level?

PEMB: It has affected them a lot. There are examples of corruption that have already taken place, and this becomes a very delicate issue. Once social structures deteriorate, it becomes very difficult to resolve the problem.

CBG: Does the PAN have a position different from the official party regarding the armed forces?

PEMB: In some ways we do. The armed forces are indoctrinated to defend the president of the republic [and] its institutions, including the official party. This has been the image in the past. We believe the armed forces ought to serve the nation's institutions but not necessarily the people in those institutions. In other words, the armed forces should defend our democratic institutions and not the people who are occupying government positions that may not rightfully belong to them. The army should never again be used to protect electoral fraud, because to do so tarnishes its image before the people. Unfortunately, this has happened in the past. The book I've given you[7] contains an account of a relevant experience I once had. I think it's important to conclude with this.

CBG: Will you allow me one additional question? Foreign relations—it's very important?

PEMB: We believe that a restrengthening of Ibero-American unity needs to take place. We enjoy membership in a community of language, customs, and traditions even though we are dispersed geographically. There is much that can be attained with other Ibero-American countries through reciprocal support. We strongly believe in this unifying Ibero-American concept. Naturally, too, we believe that the Central American countries ought to find peace. Having been on a war footing for so many years, as in the case of El Salvador, has been very painful. We must think that it's time to live in peace. Our party gives due consideration to the fact that Mexico has recommended the democratization of the region through the Contadora process in order to stop the violence.

However, we believe that, in the words of José Vasconcelos, the Mexican government may be likened to someone who is a "vegetarian abroad but a carnivore at home." It does not do what it recommends to others. We believe that democracy will bring an end to the violence in Central America. We also believe that democracy will help avoid violence in Mexico. This is why we consider it urgent for Mexican institutions to become democratized.

We further believe that a democratizing current is pushing its way up from Argentina, Brazil, Ecuador, Jamaica,
even Central America, as in the case of Honduras,
Guatemala, and El Salvador (without mentioning the countries that had already achieved democracy like Costa Rica
and Venezuela). We hope this current will continue all the
way to Mexico.

CBG: Does the PAN agree with the Reagan policy of giving support to the contras, who are presently fighting on
the Honduran-Nicaraguan border against the Sandinista
government?

PEMB: The external support of a rebel group is a very
delicate situation for us because it constitutes interference
in the internal affairs of another country. It appears to us
that the Salvadoran contras in El Salvador (the rebels fighting against President [José Napoleón] Duarte's administration) are receiving external aid too. Practicing this kind of
policy simply makes problems last longer. This is why I say
that an effort ought to be made to introduce democracy,
structurally speaking. This is something Mexico ought to
contribute to and support by setting an example. Mexico's
word takes on a hollow ring if we recommend something
there and do not practice it here.

CBG: Do you think Nicaragua is introducing democracy,
structurally speaking?

PEMB: Unfortunately, I don't think so. There ought to be
a way of convincing the Sandinista government to step in
the direction of democracy, although there's always the
chance we might not be able to succeed. Whatever the outcome, if Mexico is going to talk about democracy, it ought to
practice it too.

CBG: Beyond looking for better relations, what does the
PAN seek from the United States that the PRI does not?

PEMB: The government of the United States has supported Mexico in a systematic fashion. The Mexican government has received support from the United States in all of
its critical moments. Let me refer to two of these in the past.

Vice President Henry A. Wallace visited Mexico in 1940,
when the Almazán campaign to which I've referred was still
going on [a fraud was committed to cover up Almazán's vic-
tory]. Nonetheless, Wallace came and toured the country at
the side of outgoing President Lázaro Cárdenas, and he said

nothing. In effect, his trip announced to the whole world that the U.S. government supported the fraud that had taken place. And, in the 1982 presidential elections, I received the honor of being nominated as my party's candidate. On election day and before the first electoral results were made public, the U.S. secretary of state was already congratulating Miguel de la Madrid for his victory.

What we ask of the North Americans is respect. We wish to be good neighbors and enjoy a relationship based on our independence. We don't want to be subordinate to anyone, but we do want to be friends. I don't think it is in the best interests of the United States to keep on having a group of subordinates here who stay in power by resorting to brute force. We think that a real process of democratization ought to be in the best interests of the United States. But don't come and intervene here in order to help achieve it! Don't give blind support as in the past either. That's mostly what we ask.

CBG: Does the PAN advocate anything specifically regarding the "undocumented" Mexicans in the United States?

PEMB: Yes, of course. We believe they are our problem! They go to the United States because they can't find work here, unfortunately. It is our problem, and we know we must resolve it. We also know, however, that the United States creates a demand for Mexican labor, and we acknowledge this demand as reasonable, because we believe the United States has a genuine need for [the labor]. What we ask for is a procedure that would make it possible to allow migratory workers to go there legally and then return. If something like this could be worked out, it would be beneficial for both sides.

Notes

1. The interview was held March 6, 1986, in the offices of the PAN's National Executive Committee, Mexico City.

2. *Unomasuno*, February 27, 1986.

3. Madero is undoubtedly referring to Alvaro Obregón, who was assassinated in 1928.

4. Rogelio Sada Zambrano, Vitro general director, was fired from his job allegedly because he openly supported the *panista*

mayoral candidate for Monterrey. See *La Jornada,* December 14, 1985.

5. Ibid., February 24, 1986.

6. President Miguel de la Madrid gave a speech on February 21, 1986, that was heralded as a change of policy. For example, the next day *La Jornada* headlined an article: "Ajuste de la Deuda Externa a la Capacidad Real de Pago: MMH."

7. Pablo Emilio Madero, *500 horas de hielo* (Mexico City: n.p., 1985).

The Center

CHAPTER 6

Cuauhtémoc Cárdenas Solórzano

Cuauhtémoc Cárdenas Solórzano is the son of Lázaro Cárdenas, Mexico's most revolutionary president. This fact alone helped propel him into national and international prominence once he had separated from the PRI in 1987. Ironically, he felt obligated to leave a party his own father had helped strengthen. He discusses this seeming contradiction here.

Like many other student leaders of his generation, Cuauhtémoc Cárdenas first demonstrated his progressive spirit when he took part in public activities condemning the U.S. role in Guatemala in 1954. He trained as a civil engineer and received his degree in 1957 from the UNAM. He spent most of his nonpolitical years working in the technical field; in the early 1970s he began pursuing reforms within the PRI. He was elected senator for Michoacán and finally governor of his father's home state in 1980. In 1988 he led the most powerful political movement ever to compete with the PRI for the direction of the nation's future.

CBG: Tell us when and where you were born and offer us some information about your family.[1]

CCS: I was born on May 1, 1934, here in Mexico City. My father was General Lázaro Cárdenas and my mother Amalia Solórzano.

CBG: Everyone knows about your father. Can you tell us something about what he might have represented in your life in terms of a role model?

CCS: Besides his being my father and our having a very close relationship (he was a friend, too), I believe that the ideas and principles for which he fought are still valid today. They continue to point out the way the nation's biggest problems

ought to be resolved. My pride in being the son of Lázaro
Cárdenas runs deeply within me; I identify with his work and
his ideas. I try to put them into practice, even though I am
totally aware that we live in a Mexico that is different from
the one in which he lived. However, his ideas, principles, and
objectives continue to be valid as we try to improve the political, social, and economic organization of the country.

CBG: So you accept that these are different times, but
you believe nonetheless that it's possible to maintain your
father's ideas as long as they are adapted?

CCS: This may be done within a wider framework of
thought. In other words, this may be done using the same
sources, which is what happens with other great ideological
movements.

CBG: Is there a difference between what Lázaro
Cárdenas represents to you and what he might represent to
the Mexican people?

CCS: I don't think there is a difference between what he
means to me, aside from the fact that I am his son, and
what he means to the Mexican people.

CBG: Tell us something about your political career.
When did it begin? What steps did it take?

CCS: I took my first political steps as a university student.

CBG: Tell us about your education.

CCS: I graduated as a civil engineer from the UNAM. I
attended what was known as the National Engineering
School from 1951 to 1955, and I graduated in 1957. I did
some further study outside of the country, mostly in the
form of visits I made to different projects connected with
regional urban development, my specialty. This took me to
France, Germany, and Italy.

I took part in university politics, especially when a student movement arose protesting U.S. intervention in
Guatemala in 1954.[2] Later, I participated in the National
Movement for Liberation born out of the Latin American
Conference on National Sovereignty, Peace, and Economic
Emancipation. This conference took place in March 1961,
and I became a member of its Executive Committee from
1961 to 1962. I then stepped down and simply served as a
member until 1964, when it finally disappeared.

CBG: When did you join the party?

CCS: I joined the PRI in 1967 when the CNC, the
Confederación Nacional de Campesinos, invited me to take

part in its Technical Advisory Committee; I served as president of this committee for about a year. During the 1970 presidential campaign, I became a part of the party's IEPES [Instituto de Estudios Políticos, Económicos y Sociales].

In 1973–74, I became a precandidate and thus took part in an intraparty campaign to become PRI candidate for the post of governor of Michoacán. The president and high-level party officials had promised the democratic selection of a candidate for that post, so I stepped forward as a precandidate. Despite promises to the contrary, undemocratic procedures were followed which I publicly denounced; I did not get the party's nomination either. I continued on as a member of the party, nonetheless. In 1976, I became the PRI candidate for the senate, representing the state of Michoacán. I campaigned for that position, and on September 1 of that year, I became a member of the senate. Shortly after I took the senatorial oath, President López Portillo invited me to serve in his Ministry of Agriculture as subsecretary for forestry and wildlife, so I took leave of my senate duties. I served in that capacity for a little more than three years, at which time I was chosen to serve as the party's candidate for the governorship of Michoacán, at the beginning of 1980. And I served as governor of Michoacán from 1980 to 1986 (my term ended on September 15). The rise of the Corriente Democrática, around August of 1986, coincided with the last days of my governorship.

CBG: You stated that you had become a precandidate for the governorship of Michoacán and that you were backed by a—

CCS: I was backed by an important group of people within the PRI.

CBG: Can you tell us more about this? Was it something similar to the Corriente Democrática?

CCS: One could say that it was an independent movement that offered to support my candidacy. I accepted the challenge of seeking the candidacy [within the party]. As I said, the PRI and the president had promised a democratic contest within the party; we did our best to make this a reality. This didn't happen, and so I denounced this fact, but we continued to function within the party.

CBG: I asked you this question because I'm interested to know when you began your dissent with the party.

CCS: I have had a critical posture ever since I joined the party. My entry into the party was a result of a conscious sense of responsibility aimed at helping transform the country. I can also tell you that, from 1969 to 1974, I served as assistant director of the Lázaro Cárdenas-Las Truchas Steel Mill. Moreover, from 1971 to 1976, I also served as trust manager of the mill's community, named after my father, where I oversaw the region's urban and economic development. Those were the technical duties I had at the time.

CBG: The question that comes to my mind, *ingeniero*, is the following: Your father is famous in most of the history books because he molded the party into its present form. This is to say that it was founded [corporatively] on labor, peasant, and middle-class [constituencies]. The PRI is severely criticized today because of these overly centralized foundations.

CCS: The official party, especially the PRI version, which began in 1945, represents a party which is radically different from the party that developed during my father's term of office. Don't forget that the party transformed itself from the PNR to the PMR in 1938. If you compare the PMR's Declaration of Principles with the PRI's, even in 1945, along with later modifications of those principles, you will see for yourself that the PRI is radically different [from the PMR]. There's a difference between the democracy that was practiced during my father's administration, in the selection of party candidates and in the participation of the lower party ranks in party decisions, and the authoritarianism which I believe has reached its peak during the present administration.

CBG: You maintain, then, that the party's authoritarianism has grown since 1940, more or less?

CCS: That is what I affirm; that's the way I see things.

CBG: Would you describe the democratic method you claim existed within the party? I suppose too that this is what you folks wish to see anew within the party.

CCS: May I remind you that we are now out of the party.

CBG: Yes, of course.

CCS: During my father's administration, internal plebiscites were organized for the purpose of selecting party candidates for the senate or the Chamber of Deputies. There was interplay between the precandidates within the party itself; this provided for the selection of party candidates for state governorships too. This interplay ceased to exist later, and it simply does not exist now.

CBG: Regarding your term as governor of Michoacán, can you identify both positive and negative aspects about it?

CCS: My term of office went from 1980 to 1986. The beginning of my administration coincided with the start of the economic crisis which is still affecting us. It began in earnest in 1982, López Portillo's last year in office, bringing with it the reduction of state budgets, irregular funding, and the limitation of many programs.

Nevertheless, the most important achievement connected with my administrative term was the constant communication I was able to have with everyone in the state. I was able to travel throughout the state, over and above the campaign trips I made. I believe I was able to visit perhaps as many as 800 communities in the 113 *municipios* as a result of the three rounds that I gave to the state during my term, because I considered it very important to talk to the people. I thus came to know the problems they were facing and the development programs that were being carried out in their areas and how these were turning out. This kind of contact with the state, its territory, and its people allowed me to adjust certain projects and thus help resolve key problems in the state. A lot of people helped me get certain projects finished; given the economic limitations, a lot of small projects were finished this way. This permitted us to do more than the restricted budgets allowed.

In another area, with the aid of the state congress, we passed specific legislation, initiated by the executive branch, designed to make life better in Michoacán. For example, we modified the penal code in order to penalize prostitution. With this measure we wiped out this practice throughout the state and thus reduced the crimes of passion normally connected with it. State permits were denied to people wanting to hold cockfights, because they represented an activity that not only encouraged betting but also encouraged acts of violence. I also consider the state ownership of public transportation an accomplishment, something that we encouraged in the capital city of Morelia. We also passed laws on rent control and legislation that opened up and democratized the university.

CBG: In asking you about your governorship, I was trying to catch an essence about it. What do you think that would be?

CCS: In public works it would be the opening up of roads into many corners of the state, although we didn't do all we wanted to, because of budgetary limitations. We tried to coordinate certain projects with the federal government, but it too was unable to help us.

CBG: You were born in Mexico City?

CCS: I was born in Mexico City, but I am nonetheless a citizen of the state of Michoacán because its constitution affords state citizenship to all children of *michoacanos* no matter where they are born in Mexico. This is one of the reasons why I have always maintained links with the people of Michoacán, but also because both my parents were *michoacanos*. I went to school there too (I finished high school at the Colegio San Nicolás), and I worked professionally there too, as I've already stated. I resided in the state from 1964 to 1969, overseeing the construction of the José María Morelos Dam over the Balsas River in Melchor Ocampo, now renamed Lázaro Cárdenas, Michoacán. I also worked at Las Truchas, and this kept me in touch with affairs in the state between 1969 and 1976. I spent part, if not most, of my time there. I then joined the senate and thus [continued to] develop strong political ties with the state.

CBG: Your father, if I recall correctly, enjoyed a very influential role within the state even after he served as governor. Am I right?

CCS: He came to represent the moral force of the state, yet he never employed his influence on behalf of himself, nor his friends.

CBG: But he was influential!

CCS: His influence was ideological. I would say he came to embody the revolutionary conscience of Mexico.

CBG: I meant in Michoacán.

CCS: His presence was important in Michoacán, but I can assure you he never intervened in electoral issues nor in appointing public officials, once he finished his term of office.

CBG: Even though you're not governor of Michoacán, do you still enjoy a certain influence there? Do people consult with you about state matters?

CCS: No, absolutely not. I feel very close to the people there, but that is all.

CBG: I note that your successor, Governor Luis Martínez Villicaña, has taken on the role as your archdetractor with enthusiasm. It seems so strange to me! Can you explain his role?

CCS: All I can say here is that we occupy opposing political positions.

CBG: But there are others who occupy similar positions, and they don't treat you the same way!

CCS: Well, all I can say is that everybody has their own personal style of doing things. We have a different view of how we can serve the people of Michoacán and how to serve as public servants.

CBG: You might appreciate that there are a lot of people like me trying to understand what is going on here, and it all seems—

CCS: I think personal differences enter into this equation too, but I don't feel I ought to discuss them.

CBG: I reached the point of suspecting that perhaps the present federal administration might have assigned him as your hatchet man.

CCS: It's quite possible, but I don't have evidence to back it up. I insist that we hold opposing political and personal views as well as contrasting visions of what we ought to be.

CBG: Can you explain how your critical posture developed, step by step, to the point you decided to separate yourself from the party?

CCS: The Corriente Democratizadora [another name for the Corriente Democrática] began by calling for some fundamental changes in the government's economic policies, including a different way of handling the foreign debt problem: employing resources to raise employment levels and thus reactivate the economy. We came to believe that, in order to bring about these changes and thus come to the aid of the people, the politics of the nation had to be democratized. We thus concluded that the party itself needed to become the instrument for the political reorientation of the state. We believe that, among the ways in which this democratization could take place within the party was to insist that it honor its own statutes and its own Declaration of Principles. We also believed this needed to be reflected in the most important decisions the party had to make: the selection of a candidate to the nation's presidency. We asked the party president to insist upon this. In a more public way, we requested this of other party members too when we participated in open party meetings and in private discussions.

CBG: What are you referring to, specifically?

CCS: The party statutes, for example, call for an invitation to a meeting that is supposed to lay down the rules for a national convention aimed at designating the official candidate. We requested that this invitation be made with ample time to do what the statutes themselves call for: the internal campaigns to gain rank-and-file support and thus arrive, through democratically elected delegates, at a common candidate at the convention itself.

CBG: This preceded the "uncovering" of the six precandidates?

CCS: Of course. We requested this in August 1986, a full year before the six precandidates were announced.

CBG: All of you were aware that this succession was coming up in 1989?

CCS: We were conscious that the gravity of the nation demanded the democratization of the country and that democratizing the party was a way to begin. Our proposals fell on deaf ears. The invitation was not made. In the course of the 13th Party Congress, held in March 1987, we were bitterly criticized. I would say that, from that moment on, the Corriente grew even as we strongly rejected the party's authoritarianism. We broke relations with the party and devoted our efforts to strengthening our movement throughout the country at the same time that we continued to demand a call for a national convention and for the opening of the precandidate registry. We did this in July, even when the Corriente declared me a precandidate, so that I could begin to earn support within the PRI, but these efforts ended in the last days of August 1987. This is when the authorities organized their political circus consisting of "uncovering" six party precandidates, and each one thereafter began giving speeches as a way to distract the people.

CBG: Didn't that procedure exist in the party statutes?

CCS: It doesn't exist, and I don't believe it will ever exist, because it is nothing but a mere political circus. The farce blundered to an end too, because [at one point] miscommunication led many high-level officials to congratulate and express their loyalty to the wrong precandidate.

When this blunder was cleared up, and the government announced the candidate it had sought to impose to begin with, the members of the Corriente Democrática gathered once more. They decided to continue to look for alternate ways of participating in the 1988 election, and they opted to do this by encouraging the convergence of various democratic forces.

CBG: You presented a position paper at the 13th Congress?

CCS: During the course of the 13th Party Congress, held in March 1987, I formally presented the Corriente proposals regarding the democratic selection of the party candidate, including the opening of the precandidate registry, as I've said before. All of this was rejected. In his closing speech, the party president specifically referred to our proposals and attacked us bitterly. A counterattack was prepared and delivered.

CBG: How were the proposals rejected? Were they voted on?

CCS: They were rejected artfully during a working session of one of the committees. As I said earlier, the party president then attacked us in his closing speech.

CBG: After that closing speech, then—

CCS: On March 9 a letter was written and made public which criticized the party president.

CBG: You wrote a famous letter?

CCS: That's the letter, yes. In it, I reject the party president's authoritarianism and the party's lack of democracy; I point out the violation of party statutes as well, and I state that we will continue the fight.

CBG: You were conscious this step could lead to a complete rupture with the party?

CCS: Yes, of course, but the principles involved were more important than anything else.

CBG: I understand that the central offices of the PRI announced, the day following your letter, that you had resigned from the party. Is this true?

CCS: They issued a communiqué stating that I had refused to collaborate with the party leadership, as I had written in the letter. They simply reiterated what I had stated, but they also gave the impression that I had simply resigned, which I did not.

CBG: When were you formally expelled from the party?

CCS: I decided to leave the party when I accepted to run as the presidential candidate for the PARM. A little later too, they said I was out of the party, which I realized already. Nonetheless, I continue to believe that the present party leadership lacks legitimacy because it trampled on the statutes of the party. It lost the necessary credibility to represent the party, and I don't recognize its decisions at all.

CBG: Your decision to accept the PARM's candidacy must have been a very tough decision to make.

CCS: It was a conscientious decision. It also represented another step in the direction which I had already taken earlier. It's been part of my life. If anyone was left out of a political current, it was they, not I.

CBG: Everyone has been asking: Why the PARM?

CCS: The PARM decision came out of our talks with many political groups. We had been in discussion with groups that included the PARM, the PST, the PPS, and others.

CBG: I understand that there are certain ideological similarities between the PARM—

CCS: The Corriente Democrática made the decision to participate in the coming elections, and it did so by seeking the convergence of nationalist, revolutionary, and democratic forces. My being the PARM candidate simply represented one of several measures leading to the implementation of decisions made by the Corriente in connection with other political groups.

CBG: Who makes up the Corriente Democrática?

CCS: A lot of people spread throughout the country make up the Corriente. It includes mostly former members of the PRI with whom we have been in contact.

CBG: Do you mean they are still in the party?

CCS: They may not have torn themselves from the party, but, in their supporting a candidate opposed to the PRI, one can say that they are out of the party.

CBG: So, when you talk about people in the Corriente, you are speaking of people who belong to the PRI?

CCS: I am referring to people who belonged to the party. The Corriente also includes a lot of people who did not belong to any party but simply decided to join our cause, many of them from the start.

CBG: I mentioned to you that I have interviewed Porfirio Muñoz Ledo. When did you begin speaking to him for the purpose of organizing the Corriente?

CCS: I can't specify dates exactly, but it must have been between May and July of 1986.

CBG: Did you know each other before?

CCS: Yes, from our student days, but we had little contact. Professionally, he was in one area, and I was in another.

CBG: Did you discern a certain ideology in Muñoz Ledo that you felt you could accept?

CCS: We have had and continue to have many ideas in common. This was so earlier, even though we operated in different arenas.

CBG: Who might you say constitutes the "staff" of the Corriente?

CCS: We have a Coordinating Group that is made up of Cesar Buenrostro, an engineer; Leonel Durán, an anthropologist; Ignacio Castillo Mena, a lawyer; and Ifigenia Martínez, a historian. We are the ones who lead the Corriente.

CBG: Did the Corriente set down a strategy (I use the word purposefully here) to reach certain goals?

CCS: We developed certain strategies, but generally these consisted in achieving the widest possible convergence of supporters within certain political limits, organizing them, and so on. We had to be convinced of the need for change in this country and to recognize the great challenges awaiting us.

CBG: My understanding tells me that, of the parties that were formerly referred to as *partidos paleros*, none remains as such today.[3]

CCS: My view is that, at the moment they decided to converge with other political groups in the country by striking up agreements with the Corriente Democrática and helping launch my candidacy for president, they did so first as autonomous organizations. They did this, resisting the many pressures they have had and continue to have coming from the government. I believe this represents the unraveling of a system. It also means that their convergence with a national front like ours has helped them discern new opportunities. They now have the chance of acting as real factors in the political life of the nation on behalf of democracy. They had not experienced this before. Given the combined forces, they now have the chance of becoming part of an electoral majority today.

CBG: They really have a chance?

CCS: From my point of view, we are already the majority among the voters. I am totally convinced of this.

CBG: Please identify the groups that have come to support the Corriente, registered as parties or not.

CCS: In order of their agreement to make me their candidate, the registered parties are the PARM (October 14, 1987), the PST (which became the PFCRN, or Partido del Frente Cardenista de la Reconstrucción Nacional, on November 22, 1987), and the PPS (December 13, 1987). Among the nonregistered parties and political groups that have rushed to support my candidacy, we have the PSD [Partido Socialista Democrático] (whose registration was canceled in 1982 after a bitter clash with the de la Madrid administration), the PSR [Partido Socialista Revolucionario], the Partido Nacional del Pueblo (which is made up mostly of the Comité de Defensa Popular de Chihuahua), the Confederación de Comerciantes y Organizaciones Populares (made up mostly of nonsalaried workers living in the federal district), the Consejo Nacional de Obreros y Campesinos de México (which brings together thirty to forty unions located in the federal district and in the states of México and Morelos mostly), the Unidad Democrática (an organization whose president is Evaristo Pérez Arreola, who also serves as the secretary general of the university workers union at the national university based in the state of Coahuila and in different universities throughout the country), the Partido Verde Mexicano (a group of ecologists), and so on.

CBG: How many people does this represent?

CCS: The actual numbers involved right now may not only be added up but multiplied as well, because these groups, especially the registered ones, have been busy adding new members ever since they collectively launched my candidacy. I say the numbers may be multiplied, because the groups I have mentioned are now attracting many popular organizations, including the Consejo Nacional Cardenista (made up of peasants mostly), which joined us just two days ago. We are now talking to another small organization known as the Partido Liberal, whose leaders have stated their wish to join us. Many individuals are joining the Corriente too, which maintains its own identity, and it plays its own role within the Frente Democrático Nacional (FDN), which incorporates all of these groups.

CBG: What are the possibilities of forming an alliance with the PMS? It seems like such a critical thing to do.

CCS: We are open to any possibility. When the PMS proposed that I take part in a primary election, as part of an
effort to join the two groups under the candidate who would
win the primary election, I accepted without condition. Soon
afterward, however, the PMS placed conditions on the primary election itself by requiring that the PRT take part in
those primaries, despite the fact that the PRT had already
announced it would not collaborate with the Corriente nor
with me personally. This means that the PMS set down a
condition it knew could not be satisfied. Nonetheless, we
continue to be open to any effort that will foster the strength
of the democratic forces in the country. We also believe that
the possibility of allying ourselves with the PMS will not be
eclipsed until March, when the legal registry for the various
candidacies (to the presidency, the senate, the House of
Deputies) is finally closed. So we have kept contact with the
PMS, and we hope something can be done with them.[4]

CBG: Do you think something will come of this?

CCS: I am not very optimistic, frankly, but I see it as a
possibility.

CBG: In my interviews with Heberto Castillo, I came
away impressed with his dogged intent to unite the Left.
He also seemed willing to step down if someone else who
could really win the presidency appeared on the scene.

CCS: Well, that's what he says, but he doesn't do it.

CBG: Any relations with the PDM?

CCS: None.

CBG: With the PAN?

CCS: None outside of a certain amount of work that is
being done by selected groups in an organization known as
Defensa del Sufragio [Defend your vote], where individuals
have come together, including members of the PMS, the
PAN, the Corriente Democrática, and others who don't have
party affiliations.

CBG: A strategy to work with the PAN does not exist?

CCS: Only in the Defend Your Vote organization.

CBG: What percentage of the PRI will vote for you [in
July 1988]?

CCS: It is very hard to say. We don't know the real figures, but I can tell you that a lot of them will do so, because
the people who are supporting us and showing up at our
meetings are mostly people who have voted for the PRI,
party members or not.

CBG: What does the candidacy of Carlos Salinas de Gortari mean to you?

CCS: It means the continuation of the policies applied by the Miguel de la Madrid administration. It also means policies that cede national sovereignty, lose autonomy, and encourage the submission of the country to decisions made abroad concerning our interest and our welfare; it means the [continued] impoverishment of the working classes of this country. It means six more years of what we have had in the last six.

CBG: Salinas de Gortari played an important role in the formulation of economic policies.

CCS: The policies of the outgoing administration reflect the decisions taken by the head of government, of course, but the official in charge of applying those policies is co-responsible, just as any other member of the president's cabinet is likewise responsible. As secretary of budget and planning, Salinas was in charge of implementing these economic policies, the same ones that have become a carbon copy of the "recommendations" made to us by the International Monetary Fund.

CBG: I read in the newspapers that Salinas is willing to change his ways.

CCS: To change form and method but not the basis of it all. As long as you maintain the same objective, there is no real change.

CBG: What is the main objective?

CCS: Their objective is to give away the country and to dismantle the Mexican economy and subject the masses to ever-greater levels of exploitation.

CBG: What is the Corriente Democrática's economic platform?

CCS: Economically speaking, our platform calls for priorities which differ from those made by the outgoing administration. In the allocation of public revenue, we believe priority should be given to the reactivation of our national economy and to social welfare programs and not to pay our foreign debt.

CBG: Not to pay?

CCS: Right now, the de la Madrid administration is setting aside 60 percent of the Mexican federal budget to the payment of our foreign debt. This means that we have no funds to reactivate our economy, increase employment and salaries, and take care of our social problems. We therefore think that a policy which is different from the present one is sorely needed. This requires giving a different priority to the payment of the foreign debt; it means suspending payment until we renegotiate under different terms. The banks have already recognized that the Mexican debt has a lower value than the one they have been insisting on, yet we continue paying as if the debt value were still worth 100 percent. It is thus necessary to agree on new terms and new interest rates; it is necessary to differentiate between the debt that was contracted when we were in a position to pay and that which was contracted merely for political reasons when it was obvious we couldn't pay. These two types of debt contracts need to be treated separately.

We do not believe it is right either to extend privileges to speculative investments. I have the stock market exchange in mind that has been held up and inflated by the Mexican state itself thanks to the Nacional Financiera, for example. When the stock market fell, it dragged down with it some five hundred thousand small- and medium-sized investors whose savings were wiped out. Speculation has been protected; interests are sky high, and this impedes investments into productive activities. This must change entirely.

CBG: What is your view concerning the bonds-for-debt arrangement, which became the focus of considerable publicity in early January 1988?

CCS: The bonds-for-debt proposal is not the important remedy for our economy as our government has claimed. First, the calculations which have been made by the current administration on this are wrong, just as they've been wrong on other economic projects. Second, this kind of an arrangement does not encourage new investments. Third, the idea of changing $20 billion for $10 billion, based on a special fund located in the U.S. Treasury, represents yet another opportunity for the United States to interfere with our sovereignty. The guarantees that derive from the U.S. Treasury are guarantees that the Mexican state could offer. The benefits that derive from the $2 billion which have been deposited there stay in the United States because that is where the funds will remain, despite the fact that investments earn more in Mexico right now than they do in the United States—unless Mexican government officials are expecting another economic bust, in which case they ought to be more considerate of Mexicans with savings deposits.

CBG: Are you offering alternatives which are clearer than the ones the Corriente published recently in pamphlet form?

CCS: We are about to publish a common platform on January 12, 1989, that contains many of the ideas that were set out in publications issued by the Corriente and allied organizations, all of which have a lot in common.

CBG: What do you and your backers think about government-owned industries?

CCS: Our policy toward government-owned industries requires defining them first, because the law itself is not entirely clear at present. I believe that both the areas and the industries which are strategic to our economy should be further developed by the state. Some of these state-owned enterprises ought to be integrated, as in the case of petro-chemicals. They ought to be reviewed, including why they came to be in the first place. Many of them became state industries when the private companies that owned them went bankrupt. The plants had served as collateral for state credit. This kind of enterprise has to be looked at separately from the others; they ought not be viewed as equal. Nonetheless, I consider that strategic areas of the economy need to be commanded and impelled forward by the state in association with certain social sectors, including cooperatives and *ejidos*.

CBG: Isn't this what the government is already doing?

CCS: The government is doing away, practically speaking, with all kinds of *paraestatales*. I would say it is going beyond the demands of the IMF. The government is tearing apart economic enterprises that could be used by the state in its role as manager of the national economy. The state-owned banking system has not been used as it ought to be either. Certain capabilities have been given to the parallel banking system [privately run banks], which has itself resulted in extending privileges to special private interests, ex-bankers mainly. The state-owned banking system has not been employed as an effective mechanism to promote economic growth and social well-being.

CBG: Within this general subject, you recently identified agricultural properties ranging in amounts of several million hectares.

CCS: Certain official peasant associations have identified about five million hectares of agricultural land liable for expropriation under the law. Some estimates go as high as ten million. I think that all lands liable for distribution under the law ought to be given to landless peasants simply because it is the law.

CBG: How would this affect Mexico's present need to import grains and other foodstuffs?

CCS: My proposal here would not increase Mexico's need to import foodstuffs, because the lands to which I refer are not being used for production right now. The need to import merely reflects long-standing neglect of the agricultural sector. Existing policies simply do not add up to a systematic effort aimed at organizing the various units of production. Right now, for example, agricultural credit is practically nonexistent. All of the things I've discussed make it impossible to have a working policy promoting rural production. The rural sector deserves priority as part of a general reorientation of the nation's economic policies.

CBG: In your view, further dividing up of the land would not imply—

CCS: A policy of land distribution needs to be accompanied by credit and technical and organizational assistance. There are regions in the country where *ejido* production, based on farming and cattle raising, is flourishing. It may be said, in fact, that *ejidos* are doing better in these areas than privately owned lands.

CBG: Can you identify some examples of this?

CCS: I'm thinking of the Yaqui River region, certain areas in Baja California, and in Sinaloa. One can find examples throughout the country.

CBG: Would you comment on the Economic Solidarity Pact, which was announced by the Miguel de la Madrid administration in the last days of 1987?[5]

CCS: We've said it several times already. The pact is not a pact at all. It is instead an aggression against the working classes of the country.

CBG: What was the purpose of the pact?

CCS: Via union representatives who have not defended the interests of the workers, the pact sought to impose restrictions on wage increases. These restrictions were already figured at 15 percent in December and 20 percent in January in exchange for a promise that inflation was supposed to be controlled by March 1988. The pact does not allow any other wage or benefit increase for the workers after March. As I said earlier, this is an attack on the economy of the workers which reduces the legitimacy of the state because the policy flies against the interests of the majority. Moreover, the purchasing power of the workers has already been annulled by government-ordered raises affecting certain fees and services [gasoline and transportation fees were increased by 85 percent, natural gas by 100 percent, and taxes by 100 percent].

Moreover, the pact does not include any formal agreement on the part of the business community to keep a lid on prices. Members of this community do not feel committed to any restraints. This is why I believe that the pact merely represents one more link in a chain of economic policies implemented since 1982, when the de la Madrid administration began. These measures merely represent policies of imposition fashioned by leaders who no longer communicate with the people they are supposed to be representing; they have the net effect of giving the appearance that solutions are being worked out, when everybody knows nothing will be resolved.

CBG: Does your party belong to the antipact coalition that was formed?

CCS: Members of the Corriente have been taking part in it; I took part in some of its early meetings.

CBG: What could be a better alternative?

CCS: We offered our proposals in the last days of December [1987]. These included the scaling back of the prices and fee rates to what they were before December 15, 1987, when the pact was announced. We proposed the establishment of a fixed exchange rate, controls on capital transfers going out of the country, and so on.

CBG: How do you think your proposals will be seen in the United States?

CCS: I think the American people will view our proposals in a realistic way. Our country simply has to improve. Since 1982 the great majority of the Mexican people have lost more than 60 percent of their real purchasing power, including the last devaluation and the limitations imposed by the pact. We are living with 15 percent unemployment, which represents the highest rate anyone can remember. Estimates tell us that there are between five and six million people without a job and eleven to fifteen million who are underemployed. This represents a situation demanding objectivity; it requires conscientious measures to correct the situation, even if they are drastic. If Americans take a close look at the grave reality that faces us, then they will better understand our proposals. These include the freezing of prices, raising wages, reactivating the economy by strengthening internal markets, lowering interest rates, and generally supporting industry, agriculture, and transportation instead of undermining our own economic strength as we have been doing in the last few years.

CBG: By what you've said, I presume you and your supporters would not have favored Mexico's membership in GATT?

CCS: Not the way it has been done by the de la Madrid administration. On the one hand, the administration's approach makes it very difficult for the Mexican industrial sector, especially for the owners of small- and medium-sized industries. On the other, it gives many advantages to the multinational corporations in Mexico.

CBG: What changes do you wish to see in the political arena?

CCS: In the political area we urge respect for electoral results. The electoral processes of the country need to be rectified, and their credibility upheld; this is something that has been demanded since 1910. We want democracy to enjoy an expression not only in the political area but also in the economic, as well as in the distribution of wealth. We simply want equal opportunities for all Mexicans.

CBG: Do you see the need for constitutional amendments?

CCS: We ought to begin by applying what is written already and later consider what might have to be reformed. It may be necessary to make amendments in those cases where inappropriate changes have been applied to Article 27, for example, or to Article 123, where distinctions are made between state workers and others who are not.

CBG: I presume this kind of review might apply to labor unions too.

CCS: We believe that, in an effort to democratize the country, attention should be paid not only to political parties or electoral processes but also to the social sector. Labor unions and peasant organizations need to be included so that the process of democratization can be applied broadly.

CBG: Do you foresee special programs concerning birth control?

CCS: Well, I would say: Give to everyone the right to regulate the number of children they may wish to have. We don't have anything beyond this at present.

CBG: I ask you this because demographic issues are important too.

CCS: Of course they are.

CBG: Has your organization discussed, up until now, the kind of national structure you would require in case you were to win the coming elections? It seems to me that you need a lot of help to organize a national government.

CCS: We have the people. That's the most important thing.

CBG: In the parties that are supporting you?

CCS: Among the parties and in the other groups that are helping us. There are many people in the administration too who have a lot of sympathy for us. We have university people too. What is obvious is the inability of those who are in charge right now to foresee economic problems. This has led them to fashion policies that are completely unpopular. We don't want to govern with that kind of people.

CBG: I read very negative comments about you in the press, uttered by high-level people in Mexico.

CCS: That's just part of the political struggle.

CBG: What pressures have been brought to bear on you now that you are campaigning against the government? Are they obvious?

CCS: Many people who have expressed support for us have been fired from their jobs. Pressures, temptations, and even threats have been brought to bear against our political leaders, both national and local. Repression has been brought against workers who support us, et cetera. Nothing has been done against me, however.

CBG: I am greatly surprised to know that you don't have any bodyguards.

CCS: I do not think I ought to have any, whether they are supplied to me by the government or by anybody else, because it doesn't serve any purpose.

CBG: This is so unusual.

CCS: I have never had bodyguards, and it would be the last thing I would ever accept.

CBG: You're now a national and international figure.

CCS: One should be careful not to lose certain individual rights.

CBG: If something were to happen to you, it could create a lot of conflict for the country.

CCS: Whoever was responsible would be caught quickly. I am not fearful.

CBG: You said recently that the people supporting you need to be prepared for any "irregularities" that may be planned against you on election day.

CCS: We have to figure out how we might be prepared if moves are made against us on that day and afterward.

CBG: In an organized sort of way?

CCS: We'll have to see that.

CBG: How do think July 6th [1988] will turn out?

CCS: On that day we shall have to show that we do represent the biggest electoral force in the country, that we have an ability to mobilize ourselves in order to show our presence throughout the country for the purpose of making the necessary changes less difficult. We will have to show a wide margin of votes so that our success is incontrovertible and otherwise manifest an ability to defend what we have earned through the ballot box.

CBG: Does your organization have an alternate plan just in case you don't attain that wide margin?

CCS: We would just continue with our struggle in order to achieve the kind of changes the country requires.

CBG: So, between 1988 and 1994, you folks speak in terms of continuing with the struggle?

CCS: Even after 1994.

CBG: You think the PRI will be defeated in the coming elections?

CCS: The PRI will be defeated in the coming election.

CBG: Do you and your supporters propose any changes in Mexico's relations with the United States?

CCS: We think that our relations should be advantageous to both countries. We have to recognize the long border between us, from which all kinds of interrelationships have developed. These fall into the areas of economics, labor, social relations, family, et cetera. We believe that, if the United States has developed advantageous relations with other countries, there is no reason why it can't have the same kind of relationship with us.

CBG: Are you saying that this kind of relationship does not exist now?

CCS: There are some [aspects] that are favorable to us, but most are not.

CBG: Especially the economic ones?

CCS: Especially the economic ones.

CBG: Certain people in the United States have recently expressed their willingness to support your campaign. This is as unusual as it is important.

CCS: I don't recall anything like it either. We think that our relations with Mexicans residing in the United States and with Americans of Mexican origin need to be strengthened. We think the Mexican government has practically abandoned the Mexicans living there. It could have employed the Mexican consulates to defend the human rights of the Mexicans or simply their rights as workers there. This could have been done vigorously. Some consulates have done this; many have not. Doing so could bring solidarity to our people. The government could have developed cultural ties with them, which may have been useful as a political asset to the organizations functioning there. It might have been possible to do this without interfering in our neighbor's life, of course, because residents in the United States have a right to activities of this sort. The support of social, educational, and cultural organizations for the benefit of the bilingual immigrant population could have been an important activity for the Mexican government.

CBG: Do you think the Mexican-American organizations that have promised to gather funds for your campaign will succeed?

CCS: I can tell you that the effort has already been successful! Most important is that different organizations made up of Mexicans residing in the United States have already decided to work together politically on behalf of an objective which we consider positive: support the changes that must come to Mexico. Any Mexican living in the United States can help us a lot. Any Mexican residing there should have the right to vote in Mexico for a presidential candidate, at least. [In the meantime,] if Mexicans can travel to their places of origin to vote for a president, senators, and deputies, they should do so. In their own places of origin, they can also speak with friends or relatives about their views concerning Mexico generally.

If Mexicans living in the United States and Mexican-Americans choose to help us out with funds, this will be of great value to us. I see this as something secondary, however. The most important thing is the political relationship that we might be able to establish with Mexicans living in the United States.

CBG: Isn't your organization promoting absentee balloting?

CCS: We are proposing that Mexicans enjoy the right to vote in absentee ballot form, but I frankly think it cannot be done in the short run.

CBG: Is your organization presently trying to get a message across to the American people in general?

CCS: Only to the extent available to us in existing means of communication. These have been shut against us in many cases.

CBG: You are referring to Mexican media?

CCS: Yes, but our access to the international media has not been very good either, especially if you consider the limitations which face us.

CBG: Concerning foreign relations in a broader vein, do you have a special viewpoint concerning other countries?

CCS: We believe it is necessary to eliminate foreign intervention in Central American affairs. We urge the withdrawal of U.S. bases in Honduras, an end to intervention in El Salvador and to aggressions against Nicaragua. We believe the Nicaraguans ought to be permitted to redirect their economy toward production, instead of obligating them to be on the defensive. The people of Central America ought to be given the right to self-determination.

CBG: What would your final word be to the American people?

CCS: The final message is that we are trying to resolve our own problems. In no way are we trying to fashion policies contrary to the interests of the American people. We believe we clearly understand the attitude that they have had toward Mexico. We understand this attitude to be one of collaboration and sympathy, feelings that the Mexican people hold toward the American people, speaking at the level of people to people. We want respect for our rights, but we also want to find genuine forms of collaboration so that our neighborhood, and all of the relationships that flow from it, become beneficial to both sides.

CBG: Do you have a different message for Americans of Mexican ancestry?

CCS: First, I would say to them what I said above. It is important that they too realize what our goals are. We want to be closer to all of the hispano communities, be they Mexicans living in the United States or Americans of Mexican origin. I've enjoyed contact with some of these communities, and I have seen as very valuable the kinds of organizations and social networks which provide a sense of solidarity to the newly arrived Mexicans or simply the Mexican-Americans who move from one region to another in search of work and a better life. These are important manifestations of solidarity which can be strengthened from both sides of the border.

Notes

1. The interview was held January 10, 1988, in Lomas de Chapultepec, Mexico City.
2. Employing CIA personnel, President Dwight D. Eisenhower approved the overthrow of President Jacobo Arbenz Guzmán of Guatemala in 1954. See Richard H. Immerman, *The CIA in Guatemala: The Foreign Policy of Intervention* (Austin: University of Texas Press, 1982); and Stephen Schlesinger and Stephen Kinzer, *Bitter Fruit: The Untold Story of the American Coup in Guatemala* (Garden City, NY: Anchor Books, 1983).
3. The divorce between the PRI and some of the so-called satellite parties was not long lasting. Cooperation continued between the PRI and some of the small parties after the election of 1988.
4. Cárdenas's FDN joined forces with the PMS on June 5, 1988, in an alliance that would become the Partido de la Revolución Democrática (PRD).
5. The Economic Solidarity Pact is a package of fiscal reforms produced by the Salinas administration in an attempt to resolve economic problems inherited from earlier years. In exchange for an agreement from government-controlled labor unions to control wage increases, it included adjustments to taxes and prices, a review of subsidies, and tariff revisions. See *El gobierno mexicano* 70 (September 1988): 37–38.

CHAPTER 7

Porfirio Muñoz Ledo

Porfirio Muñoz Ledo appears to have been born under a lucky star. In his early years, he received a government scholarship that enabled him to attend the best private schools in the capital. At the national university, despite his modest origins, he made friends with many potential leaders who would later pull him up to the highest national levels. Another scholarship encouraged him to study political science in Paris, where he made and took advantage of high-level connections. He thus began to pave a professional path that would impress any observer.

Due to his penchant for the right connections, Muñoz Ledo took part in the administrations of Adolfo López Mateos, Echeverría, López Portillo, and de la Madrid. He served as secretary of labor, secretary of education, president of the PRI, and ambassador to the United Nations. He believes that he nearly became president of Mexico.

Disavowing status and prestige, he conserved his reformist instincts and joined the *cardenista* movement, where he exercised a significant role in the late 1980s and in the 1990s. In late 1990 he was running as a candidate for governor of his paternal state of Guanajuato, on the PRD ticket, and as such stood a chance to become the second non-PRI governor.

CBG: Please tell us where you were born and something about your childhood.[1]

PML: I was born July 23, 1933, in Mexico City. My parents were both schoolteachers. I attended public schools in the Colonia del Valle, my neighborhood. Having obtained a scholarship from the Ministry of Education, I was able to finish junior high and high school in private schools. I then entered the UNAM to study law, and I worked in a modest position, as clerk in a government office, at the same time. I did this until I entered university politics full-time.

I was part of a student generation known as the Generación del Medio Siglo [Midcentury Generation], which includes, among others, people like Carlos Fuentes (the oldest member), Miguel de la Madrid (the youngest), and other Mexicans who likewise became very prominent. Even before I was eighteen, I became executive secretary of the student journal, *Medio Siglo*, in which a lot of us youngsters began to become known by the articles we wrote.

CBG: This was during your student years at the university?

PML: Yes, and I also became president of the Law Students' Association, and I helped to start a student federation too.

CBG: Which one?

PML: It was called the Federación de Sociedades de Alumnos. We encouraged young people with an intellectual vocation to dedicate themselves to political work. We wanted the Federación to act as an intellectual, cultural, and political purifier of the student movement.

CBG: What years were these?

PML: All of this took place between 1952 and 1955. I traveled to France afterward, where I studied at the Political Studies Institute and the Law School of the University of Paris and earned my doctorate in constitutional law and political science. In 1958, Jaime Torres Bodet, who was serving as the Mexican ambassador to France, invited me to go to the University of Toulouse to teach a course on Latin American civilization and another one on the Mexican Revolution. Having done this, I returned to Mexico and began working at the national university, where I taught the theory of the state; this was part of a plan to write a book on the Mexican political system, having already written my thesis on this topic in Paris and at Toulouse.

When I was twenty-six years old, President Adolfo López Mateos, whom I had known when he was a student activist, personally invited me to become part of his administration. He wanted me to help him fashion a progressive wing within his administration. I became his adviser for over a year, during which time I served with distinguished men of the likes of Alejandro Carrillo Marcor, Enrique Ramírez y Ramírez, José Iturriaga, and Emilio Uranga. It's important for me to stress this point; I entered government service because the president of the republic wanted me to organize progressive teams. This is when he declared that his government belonged to the "extreme Left within the constitution," as you might recall.

A year later, Torres Bodet, who was now serving as education minister, invited me to join government service in a more formal way, as assistant director of higher education. This coincided with the private sector's campaign against free government textbooks for use in public schools. As part of a plan to defend nonreligious education, which was also under attack, Torres Bodet asked me to act as a link between the Office of the Presidency and the Ministry of Education. The *escuela laica* was under attack. I did this until the end of the López Mateos period. During this time, I managed to change higher education curricula in many autonomous schools throughout the nation, in accord with ideas I had learned abroad. At about this time too the Fondo de Cultura Económica published my first work, which dealt with higher education. You could say it represented my first specialty area.

Feeling incompatible with the new administration presided over by Gustavo Díaz Ordaz, I accepted an appointment as cultural counselor of the Mexican embassy in France when the López Mateos administration ended. For an entire year, I served under Dr. Ignacio Morones Prieto, the Mexican ambassador at that time. Later, he returned to Mexico as the new director of the Social Security Institute, and he invited me to become part of his team.

CBG: So you were abroad in 1968?

PML: No, I was in Mexico working at the institute. As you know, most of the nation's doctors are connected with the institute; Dr. Morones's assignment represented part of an effort to soothe the wounds resulting from the big 1966 conflict involving young doctors. During the strife surrounding 1968 we did not have any problems at the institute at all, because we opened and maintained excellent communication with the institute's doctors and the interns. None of them found it necessary to join the 1968 student movement. I served as secretary-general of the institute during this time, from 1966 to 1970. I thus avoided the problems that had shaken the various hospitals connected with the institute two years before.

When Luis Echeverría began his campaign for the presidency, he invited me to join his team. I had known him personally before, too. Following the 1968 conflict, Echeverría conveyed to me the necessity of changing the political rhetoric in the country,[2] of incorporating young people into government service, and of giving a progressive and revolutionary tone to the Mexican government. Knowing about the work that I had done up to this time, he believed I would be able to help him in this regard. Before going on, I should add that, in 1962, I was invited by Daniel Cosío Villegas of the Colegio de México to inaugurate the first course ever given on our Mexican political system, entitled "Government and Political Process in Mexico." I taught this course for nearly ten years there. I also started this same course at the Escuela Normal Superior. Hence, my second area of specialty was the Mexican political system, and this is part of what Echeverría took into consideration when he invited me. He became familiar with some of my written work, including a critique I had written about the Mexican federal system and another one concerning the issue of youth and the government. I thus became part of the Echeverría administration, and, as everybody knows, I oversaw the rewriting of school textbooks with the new political rhetoric.

At this time I also took part in an academic debate concerning the *apertura democrática* [democratic opening], as it was becoming known. In a debate with Daniel Cosío Villegas at the University of Texas in May of 1971, I applied the idea of *apertura* to international affairs, to Mexico's dependency, to social equality, and especially to our own democracy. The conference proceedings were published in both English and Spanish. In any case, I worked as Echeverria's undersecretary for two years. It was a multifaceted job. I was responsible for administrative reform, for putting together a new system of public investment and finance with José López Portillo (who served as undersecretary of Patrimonía Nacional [National Heritage]), and for the writing of the new textbooks.

In 1972, Echeverría asked me to become labor minister, which I accepted. In this job, I faced a very complex situation, because we tried to solve both economic and social issues amid high inflation. In order to reach our goal, we founded the Tripartite Commission, which I chaired for four years too. This commission brought together labor unions, employers, and key government agency heads in a permanent and public dialogue that addressed important social and economic questions which were facing all of us.

CBG: Did the commission conduct studies for the most part?

PML: No, a lot of legislation issued from this exercise, including the creation of the National Housing Institute, the Foreign Commerce Institute, and many others. At the same time, I had to do something about inflation. I put together a salary policy which, in my view and in the view of others, protected the nation's purchasing power, because we managed to keep [the policy] above the inflation rate without having it become a cause of inflation itself. I tried to modernize the Labor Ministry and, in some ways, my organizational model was adopted by the International Labor Organization. For example, we created agencies for work rehabilitation, organized the first employment agencies in Mexico, put together a system for on-the-job training, and did research on labor issues. These years were very creative years. However, many of these institutions have perished.

My name began to be mentioned as a PRI candidate for the presidency, but the effort did not materialize as I would have wished. The presidential succession took place in the traditional manner, and José López Portillo received the nod. On the day of the nomination, however, both President Echeverría and López Portillo asked me to step up to the presidency of the PRI and to the directorship of the presidential campaign. The President [Echeverría] explained to me that my being president of the PRI meant that the party's revolutionary posture would be kept high, because I enjoyed a progressive image. Obviously, all of this represented a political arrangement.

Seen more broadly, President Echeverría made two decisions aimed at maintaining a balance before his term ended in 1976. One was to select López Portillo, a man of great abilities and an outstanding personality, for the presidency. He had been minister of finance, and he enjoyed old friendship ties with Echeverría. The second decision was to continue the revolutionary line within the party.

CBG: Does this mean that Echeverría realized that his personal political line could not go on, but that it might through the party?

PML: Some historians see a parallel with Cárdenas when he selected Avila Camacho.

CBG: But you feel that López Portillo selected you to become president of PRI?

PML: The decision was reached between the two of them.

CBG: In order for the previous line to continue?

PML: In order to maintain an equilibrium. In any case, a balance was struck within the government between the revolutionary and conservative forces, both of which were very much at the surface. I became PRI president, and I directed López Portillo's campaign. In doing so, I came to feel a lot of satisfaction. I was able to make some substantial changes for the first time. Via consultations I had with lower-level organizations of the party, afforded by campaign traveling, I changed the makeup of both the legislative chambers, the house of representatives and the senate. For example, the number of worker representatives was nearly tripled. Peasant representatives were doubled. Women and popular organizations were also brought in. All of which signified a clear step toward democratization. Moreover, economists, ideologists, and other intellectuals were selected, in combination with lower-level leaders, in order to form a group of more than ninety congress members who upheld the progressive spirit within the party and voted independently against government bills.

CBG: They voted independently?

PML: Yes, they voted independently and, above all, maintained a progressive line. In a word, I made every attempt to create a progressive wing within the party. I can add too that I was able to connect the PRI to the Social Democracy movement, although I didn't do it formally because laws prohibit this. Close ties were established via a meeting in Caracas, organized with the aid of Carlos Sansores Pérez, of seventy-some parties and organizations from Europe and Latin America. Right in the middle of the presidential campaign, I invited the most important leaders of Social Democracy to visit Mexico. Just in one session, for example, I brought together Willy Brandt, Olof Palme, Felipe González, Mário Soares, Bruno Kreisky, and Anker Jørgensen. Víctor Raúl Haya de la Torre and François Mitterrand visited later. This represented not only an important link between Social Democracy and our party but also my attempt to modernize the party's ideology and make it compatible with the world's great international democratic movements even while its own revolutionary roots were reaffirmed.

Toward the end of my appointment, I became more clearly aware of *cupulismo, verticalismo,* and other deficiencies of my party. I was then invited by other distinguished members of the party's progressive wing, particularly Rodolfo González Guevara, to study the structure and function of the party itself. This was done by a committee of us, which produced several volumes of information many months later. These data are available to any interested investigator. In fact, what we are now saying about the PRI was affirmed in these studies: the need to communicate with lower-level party organizations, to have internal elections, to define party ideology more clearly, et cetera. This committee left behind an entire structure of ideas, some of which were later transformed into statutory reforms which give the PRI the democratic structure it has on paper today. As outgoing PRI president, I handed this information to my successor, and the party decided to implement only some of these solutions. This partial implementation gave rise to talk about the need for "transparent democracy" and for communicating with lower-level people in the party.

Since I had helped in the study of Mexico's political reforms (which included reforms in the campaign itself and the need to bring change both to the legislature and to the party), it was assumed that I would become López Portillo's interior minister. But things changed, most probably because he decided to separate himself from his predecessor more than ever. As a result, he invited Jesús Reyes Heroles, an old classmate of his, to become the interior minister.

He offered me the Education Ministry instead, which I readily accepted because of my lifelong vocation for education. I consider it the most important task in a developing country. In Mexico the Education Ministry is very big. It includes not only education, but culture, sports, and relations between the federal government and the nation's universities. It also includes presiding over CONACYT [Consejo Nacional de Ciencia y Tecnología], or the Council on Science and Technology. The Education Ministry is equal in size to four regular government ministries. When I took it over, something else happened too. Despite its enormous size and its impact on society, it had not been directed by a politician since José Vasconcelos's time. Given my political approach, I forged strong links between the ministry and President López Portillo, and, in doing so, I laid out my ideas. I explained to him that the greatest challenge he faced was to duplicate the funds going to education within his six years (instead of 4 percent of the GNP, 8 percent ought to go to education).

CBG: Was this done?

PML: No, I was there no longer than a year. I explained my plans regarding the cultural issues. I also revealed my ideas concerning the importance of university workers unions, mass communication, adult education, bilingual education, the transformation of high-school education, and, above all, the obligation of the state to give ten years of free education to every Mexican. This meant extending free textbooks up to the level of junior high school, at least.

CBG: Was this done?

PML: No, it couldn't be done in one year. López Portillo was on the verge of becoming Mexico's "oil president," and I wanted him to become Mexico's "education president" as well, since he had been a schoolteacher most of his life.

I proposed bilingual and bicultural education and a constitutional recognition of Mexico's cultural pluralism. A couple of months into my job, I presented a bill addressing two outstanding issues: constitutional recognition of university autonomy and Mexico's cultural pluralism. It also had a clause concerning the problem of university unions. The constitution should state that Mexico is a multiethnic and multicultural country, and this is why we have made this part of the Corriente [Democrática] platform. We need to realize that national unity is not frayed by the development of these various cultures. We even proposed the transformation of military service to social service.

It was a grand and ambitious proposal, but it was not realized for many reasons. It could have greatly transformed the country. I told López Portillo that I would limit myself to these projects and then return to my private life. He agreed. However, the political profile that I had formed by this time began to weigh heavily. I had been a labor minister and president of the PRI. I had begun to change the legislature. I created a progressive wing within the party itself and expanded the role of the Education Ministry, giving it a higher profile than ever before, just within six months. All of this made me appear incompatible with the need for a balance. In fact, the president told me that there was a "lack of balance within the government," and he asked me to resign, which I accepted. It was all part of a political adjustment, I thought. However, I also believed I would now have time to write my book about the Mexican political system and perhaps get into other political activities later, when the waters had calmed down once more. In 1978 and 1979, I traveled outside of Mexico, visiting foreign universities and attending international congresses.

CBG: In what year did you retire?

PML: In December of 1977. I traveled in 1978 and 1979. I updated myself on the international issues of the day, including the oil conflict then going on, the North-South dialogue, which was just beginning,[3] and other issues that were affecting the life of the nation on the outside. I studied and wrote memoranda at such places as the Brookings Institution, Stanford University, University of California at Berkeley, Harvard University, Oxford University, and so on. During this year and a half, I spent most of my time outside of the country.

CBG: Did you publish anything during this time?

PML: While I didn't publish anything at this time, I did continue to gather both material and my own thoughts on the various subjects in which I was interested. When I regained contact with the Mexican government, President López Portillo appointed me presidential counselor for special affairs. I didn't refuse the job, because I didn't want to rupture my relations with the Mexican system, and because I thought it would help my own thinking on a lot of things.

President López Portillo soon appointed me as Mexico's ambassador to the United Nations. He had conceived the idea of proposing an international energy plan; and, since I had been analyzing those issues while participating in the North-South dialogue during the Echeverría years (I was the main proponent of the Economic Rights of States), he decided to take advantage of my knowledge and experience. I considered it a dignified and useful opportunity because I knew that international problems were going to be critical, that a major economic crisis was ahead, and that North-South relations were going to be critical for the country. I concluded that the president's proposal was quite relevant, since it meant advocating the New International Economic Order, once again, to which I had dedicated many years earlier. Moreover, the ambassadorship would allow me to update myself by learning more about oil and international finances, which I already knew something about. I also concluded that the administration's foreign policy represented the most progressive of policies within the government. So the post offered to me appeared as the most appropriate in that six-year period. The United Nations assignment fitted me best because I could do a good job there. It needs to be said that López Portillo held up Mexico's foreign affairs as one of the more progressive dimensions of his government, when you consider his policies toward Central America, toward the North-South dialogue, and so on.

After I arrived at the United Nations, something unexpected took place. A vacancy arose in the UN Security Council, triggering a conflict between Cuba and Colombia for the seat in November and December of 1979. Mexico received the seat as a mediational move. It was a terribly critical moment; the fall of the shah in Iran was taking place; the fundamentalist revolution led by the ayatollah was likewise beginning; the Sandinista victory in Nicaragua was unfolding, along with the invasion of Afghanistan, while the Republicans arrived in the White House. The year 1979 was a turning point indeed, and I walked into the thick of things at the United Nations.

My turn to preside over the Security Council arrived, and I acquired a very high international profile during certain events. These events included the taking of U.S. hostages in Iran, the beginning of the Iraq-Iran War, the bombing of the nuclear reactors in Iraq, and so on. I delivered a scathing denunciation of the Soviet invasion of Afghanistan. I defended Nicaragua and condemned intervention of any kind there. When the members of the United Nations were looking to fill the secretary-general position that Kurt Waldheim eventually took up, my name was mentioned as a possible candidate. I became part of the group of people who could fill the post if the African representative, Salim Salim, was not elected to that position. A caucus in favor of a Latin American was thus formed, and my name appeared at the top of the list of Latin Americans because I was president of the Security Council.

President López Portillo offered me his complete support when I presented my candidacy. In fact, he invited me to accompany him to a special meeting in Cancún to receive

certain heads of state at the airport there. He authorized
me to hold conversations with certain government representatives, and he was aware of my conversations concerning
my candidacy with heads of state, including President
Mitterrand and others.

Despite all this, mere days before the United Nations
elections, I received instructions not to go ahead with my
candidacy. To this day, I've never received a satisfactory
explanation for this. But I do know for a fact that someone
stated at Los Pinos [the president's residence] that "the
Mexican political system was not big enough for a Mexican
pope." Perhaps this statement reflected fear that I could
take on an international role that would give me more influence at home, or perhaps it was mere political intrigue. I
really don't know what the reason for this change was. What
is certain is that I was a candidate for the United Nations
post, that I had the full support of the president, and that,
three days before the elections, I received instructions to
withdraw. As a diplomatic representative, I had to obey
them.

CBG: All of this took place in 1979?

PML: No, it took place in November 1981. I then considered leaving government service. However, I decided to
finish out my appointment until the end of the López
Portillo administration.

A little later, Miguel de la Madrid, a friend from my
younger days, asked me, during his campaign for the
Mexican presidency, to study the Central American situa-
tion. Consequently, I traveled to that region and to South
America as well and spoke with key political leaders. With
the aid of President [Luis] Herrera Campíns of Venezuela,
Colombian President-elect [Belisario] Betancur [Cuartas],
and the Central American heads of state (Commander
Daniel Ortega of Nicaragua, President Luis Alberto Monge
[Alvarez] of Costa Rica, President Aristides Royo of
Panama), we put together what was later called Contadora.

CBG: Contadora was initiated in this way?

PML: In other words, the so-called Contadora process
was started by my trip in June 1982 when I spoke to the
leaders I've mentioned and to whom I explained my plan
for the region. All of them are my personal friends, by the
way.

CBG: Tell us again who assigned you to do this work.

PML: With the authorization of the president who was leaving, the other who was coming in at the time, and with permission of the ministry, I assigned myself.

CBG: But de la Madrid had already assigned you—

PML: Yes, a month before the elections. When the administration changed, newly elected President de la Madrid did not give me the impression that I was being considered for a new government appointment. So I asked permission to leave the United Nations and return to private life. I wanted to return to university life to finally accomplish my lifelong dream to write the book which I had so often postponed. In response, the president asked me to stay a little bit longer at the United Nations and help him with the North-South dialogue, which continued to be important. So I stayed on in order to comply with his wishes. However, I also presented my candidacy [for] the presidency of the Group of 77, which sought to negotiate a better economic situation for the developing countries.[4] When I became the group's president, I traveled the whole world, visiting with important leaders about this issue [the need for North-South cooperation]. I visited Japan, Britain, and the OECD [Organization for Economic Cooperation and Development]. I organized a meeting with the European Parliament concerning issues affecting developing countries, and I worked intensively in the North-South dialogue. Unfortunately, we didn't get anywhere due to the [Ronald] Reagan administration, although we did manage to present a document outlining the group's proposals to the seven most industrialized countries, which met in London. But with that document we had reached our limit. I hate to say it; but, since I left the Group of 77, no other attempt has been made along these lines.

As president of the Group of 77, I put in my last effort on behalf of the Mexican government, and then I finally went home. My return home was delayed a bit because some people thought I ought to continue to stay outside the country. Important ambassadorships were offered to me very generously, which I declined. I insisted on returning home.

The incompatibility that had grown between the government and me became clearer than ever by this time. I had already begun to notice this as I took part in the North-South dialogue. The men in charge of the Banco de México, who came to power with Miguel de la Madrid, acted con-

trary to my role abroad. This group was led by Antonio Ortiz
Mena at the start. The people who are there now are his
students, and President de la Madrid sits at its apex.
Salinas de Gortari was formed by this group, and most of
them studied at Harvard and Yale. This is a dozen or so people who support each other. In any case, this financial group
opposed the Bank of the South, an idea I had presented as
part of the North-South discussions. In fact, things got so
bad that I had to insist on a gentleman's agreement with
the minister of finance, then Jesús Silva Herzog, to the
effect that, if I became president of the Group of 77, they
would not attack my ideas publicly. They were kind enough
to agree, but they didn't support me. What this means is
that the internal conduct of the Mexican government dif-
fered from what we upheld in international forums. In fact,
the Contadora process itself gradually became separated
from the original objectives which we pursued at the United
Nations. The result was that my work became more
autonomous from the Mexican government with each passing day, and this created a problem for the conduct of the
nation's foreign policy. So my role in the United Nations
weakened toward the end. Once back home, I began to study
the domestic scene and became acutely aware of the limitations of our economic policies.

Miguel de la Madrid made everybody understand that
he would come in with a financial team ready to implement
a fiscal adjustment policy to the economic crisis the nation
was experiencing in the first two years of his term. He said
he would dedicate himself to a program of national recovery
and development. But he didn't do it. Different labels were
applied to the same fiscal policy, and they simply continued
the same thing, up to this last decision to select Salinas de
Gortari as the PRI candidate for the presidency. In fact, he
is the author of this policy, which consists of opening up
Mexico and tying it to the decisions of the great financial
and international centers of the world. This tendency gained
strength in the very centers of the de la Madrid administration as it matured. It was made very clear that he was going
to confront the crisis with a financial team during the first
two years.

CBG: You saw all this going on?

PML: Yes, of course; I saw it all. He led people to believe
that he would change his tack and begin addressing economic

problems at their root by pursuing a national recovery program. This did not happen. What did happen is that the financial group, to which I've referred, took over the party, and the administration and it gradually dominated the political scene.

CBG: Who led the financial group?

PML: Originally, Antonio Ortiz Mena directed it. But now it is a group headed by the president.

CBG: Does Salinas de Gortari belong to this group?

PML: Naturally; he was created by this group. They all studied at Harvard and Yale and formed a network.

Conservativism is sweeping Mexico. The de la Madrid administration is the farthest to the right. There's no doubt about it. Without discussing its errors, the López Portillo administration seesawed ambivalently, ideologically speaking. Neither the López Portillo nor the Echeverría administration was openly counterrevolutionary. López Portillo took actions that demonstrated a certain progressivism. His nationalization of the banks and his inclusion of progressive officials within his administration demonstrates this.

De la Madrid's conservativism partly reflects his own thinking. It also reflects the thinking of the team to which he belonged. I remember that, when de la Madrid became the PRI candidate, and differences of opinion began to show up between outgoing President López Portillo and him, López Portillo made a now widely known public statement revealing this. He said: "They have seized his will" ["Le han ocupado la voluntad"]. "They" refers to people in whom de la Madrid believed blindly. You could say that he practically abandoned the kind of person he was at the university: a constructionalist, a political scientist, someone with an open mind. Further proof of this may be seen in the final candidate picked from the six precandidates he presented to the bar of public opinion in the middle of 1987. There were three lawyers and three finance specialists. Those of us who have been following the country's developments already knew that the finalist would not be a lawyer. It had to be one of the financial experts. And the one selected, Carlos Salinas de Gortari, was the one who best portrayed the technocratic approach to government! His selection represents a kind of bloodless coup d'état.

During 1978, when I visited various universities in the United States and in Europe, I kept thinking about my

situation. While visiting Princeton University, I stopped to
see Carlos Fuentes, who was living there at the time, and he
asked me why I didn't start a new party. I gave him two
reasons why I wouldn't do it. One was that I didn't think the
country was ready for the splitting of the PRI. Due to López
Portillo's own ambivalence, I still thought that a consensus
between the different wings of the party was possible.
(Ambivalence leaves room, doesn't it? López Portillo selected
de la Madrid, who also reflected this ambivalence at the
start. He might have been a Banco de México economist,
but he was also a university professor. Parenthetically,
Fuentes was very critical of the López Portillo administration.) The second reason why I didn't try to found a new
party in 1978 is that Mexico faced a different struggle at
the time. It was engaged in making a major effort to take off
economically. I believed that my helping out in the international arena represented the best way I could contribute to
this takeoff.

However, the situation began to erode. Even while I was
serving as United Nations ambassador, I thought of doing
something, but I didn't think of forming a new party at this
time. My original idea was to create a converging democratic
center, perhaps something like a foundation for democracy
that would encourage new ideas from people located in different political streams. I became convinced, however, that
the country could not resolve its problems without major
political change, and it was going to be necessary to promote change.

In other words, the doors began closing slowly. The
opportunities for change began to vanish slowly too. This
technocratic group at the Banco Central gradually consoli-
dated itself in power. The possibilities against change hard-
ened gradually.

A major decision does not happen from one day to the
next. You do not know the final implications of what you
pursue day by day, although the orientation is present. We
have been separating ourselves each day as the government
has been closing itself off. Its own decisions have taken on a
more definitive or more irreversible character for the future
of the nation. It is very hard for someone who has been
faithful to the symbols of the party (I call it "love of the T-
shirt") to say one day: "I'm bolting from the party." People
don't understand what we're doing; they see it as a simple

defection. All rescissions begin with a long period of dissidence. Martin Luther's example is apropos because he did not decide to create a reformed church overnight. It took him a long time to make the decision. The more the institutions close their doors, the more the reformer is pressed to the doorway. And, as the struggle becomes radicalized, the positions taken become more contrary. We initiated a dissidence which is turning out to be a rescission.

A few months before I returned to Mexico, I held conversations abroad with friends of mine, many of them ambassadors and political appointees. They advised me that there would be many people like themselves (they had been sent abroad for ideological reasons, and they felt out of step with the way things were going at home) who would support a well-organized *corriente* within the party. They favored something that would bring them together in a move towards internal change. This became a very seductive idea.

I don't know if you'll write this down in the end, but I am known as an honorable man, and I am that. I am known as an excellent government official, and I have been that. I developed my talents in public office. I think the children of schoolteachers are potentially good officials because what they learn represents good training for the job, right? Educators uphold republican values which one learns from childhood: honor, efficiency, respect for institutions, et cetera. I think I've been an efficient and imaginative official and a politician of high prestige in my country. Moreover, I haven't made enemies with those who have governed the country. I maintain a personal friendship with them instead. This means that I did not leave the system because of bad personal relationships nor the lack of efficiency on the job nor the lack of honor or prestige. I stepped away because of the government's ideology. In other words, the ideology of progressive men and women has become incompatible with the government's ideology.

I believe that the Mexican system did represent a system of consensus and that an internal equilibrium did exist among various political actors. Some refer to this as the "revolutionary family," an idea first coined by an American author [Frank B. Brandenburg]. I admit this sounds a little bit like the mafia or something of a tribal nature, but it is far more than that. The "family" did represent a political and ideological pluralism which did exist in fact.

CBG: Was it oligarchical up to a certain point?

PML: Look, I hail from a very modest family. I've told you that my parents were schoolteachers. I was a mere university professor for a long time too. It took me ten years to become a government minister. The system might have been oligarchical, but not in the social or classist sense. The top of the system was open to the lower parts at certain times. I served in a period when this was so. The Mexican system had its ups and downs like any other. Adolfo López Mateos took it upon himself to personally combat oligarchical tendencies. The system had built-in checks. Obviously, there are oligarchial tendencies that are visible. I would agree with the famous specialist on political parties, Michels, who argues that the iron law of all parties is to create oligarchial *cúpulas.*[5] All systems need to have their own built-in checks and balances, to be open to new elements, and to give people with new ideas a chance to try them out.

I had the chance to do something in the two great moments of my life when I served with Echeverría and López Mateos. In the United Nations, I was holding onto the most progressive corner of the government. These represented moments of great aperture in the system. I became a point of equilibrium myself, along with other distinguished Mexicans like Jesús Reyes Heroles, Flores de la Peña, Jorge Castañeda, and Carlos Tello. We are considered to be part of the corps of progressive secretaries of state in Mexico because we created an impact by dint of our ideas, our political rhetoric, and concrete government actions in order to keep a lid on those oligarchic influences. The problem is that they won in the end! That's the problem!

CBG: You are no longer a progressive?

PML: I'm a nationalist. You ask me how I came to think the way I do. In 1987 the journal *Jueves de excelsior* reprinted the first article I ever published. It comes from an article published in the student journal *Medio Siglo* entitled "La juventud universitaria ante la realidad nacional," a very sophomoric title obviously. But, in it, I say something to the effect that the Mexican system is reaching a limit, and it is urgent that it renew itself internally; otherwise, it will be recast from the outside. I am still saying this today.

CBG: I'd like to know where this tendency comes from. For example, why didn't you join the Communist Party?

PML: Why didn't I become a Socialist or a Communist? Because I am not a Marxist, and I have never been one. I think that Marx is a very important thinker and that his ideas have helped shape the evolution of history. There's no doubt about this. I also think that no educated man ought to ignore Marxism, particularly if he specializes in the social sciences. Marxology or studies about Marxism should not be ignored either. You may recall that I received a lot of my education in Europe, especially at a time when Marxist books were being rewritten and when the criticism of Stalinist dogmatism became widespread (this took place around the time of the 20th Congress of the Communist Party). Much of this criticism came to me from many sources, including Jesuit studies and studies from the liberal school as well. In any case, I maintain that Marxism represents one of the great themes of our time which we need to know. It represents an intellectual formation which we ought not be without.

However, the distance between this and actually being a Marxist is quite great. I was shaped by the ideology surrounding the Mexican Revolution. My parents were schoolteachers, and they too were formed within this ideology, which was nationalistic, social-oriented, egalitarian, and democratic. They were also *indigenistas*; they had real conviction. Don't forget that they taught during the era of General [Lázaro] Cárdenas. This means that they lived during the 1930s, and they shared the intensity of those years. My home was filled with Mexican nationalism. Moreover, during my school years, I studied broadly. I think a student needs to read the great authors of capitalism as well. I recommend that public schools rigorously stress the study of [John Maynard] Keynes as well as Marx. Although I believe that intellectual training ought to be all encompassing, I also believe each person needs to develop his or her own line of thought. For all these reasons, I never joined parties of the Left, because I always considered my place to be with the Mexican Revolution, the real Mexican Revolution, not the falsified version that we hold up today.

CBG: Who would characterize or define the true Mexican Revolution?

PML: I think that *cardenismo* represents the highest point in the Mexican Revolution. I don't think there's any doubt about this. I insist too that there ought to be a bal-

ance, because the Mexican Revolution represented a balance
as well. The constitution of 1917 also represents a balance
between individual and social interests. I repeat, the most
important thing for me is to be a nationalist, to fight for
social equality, and to have an attitude which is democratic
to its core. This is another way of saying that, in defining
Mexicanist thought, Francisco I. Madero is as important as
Emiliano Zapata or Lázaro Cárdenas. *Maderismo* represents
the fight for civil dignity and democracy, which I view as
fundamental notions which derive from the revolution itself.
This is not to discount Zapata. He represents the voice of
the people who work the soil. Cárdenas represents the con-
summation of the great reforms in our history.

CBG: Can one say that you represent *cardenismo* within
the PRI now?

PML: I represent much more.

CBG: What more than *cardenismo* do you represent?

PML: I represent the social progressive current that is
expressed in very distinctive ways. Obviously, I was too
young to take part in the epoch of *cardenismo* whose social
democratic ideals are similar to those of the Mexican
Revolution.

CBG: In the 1950s, Lombardo Toledano had a—

PML: Lombardo was formed within the Marxist school.
That's the reason why I never took part in leftist parties,
not because I didn't respect them nor appreciate the role
they played in the country, not because we do not share common concerns. I identify myself with the ideals of the
Mexican Revolution. Some say on the left or liberal side of
it, but it doesn't matter, however you want to say it.

CBG: So you represent the left wing of the PRI.

PML: To say that I represent the left wing of the party is
in itself too simple. I prefer "the progressive wing" because
in Mexico it means much more. The word "left" usually
means Marxism, and "progressive" does not necessarily; this
is why we prefer the words "the progressive wing."

CBG: What do you think of the leftist parties in Mexico
in the late 1980s?

PML: I believe that they were undergoing a very healthy
evolution which was encouraging them to set aside Marxist
symbology and old dogmatisms; they were stepping into the
most important streams of Mexican thought. They exhibited
notable flexibility, referring not only to the process of fusion

with forces less radical than they, but also with less radical individuals as well. Here I have Heberto Castillo in mind.

I also recognize, perhaps as their most meritorious actions, their unwillingness to disparage political democracy and their effort to make it their own, instead. I recognize the fact that they don't dismiss what they have called "bourgeois democracy"; this is very important. Their joining the crusade on behalf of political democracy in the country appears to me as an important step in the evolution of the Mexican Left. They were interested in talking with us [in the Corriente Democrática] because of the possibility of forming an alliance, and we were interested in this ourselves.

CBG: Do you see the role of the parties of the poor as a useful one in this era?

PML: Which parties of the poor?

CBG: The people who rose with men like Lucio Cabañas and such.

PML: When I speak of the Left here, I do not include the kind of movement represented by Lucio Cabañas in the 1970s. That was something different because it represented an insurrectional movement. However, we believe it arose from the grave social conflicts of the time, and we also believe that a democratic country ought to reabsorb its members in a peaceful way. Moreover, efforts taken on behalf of political reform, based on the efforts we expended during the López Portillo years, served as an important element helping to reincorporate these people into the mainstream of national institutions.

CBG: What do you think of the Right or of the PAN?

PML: You ask my opinions about the PAN, but I shared them in another interview, so I'll ask you to go on to another question.[6] However, I do need to say something else.

In the late 1980s it was necessary to rehabilitate the parties of the Center-Left, ones which we often forgot. Three groups which split away from the PRI existed in the 1980s. One of these was the PPS, led by Vicente Lombardo Toledano. The PARM also represents an offshoot of the PRI. Old revolutionaries and military officers of the early years of the revolution who felt unhappy with the political and economic evolution of the country took one of two options. They either joined the *henriquista* movement in 1952, which linked itself up with the Federacion de los Partidos del Pueblo, or they banded together to form a minority party

called the Authentic Party of the Mexican Revolution, or
PARM. The third splinter group is the PST, which is made
up of young advocates for social change who have confined
most of their activity to the agrarian sector. They supported
the demands of small farmers, the *ejidatarios*, because they
were abandoned by government policymakers. I need to add
the PSD, or the Social Democratic Party. It was put together
by a group of forward-looking businessmen who began to
put together ideas favoring social change. It did not obtain
its registration as a party, strictly speaking, because it dared
to present Manuel Moreno Sánchez as its presidential candidate. He is a former senator feared for his criticism. Other
organizations like the PSD have not been allowed to present independent candidates.

This group of parties making up the Center-Left was
greatly vilified. It was satellitized, and it lost the respect of
many people. These parties needed to be rehabilitated
because nobody gained as long as they continued to function in that [subordinated] condition. I believe that the
Center-Left represents the potential for change in Mexico.

Moreover, certain conservative government policies in
the late 1980s sought to liquidate the progressive wing of
the PRI (which we represented), by taking away the freedom
of speech enjoyed by members of congress and by reducing
important organizations to mere instruments of centralized
power. One of these, for example, is the National Association
of Economists, whose new president in 1987 was going to
be selected "by acclamation"; this meant that he was going
to be selected according to the wishes of the secretaries of
state, who had a lot to do with the various candidates of the
association to begin with. Another example is seen in the
pressure placed on union leaders and on people in other popular organizations, including youth groups, who hold progressive views. All of this represents a verticalism seldom
seen in the Mexican system which includes the selection of
congressional candidates, for example, from lists concocted
by technocrats in the offices of the secretaries of state. The
subordination of people who hold progressive views to those
who hold technocratic points of view goes on, and it exists
within the PRI. This is an attempt to liquidate the progressive wing and anyone else holding independent views.
[Anyone trying to understand politics in Mexico] needs to
combine this information with evidence of the drive to

weaken the parties of the Center-Left by converting them into government satellites.

With regard to the PAN in the late 1980s, we spoke with important members of the Right who had decided to really fight for democracy. This included business groups from northern Mexico as well as organizations affiliated with the PAN.

CBG: Can you name some of these people or organizations?

PML: I can identify distinguished people who belonged to the PAN executive committee, like Norberto Corella, or people referred to as neo-PAN members, like Alejandro Gurz, or businessmen from Monterrey, like Rogelio Sada Zambrano, or important members of the Left too, like Arnoldo Martínez Verdugo and Pablo Gómez. In combination with others, all of these people helped us put together what we are calling the Asamblea Democrática por Elecciones Limpias [Democratic Assembly for Honest Elections].

It's necessary to add here that the PRI system did not fear a presidential candidate of the Left before 1988 because the number of people who had voted for this type of candidate was limited to national elections. It did not fear a presidential candidate of the Right either, for the same reason. However, at the state level, like in Sinaloa, Nuevo León, or Chihuahua, the system did fear competition, naturally. What the system really feared was the formation of a Center-Left movement which could gather the small parties and thus bring about a splitting of the official party. This is why we were condemned so strongly. The system had been trying to prevent this since 1952, when Miguel Henríquez Guzmán sought the presidency.

CBG: When did you decide to have to step away from the PRI?

PML: The situation was already clear when I left the government in December 1977. When I speak of myself, I speak as someone who acts as a representative figure for others in Mexico.

CBG: Who else?

PML: I have many disciples and collaborators.

CBG: Three or four?

PML: Many. For the most part, they're in the government; they are people like Ifigenia Martínez, Armando

Labra, and Carlos Tello. My first clear ideas concerning the need for change go back to the first phase of my political career, when I worked for President López Mateos, explicitly for the construction of a progressive wing within the party. In the second phase, I was invited by President Echeverría for the same reason, to organize a progressive front within the government itself. I also accepted the presidency of the PRI in an attempt to balance it [away from the Right]. In other words, those who felt like I did never stood up conditionally; we always stood up for something. We were never bureaucratized by the system. If we stepped away, it was for ideological reasons, especially those relating to economic issues like the foreign debt.

CBG: Then, you're saying that de la Madrid's position was farthest to the Right, so you and others decided—

PML: The debt problem could have been resolved in several ways.

CBG: One also has to note that the international environment, especially what the United States represents, was an enormous factor in de la Madrid's way of thinking.

PML: I'm not suggesting to you that de la Madrid had to adopt the position taken by Alan García [Peruvian president who limited debt repayment to 10 percent of foreign earnings], because we're talking about two different countries with very different temperaments. Even so, a more independent attitude could have been fashioned, one that might have changed the balance in the relationship between Mexico and Latin America. This is very important! Mexico's decision to close ranks with the Baker Plan is something I discussed with various Latin American leaders who happen to be friends of mine, though I won't reveal their names. Closing ranks is not done so explicitly, right? Certain forms need to be maintained! The idea was not to begin selling off publicly owned enterprises from one day to another nor to accept all foreign investments. Keep in mind, however, that, in just one day alone, Mexican government officials brought down many tariff duties, something that takes years to negotiate through GATT.

CBG: What day was this?

PML: This took place in 1984 or 1985 even before Mexico entered GATT. The openhanded treatment of foreign investors has been scandalous as well. The difference between political speeches and actions is notable too. In

February 1986, Miguel de la Madrid made a speech on
Mexican television in which he said we would not continue
to borrow money abroad in order to pay old debts. He
affirmed that Mexico would change its way of doing things.
This line of argument was taken up by Finance Minister
Jesús Silva Herzog, who began to repeat it in international
financial circles. He began to say that debt issues would
have to be treated differently. In May 1986 the PRI's
National Committee held a meeting to define the party's
position on economic issues. I was present as former party
president when it resolved that Mexico needed to change its
position on the international debt. It also resolved that the
government reject new credits. All of this happened on the
eve of renegotiations.

However, neither the president's speech of February
1986 nor Silva Herzog's words nor the party resolutions
were taken into account. Silva Herzog became a sacrificial
lamb, though no one has stated it publicly. The reason was
that certain people in the government changed their minds.
They didn't want Silva Herzog to raise the banner of
change and benefit from it politically. Months later the
debt renegotiation took place, and a position was adopted
which was diametrically opposed to the president's speech
[of February 1986]. This is very serious. It tells me that an
internal political shift took place and that the technocrats
won the battle. Many people think that Salinas de Gortari,
who stood as Silva Herzog's political rival, engineered his
downfall. They attribute the refashioning of the nation's
economic policy, which we refer to as a "giveaway" policy, to
Salinas. All of this precipitated matters, and it radicalized
the situation.

This is the way the Corriente Democrática was born.
The name "Corriente" ["current"] was suggested by
Ambassador Rodolfo González Guevara when he was in
Madrid. The ambassador took the label from the European
political scene, where currents exist from time to time.
Spain has its Corriente Crítica, for example, and it was
thought that we could do something akin to that. The
ambassador suggested the idea that perhaps we could
require a fee from people in the system who supported our
ideas. He thought that we could formally petition the PRI
for fees just as you find in the Spanish system. I discussed
this with Felipe González (the [Spanish] prime minister and

my friend), and he explained to me that they handle their currents this way because they recognize independent critiques within a larger party. We were looking for ways to function within the system, and perhaps even to begin fielding candidates all the way from the presidency to the lowest elected posts in the nation.

The PRI leadership did not accept our proposal to form a *corriente*. A very strong discussion resulted from it, though it didn't reach the point of confrontation. When we proposed the idea in detail, the response given to me in a famous interview with Adolfo Lugo Verduzco, then party president, was that the PRI was a "pluri-classist" party but not "pluri-ideological." Even then I pointed out that there were indeed different currents of thought within the party. This response to our proposal may be described as being Stalinistic. It was like a papal response too; there is only one doctrine, and only the pope can interpret it properly. The PRI denied freedom of thought within the party, including the right to interpret party doctrine freely.

When Lugo Verduzco stepped down from the PRI presidency, we all thought that things would change. We thought we would be able to negotiate matters, because friends of ours were brought in with the new president, Jorge de la Vega. We spent two months discussing the matter in about eight or nine sessions with de la Vega, and we all agreed that we would continue to discuss our plans at the 13th Party Congress. I discussed the matter with President Miguel de la Madrid, and Cuauhtémoc Cárdenas did it too. I should add that, in my conversations with the president in 1986 and 1987, he never cast a negative opinion on our plans. I would even say that he looked satisfied with the idea the first time I spoke with him concerning the need for a democratic opening. It's possible he didn't think we would go as far as we did. In any case, I said what I had to say, and he didn't refute it, though he asked many questions. The second time we saw him about our plans, we went over the matter again, explaining everything. We went over erroneous interpretations which had already begun to circulate (i.e., that we were politicking during the preelectoral phase with hidden goals), and we clarified everything. We agreed in the end that we would take part in the congress, that our opinions would be respected, and that we would continue our role within the party. Doubts existed about our calling

ourselves a current, but that was mere semantics. The idea
itself was clear, however.

At the 13th Party Congress, which gathered in the first
days of March 1987, more than twenty-five of us took part
with prepared statements. No decisions were made at this
point. The day the congress closed, a surprising event took
place when former Presidents Echeverría and López Portillo
were brought in. Their presence, however, did not prevent a
final reckoning with us. We were condemned in front of
everyone present. We were accused of forming a fifth col-
umn and acting as a Trojan horse within the party. They
called us traitors, practically speaking, and we were asked
to knuckle under. Cuauhtémoc Cárdenas felt betrayed
because he had represented our views at a special
roundtable discussion with a presentation entitled "Internal
Procedures and the Selection of Candidates," which was not
rejected, nor was it discussed either. That was the way they
honored their own statute—by doing nothing. We were told,
in any case, that our theses had already been rejected, that
the majority had smashed the minority, and that we had
nothing to say as a consequence. This too was a Stalinist
procedure.

We were obligated to respond. Cárdenas reacted in a
vivid manner, in part because he had been attacked directly.
He wrote and publicized a letter in which he denied the
moral authority and the legitimacy of the party president.
This became the reason why some people said later that he
removed himself from the party. I too sent a letter, later, in
which I denounced the fact that the accusations against us
had been done on the eve of the refinancing of the international debt.

It turned out I was being prophetic, because I stated in
the letter that, each time a major refinancing took place,
certain postures were taken by the government to assure
its creditors. As evidence, I cited a very important article
published by the *Wall Street Journal* on October 9, 1986. It
was an editorial which stated that, since President Reagan
had assured American bankers that Mexico's debt position
was going to continue unchanged, the bankers had acquiesced to refinancing. However, the banking establishment
felt "hyper-nervous," the article continued, because a "group
of leftist nationalizers of banks, land, and oil" had appeared
within the party and challenged the Mexican government.

Since bankers did not know very much about Mexican politics, the article expressed concern over de la Madrid's assurances to Reagan that Mexico would continue to pay. The fear of problems arising within the PRI began to grow within banking circles. This is why I said earlier that the condemnation which we received in the 13th Party Congress represented a way to assure the international banking community.

In the letter I sent, I stated that this situation [refinancing] represented the bondage of our sovereignty and that authoritarianism was being offered as a guarantee of payment. Although I didn't say this outright, I implied that we were approaching a [Augusto] Pinochet-like situation wherein the collateral for an international economy was authoritarianism itself. This represented a grave denunciation. The government and the president himself became very irritated. I was speaking the truth, however, and I was also forecasting what occurred later.

We of the Corriente decided to take our message out to the country so that we could grow stronger. We appeared before local television, and we also began forming grassroots organizations throughout the country. I visited many provisional PRI party headquarters to talk with my supporters, and this caused a lot of friction. Finally, a political committee of the party expelled us. It did so in a hypocritical manner, because the statutory method of expulsion was not followed. This method requires a decision, by a Committee of Honor and Justice, arrived at in an open meeting. However, the party stalwarts avoided this. In the resolution written by the political committee, we are "marginalized" from the party, condemned, prohibited from using the party logo, and denied from presenting ourselves as party members. We are also excluded from all party functions. This was done illegally, as I say. In response, we took the indispensable step of registering Cuauhtémoc Cárdenas as a PRI candidate for the presidency.

CBG: How was it decided that he would be the candidate and not you?

PML: The most adequate thing for us to do was to have Cuauhtémoc become a candidate. Of the three most visible leaders at the time, Ambassador González Guevara, Cuauhtémoc, and I, we had to discount the ambassador because he was outside the country and because he was beyond a certain age (even though his faculties are complete). In any case, the ambassador urged that Cuauhtémoc be the candidate. He spoke to Cuauhtémoc and suggested he become a candidate. Many months later, I too urged Cuauhtémoc to do the same thing, in part because time was pressing too. Nevertheless, one day I came to realize fully the kind of popularity that Cuauhtémoc could attract. This was after the 13th Congress, when he sent the tough-worded letter to the newspaper, as I stated already, which immediately catapulted his image. His firmness did it. Several of us then quickly realized Cuauhtémoc's capacity to grow, because he became a national figure rather than a mere ex-governor in just a few weeks.

CBG: Did it continue to grow?

PML: Yes. Besides his name, other reasons existed as well. His name and what he has done all of his life together meant a lot to many people in Mexico. With Cuauhtémoc, I visited the Laguna District in northern Mexico, where General Cárdenas distributed land in the early years, and I was witness to the amazing devotion that Cuauhtémoc commands there.

CBG: Did he have support in the agrarian sector, among the campesinos?

PML: He enjoyed enormous support among the people who made up the agrarian sector. Another reason is that his candidacy provided the best balance within the Corriente itself in 1987.

CBG: Balance?

PML: What I do in the areas of organizing and strategy balances quite well with his promotional activity. Moreover, what I did in the last administrations was too noticeable, and very strong criticism concerning these administrations (Echeverría and López Portillo) still lingered in the country.

CBG: Did Echeverría have anything to do with the Corriente?

PML: Nothing.

CBG: What position did he take?

PML: If he said anything concerning our activity, it was to side with the government and the official party. For example, he eulogized Salinas, the elections of 1988, the PRI president, et cetera. However, he did not criticize us. He played the role of a man who belongs to the system.

CBG: Did he say anything to you?

PML: No, he may have had some ideological sympathies with us, but, politically, he was a man of the system, and he respected the system which we want to change. It's entirely possible that, as with López Portillo, when we criticized the *dedazo* method of selecting leaders, we also criticized him.

CBG: Have you communicated with López Portillo?

PML: No, they are playing traditional roles; they have interests to defend. Moreover, things have not gone well with them, because they did not receive the respect they expected; their successors treated them poorly. In any case, they do not represent a political factor at all. I ought to add that young supporters of both men have shown us a lot of sympathy, but they can't do more than that.

You say that I am identified with Echeverría and López Portillo, and this is true. This is one of the reasons why I didn't step forward at the time. It would take too much time to explain why I did certain things, my attitude, and so on. This would weaken our movement. Cuauhtémoc represents a newer figure than I do. My coattails are tied to positive elements, but there are some negative ones too, which were manipulated by the government. I was the object of a terrible campaign that cast me as Echeverría's instrument, as you have stated. People react in a very torpid way about these things because their political sensitivity is not well developed. I have already referred to the example of Martin Luther. It's like faulting George Washington because he was a subject of the British Crown once, or Miguel Hidalgo, Mexico's "father of independence," because he held a viceroyal appointment at one time too. If those who pursue social change had not taken part in prior regimes, revolution would have to arise out of kindergartens! Every great rupture begins with dissidence. When systems decay, internal balances go awry and someone has to interpret the need for change.

Let me return to our attempt to register Cuauhtémoc as a PRI candidate despite official opposition. We had to gather signatures to register him as a precandidate. We ended up with 780,000 signatures from around the country, petitioning the PRI to invite party members to a convention. We did this because precandidates may only be registered as such, only after a convention invitation has been issued and the register itself has been opened to internal party nominations. We

thus petitioned that this invitation be made with at least
150 days' notice (five months), because we calculated that
internal campaigns or primaries for a country with eighty
million people ought to last at least that long. In the United
States, for example, they last one year, and, in Venezuela
and Costa Rica, they last as long as two years. We asked
for party facilities in order to compete within the party too.

All of this was denied, of course. No one paid any mind
to us; they acted as if we didn't exist, and a negative position was upheld. Our supporters began to feel the pressure
too. Government employees who were seen with us were
fired. Credit requests by peasants who supported us by
attending our meetings were denied by governmental
authorities. Boats owned by fishing cooperative members
who identified with us by showing up at our meetings were
likewise denied access to port, and so on. In fact, in some
ways we had to fight more than the regular opposition did.
Persecutions against us were felt most in the state of
Michoacán, where Cuauhtémoc Cárdenas served as state
governor, and where the current governor, Martínez
Villicaña, rescinded Cárdenas's accomplishments and has
acted as a hatchet man.

In Mexico City, on September 21, 1987, we organized a
demonstration to bolster our position. On our way to party
headquarters, we had to stop at the Monument to the
Revolution because we learned that unidentified shock
troops or thugs recruited from progovernment labor unions
(also known as *halcones*), police forces, and mobile anti-
crowd water tanks were waiting for us farther along the
route. We then sent a delegation to talk matters over, and I
had to make a speech to our demonstrators in order to ask
them to disperse. If we had not exercised the prudence to
stop the demonstration, another Tlaltelolco would have
taken place.

In what I consider to be a farce, six precandidates were
identified by the government afterward. They weren't registered anywhere and they didn't compete for support openly
within the party. The uncovering of these six men simply
turned into a speech-making contest that only served to distract public opinion and to try to counter our own efforts.

On October 4, 1987, Carlos Salinas de Gortari was
selected as presidential PRI candidate. Although he is a
well-known talented young man, to party stalwarts he

nonetheless symbolizes the economic policies which have
been attacked, for some time now, by labor unions and even
by Fidel Velázquez, the progovernment labor czar.

Even so, a long-standing tradition of party discipline and
a tightly enacted government maneuver, which gave the
impression that the system was being opened up when it
really wasn't, helped cover up the ruse. This was done so
well that, an hour before Salinas de Gortari was uncovered,
the name of another precandidate, Sergio García Ramírez
(attorney general), was announced as the anointed one. The
press and the hangers-on then rushed to García's home to
congratulate him.

CBG: What significance did this hold?

PML: What this mistake revealed was a lot of nervous-
ness due to the hermetic character of the system. It also
reflected the dashed hope of many people that the official
candidate wouldn't be someone from the technocratic team
already mentioned. It needs to be said too that García
Ramírez's name was received very favorably throughout, not
because people believed in the hidden methods of candidate
selection, but because he symbolized a change in economic
policy. The people may have thought intuitively that the
government had recovered its missteps and the people's
voice was somehow heard. But things didn't turn out this ·
way.

On the same day, I delivered a statement to the press in
which I charged that all these events were part of a simu-
lated election. I said, furthermore, that it represented the
efforts of the same technocratic group to stay in power. I
also invited members of the PRI to reject the Salinas candidacy by regarding it as illegal. Cuauhtémoc Cárdenas made
a declaration similar to mine which emphasized the irregularities of the party procedure. Three days later we issued
another document charging the chief of state with manipulating the upper echelons of the party in order to impose a
close supporter of his for many years as his successor. Again
we invited the grass-roots members of the party to recapture
the legitimacy of that procedure, and we tagged its leadership as illegal as well. Days later, several representatives
of the Center-Left political parties came to us.

CBG: They approached you?

PML: Yes, they came to us. We had already talked with
them, especially with members of the PARM, the PST, and

the PPS. They all said to us that, given the nature of the
decision taken by the government, they wanted to take
advantage of Cárdenas's charisma and the interest the situation was creating in order to increase their showing at the
polls. More to the left of the PARM, the PPS and the PST
felt wounded by the selection of a technocrat whom they
considered a conservative. The PARM itself felt little connection with the economic leaders of the government. Given
the circumstances, they all felt the need for a more independent posture. One reason we selected the PARM as the
lead party and did it so suddenly that *Proceso* calls it the
madruguete, or "the early morning surprise," is because we
feared the government would have done something to head
it off.

CBG: So that's why you chose the PARM?

PML: We also selected the PARM because its ideology
was closest to the PRI's. Actually, it didn't have a distinct
ideology.

CBG: It was the weakest of all.

PML: You say that the party was the weakest of all of
the opposition parties, but that wasn't bad either. It may
not have had a national structure, but it had strength in
certain areas, and its candidates had definitely won elections, in the north especially. The president of the PARM
was the only Mexican who had outvoted the PRI three times
in a row in the city of Nuevo Laredo.

CBG: Who was the president?

PML: Carlos Cantú Rosas. Our group was not concerned
about the PARM's lack of a national structure, because we
felt that all of us together could gain something from it. We
already had other supporters, so the PARM people simply
enriched us. The PARM does not represent a dogmatic party,
either. It isn't a Marxist organization nor a leftist party. It is
a center party. The Corriente could not have become an
appendage of the Left.

We received a lot of criticism for allying ourselves with
the PARM, because it was seen as a dummy party. Our
response was that it might have been that; however, the
moment it turned insurgent against the government, it was
no longer a dummy. No one is a slave by choice. Cuauhtémoc
Cárdenas took the role of Abraham Lincoln with regard to
Mexico's political parties! They joined us because they
lacked power, just as they supported national PRI

candidates because it meant they could continue to hold on to their local districts. This is not really immoral. These parties experienced some difficult times when they were saddled with very poor leaders, but they were thrown out around 1984 or so.

We selected the PARM too because its party symbols belonged to the Mexican Revolution. The Monument of the Revolution, here in Mexico City, is its major symbol. They claim Zapata, Villa, Madero, and Carranza too. Their Declaration of Principles was similar to ours and it also tried to recuperate the vigor of the Mexican Revolution, as the Corriente did.

Regarding the PMS, we had conversations with its leaders, whom I consider of very high political calibre. It was led by men who are prestigious, without a doubt, and we respected them as friends too. I would not dream of trying to tarnish the PMS, because it was held in the highest regard in Mexico, at that point, particularly by members of intellectual and journalistic circles. The PMS enjoyed this prestige because its leaders expended a lot of effort to fuse together six political organizations in the full light of public opinion. They put together a veritable popular front, which is not too far left, by virtue of their vocation to democracy. They demonstrated this by holding primary elections and thus elected their presidential candidate, Heberto Castillo.

CBG: What plans do you have with the PMS?

PML: We negotiated with the PMS about possible mutual support. When this book comes out, the whole world will know what happened as a result.[7] They sent us a letter in 1987 requesting Cárdenas to take part in another [PMS] primary, in which he would compete against Heberto Castillo.

I should add that the PPS did not support us directly.[8] It had already identified a modest worker as a candidate, but it nonetheless expressed interest in fusing with us in 1987 if it could be worked out. The PSD, a nonregistered party, also offered us their support, and they suggested an interparty assembly instead of primary elections, in order to arrive at a common presidential candidate. In any case, various groups wanted to find a common candidate.

I already said that we held contacts with the PAN and that these contacts increased each day, especially in looking for ways to defend the people's vote. We had some problems here because some commentators, paid by the government, accused the so-called neo-PAN wing of having an office in the United States (Mexico-United States Information, or MUSI) financed by the Foundation for Democracy (an excessively anti-Communist organization linked to the Philippines and Central America). I spoke with them; this was in fact the case, and we asked them to keep those connections away from our group.

CBG: In the final order of things, did you seek to create a new party in 1987?

PML: Not exactly. Here, I am giving you my own personal opinion without compromising anybody else. We look for a change in the balance of political forces, and this change can only rise from democracy itself. This change implies a transformation of the party system in Mexico! What we have to hurry up and do is to press the traditional and sclerotic PRI into becoming a minority party; this will take place in the next few years. When the PRI becomes simply another competitive party, many currents will arise, and from these a new center-left party may be formed.[9] I consider myself now and for all times as someone who fights for democracy in Mexico.

I don't exclude the possibility that we might win in the elections of 1988. Still, I am not like so many party militants who like to flex their institutional muscles. If all of us in the Corriente and in the opposition parties do the right things, we will gain a very strong showing, especially if we run with one candidate. We could win this way; but, if we don't, we will have gained many positions in congress. Everything depends on the way things go in the next few days.

CBG: Do you think that the imbalance that you are creating will lead to a crisis in which the military will have to intervene, as it was so close to doing in 1968?

PML: No. Even though we don't agree with the people who are now in power, they represent people who uphold modern ideas. I may disagree with many aspects of de la Madrid's policies, but I need to recognize that he has been the least repressive head of state that Mexico has had. His hands are clean in this sense. He is a modern man, and he is also an honorable one. For the same reasons, I do not believe that Salinas de Gortari would launch a repressive program in Mexico. It would be contrary to their platform, which they consider a modern one.

However, the logic of neoliberal economics may entwine itself with the logic of military neoauthoritarianism, as I've written in a book for UNESCO.[10] Both deny politics as a legitimate avenue for arriving at solutions. In my view, neoliberalism looks unfavorably at politics because it is unable to envision an economy issuing from an equilibrium of political forces. Instead, it envisions an economy issuing from unilateral decision making imposed from above. It's a curious thing to note that U.S. theorists demand more democracy from Latin America at the same time they also demand free markets. This conservative line of thinking encourages a greater gathering of natural resources for processing in the United States, a revolving credit system, and democracy too. This represents the "Bakerization" of Latin America. These theorists are wrong because their approach can only drag us in Latin America into the jaws of antidemocracy. There is no compatibility between this conservative approach and democracy itself. I believe the Reagan administration deceived us in this sense.

CBG: Have you had any run-ins with the military up to this point?

PML: No.

CBG: Only with local police forces?

PML: Yes. A democratic approach takes you along a different path toward social goals and the revindication of labor. We in the Corriente may face difficult moments, but only if a conservative and repressive policy is applied. In any case, we don't believe the military would take part in this kind of situation. On the contrary, we believe that many officers sympathize with our views.

CBG: If you formed a new party, would it reflect aspects of Social Democracy?

PML: It's hard to say at this time because I wouldn't be the only one involved in creating a new party. There would be many of us with differing points of view. If we wanted a big party, it would be as a result of party fusions. But I can say to you that, given our ideological spectrum, the party would definitely be democratic and nationalist. A parallel could be drawn between Social Democratic parties in other parts of the world and ourselves, but it would be very loose because the Mexican Revolution is basic for us. It antedates Social Democracy too. As the famous Peruvian leader Raúl Haya de la Torre once stated, "Social Democracy was

conceived for the benefit of the European industrial proletariat whereas the Mexican Revolution was conceived as an
alternative for all emerging social classes, the industrial
worker, peasants, and the middle classes." This is our view
too.

CBG: Do the other leaders of political parties generally
view the corruption of the contemporary government as an
impeding factor in the democratization of Mexico?

PML: That's the PAN's position, and I do not agree. The
PAN has waved many neopopulist flags. There is a contradiction in the philosophy of the rightist neo-*panistas.* On the
one hand, they seek to gain power through electoral means
and control the state apparatus, yet the antigovernment
criticism of the right-wing PAN is an echo of the antistatism
of the neoliberal ideology. I see this as very dangerous.

CBG: What is your position regarding the statism
question?

PML: We seek a modern state. The political chapter in
the booklet containing our platform is entitled, "The New
Democratic State and the Power of the Citizen." We want a
democratic state. We don't advocate stripping the power of
the state, but we do want it to function democratically in a
balance of government. Remember that Mexico is made up
not only of the federal government but also of state and
municipal governments too. These have lost considerable
autonomy. We want to fortify the federal system, but we also
want true state and municipal autonomy. This can come
only through free elections. We want an authentic division of
power, as well as a strong national congress (but this too is
part of the state).

CBG: What is the role of the *paraestatales,* or state-
owned industries?

PML: We want to rationalize them. We do not favor
reducing state volume, nor do we favor reducing it in order
to enrich a handful of people by virtue of foreign agreement.
May I remind you that I promoted administrative reform in
Mexico? I fashioned an entire doctrine about it and wrote a
book about it. I was the person who introduced the term *el
estado obeso,* or "the overweight state," in Mexico (I picked
up the term from Gunnar Myrdal's essay on the subject).[11]
We want a rationalization of the state so that it will become
stronger, more agile, and more responsible.

CBG: Do you advocate giving labor unions more rein?

PML: We propose the democratization of popular organizations. We oppose obligatory affiliation even as it applies to businessmen's organizations. We favor the democratic functioning of labor unions and employers' organizations. We favor self-governance and community autonomy. We favor democratic education too. We advocate the creation of a new attitude among the Mexican people in favor of representative democracy. This needs to be taught to schoolchildren in order to bring an end, once and for all, to authoritarian and caudillo traditions.

CBG: Do you want to change the senate?

PML: Yes. We propose an element of proportionality in the senate, although we haven't identified it as a possible bill yet. There are many ways to change the senate. I personally think that you could have a third senator for each state elected on a proportional basis.

CBG: Was this mentioned in the platform?

PML: Our platform would call for increasing the number of proportionally elected members and for introducing it into the senate. We also propose that we return to the original text of the constitution of 1917 in regard to the selection of the members of the supreme court. This text says that the jurors must be elected by the national congress on the basis of nominations made by the individual states. This would fortify Mexican federalism. This procedure was abolished in 1928, leaving the whole matter in the hands of the president. Other issues we favor include a new electoral code, the creation of local and regional parties, and the restoration of conditional status for emerging political parties.

CBG: Are you proposing any notable changes in foreign affairs?

PML: In foreign affairs we do not advocate new changes. Rather, we propose the recuperation of Mexico's historic approach to diplomacy as conceived by Benito Juárez, Venustiano Carranza, and Lázaro Cárdenas. We propose a restructuring of our relations with the United States. We propose returning to nonalignment status, although we do not propose to get out of GATT. Mexico should belong to all the international forums where its interests are at stake, including OPEC. It's absurd that Mexico belongs to the international organizations concerned about bananas, coffee, chilis, but not oil. We produce oil! It's absurd!

I believe we ought to continue to belong to GATT, not as a basis for the formulation of economic policies, but rather as an instrument. GATT represents an instrument for negotiation, not just an instrument to open up something. It may be used in a variety of ways. I know I am very heterodox on this; but, had we joined long ago, we could have helped out our friends in Brazil, India, and other countries like that in their own negotiations with GATT. We could have put together a united front within GATT.

CBG: Then you believe that joining GATT does not necessarily mean opening up the country to foreign merchandise?

PML: It means the ability to regulate that aperture, and this is the problem.

CBG: Do you believe that the government is doing that now?

PML: In Mexico today, GATT is synonymous with aperture. I mentioned that many tariffs were struck down even before Mexico joined GATT. We need to regulate things of this sort especially in the adverse international climate of the kind we are in now. Our position in GATT is akin to getting caught in a rainstorm without an umbrella. Many countries today are practicing differing methods of protectionism, yet Mexico is doing the opposite. The 1988 elections in the United States are going to resound with protectionist sentiments. The Democratic party is going to be raising the protectionist flag, yet in Mexico we are planning to open up. It's like going [out in the rain] without an umbrella.

Notes

1. This chapter is based on several interviews held between October 23 and 30, 1987, in Seattle.

2. Muñoz Ledo referred to the establishment of "el nuevo discurso político."

3. The North-South dialogue refers to a growing insistence by Third World countries to take part in the fashioning of economic development policies by industrial powers. Selected leaders of both industrial and developing nations met inconclusively for this purpose in Cancún on October 22–23, 1982.

4. The Group of 77 refers to the initial number of developing countries that supported an active stance vis-à-vis the industrialized nations in regard to trade, monetary policies, health,

environment, and other issues. See Brij Khindaria, "Foundation for Survival: The Desperate Need for Cooperation between North and South Nations," in *1981, Britannica Book of the Year* (Chicago: Encyclopaedia Britannica, 1981), 65–69.

5. Robert Michels, *Political Parties: A Sociological Study of the Oligarchical Tendencies of Modern Democracy* (Glencoe, IL: Free Press, 1949), 145.

6. Porfirio Muñoz Ledo, *Compromisos* (Mexico City: Editorial Pozada, 1989), 251–52.

The following is a paraphrase of Muñoz Ledo's views, as written in *Compromisos,* regarding the PAN: Ideologically forced to occupy political space on the periphery, the PAN resorted in its early years to radical posturing. It might have adopted a clearly Christian Democratic point of view in the interim, but the "hegemonic" nature of the PRI prevented it from doing so. Like Christian Democratic organizations elsewhere, it has sought to identify itself with certain groups of workers, although it has been unable to shed identification with the bosses. By virtue of a new party membership, the PAN now faces a historic opportunity to adopt a more progressivist stance. It needs to go beyond its advocacy of democracy to embrace a firm nationalist posture. In redefining its ideology, the PAN may continue to gain by upholding *maderista* ideals, but it can do the same as well by getting closer to the political ideals contained in Christian Democracy, as well as in other dimensions of the Center Right.

7. The PMS joined with the Corriente Democrática for the 1988 elections.

8. The PPS joined with the Corriente for the 1988 elections.

9. The PRD became organized after this interview and stood on the Center-Left in 1990.

10. Porfirio Muñoz Ledo, *La construcción del futuro de América Latina* (UNESCO, 1988).

11. Muñoz Ledo may have been referring to Gunnar Myrdal's *Beyond the Welfare State: Economic Planning and Its International Implications* (New Haven: Yale University Press, 1960), particularly chap. 2, "The State and the Individual," 84–107.

The Left

CHAPTER 8

Jorge Alcocer Villanueva

Jorge Alcocer Villanueva represents a new generation of Mexico's leftist leaders. Born into a middle-class family from the state of Guanajuato, he became a university professor of economics and taught prior to entering politics. Like many others in his age group, Alcocer escaped the government's repression of the Left while Mexico's authoritarian state was being erected. Even so, he became one of the strongest critics of the PRI system by the late 1980s.

He entered the Communist Party in his university years, when it was undergoing moderating transformations leading to the PSUM and finally to the PRD. Party leaders soon discovered his intellectual skills. At their request, he developed a legislative reference system in the absence of an institution akin to the U.S. Library of Congress, first for the Communist Party legislators, then for the PSUM and the PRD. Alcocer describes below not only the difficulties that opposition legislators face in trying to stay informed of legislative issues but also the legislative process and the way the opposition has been controlled by the PRI.

Alcocer became an important supporter of Cuauhtémoc Cárdenas in 1988 and 1989 but separated himself from Cárdenas and the PRD in December 1990.

CBG: Do us the favor, congressman, of giving us your name, date, and place of birth and where you were educated.[1]

JAV: My name is Jorge Alcocer. I am a native of León, Guanajuato. I am thirty years old, and at the present time, I am both a member of the Political Committee of the PSUM and a federal deputy. The elementary phase of my education took place in the public schools of Guanajuato. I attended high school and the university here in Mexico City.

By training, I am an economist, having graduated from the School of Economics at the national university.

CBG: Did you take part in university politics?

JAV: Yes, I did, especially in the last years of my university studies. I became a member of a technical committee on campus, and I thus gave formal initiation to my political experience.

CBG: Did you enter off-campus politics after you received your master's degree?

JAV: No, I joined the Communist Party in 1977 or 1978. In 1979, when I was a member of the party's Economic Studies Committee and I was working as a university instructor, I was invited by the party to organize a *grupo de asesoría*, or congressional advisory team. The party had just succeeded in electing some of its members to congress in recent elections, and they needed some help. The party thus invited me to leave the university, become a party professional, and create the advisory body. This group is still functioning today.

CBG: Why did you enlist in the Communist Party and not any other party?

JAV: I joined the Communist Party in 1977–78 because it looked like the party that best coincided with my own political perspective. To begin with, it was the best organized at the university. Its presence within the School of Economics was unquestionable: It represented one of the strongest forces operating there. I was a candidate to the position of university adviser, and I remember having been supported by the Communist Party without my being a member.

Another reason I joined is that my classmates and professors were also members of the Communist Party, and I had discussed lots of things with them already concerning politics and economics. I think these contacts led me to it, not to mention the choice of literature a student develops as he goes along. These represent the major forces that led me to the Communist Party.

It would have been difficult to join the PRI or the PAN, because these parties didn't operate openly. They operated openly in other schools, but not in economics, and much less in those years when the Left functioned like a steamroller. So the options were confined to the Left, the Communist Party, and other smaller groups (the atomization of these groups took place within the university too). I think this led me to join the Communist Party too.

CBG: Did you respond positively to their ideology?

JAV: Of course. But rather than enjoying the ideological agility involved in party discussions, what attracted me the most was knowing that party members shared my vision of the country, especially the members who belonged to the School of Economics. We thirsted to study Mexico, to understand what was going on in the country beyond doctrinal questions.

We formed a circle of economists, and we were actually quite open to other currents of thought. For example, we studied Keynes to the marrow. We studied him because we needed to understand him and not reject him outright for ideological reasons, plain and simple. I can say now, without embarrassment, that Keynes is one of my favorite economists. We also studied [Michal] Kalecki because he impressed us a lot. In fact, we studied Kalecki more than we did Keynes. We became quite heterodox because we used economic theory to help us understand reality rather than using it merely as a basis for ideological argument.

CBG: Had anyone in your family ever been a Socialist?

JAV: No, no one.

CBG: Forgive my asking, but what did your father do for a living? Was he middle class?

JAV: He was a photographer. He died long ago, in 1963.

CBG: You said earlier that you worked for the Political Committee.

JAV: I am a member of the Political Committee of the PSUM.

CBG: What does that mean?

JAV: The PSUM party structure is made up of the Central Committee composed of seventy-five members who are elected to that body by a national party congress which meets every three years. These elected members act as national directors between congresses. Among themselves the Central Committee members elect those who make up the Political Committee and the Secretariat. I was elected a member of the Central Commmittee. I need to clarify that I was never a member of the Communist Party Central Committee. I served as a member of one of its study committees but never as a member of its Central Committee.

I enjoyed several positions within the PSUM after the Communist Party merged into it in 1981. In addition to

directing the advisory-research group, I was elected into the
PSUM's Central Committee, as I've said. In 1982, I was
elected a member of the Secretariat, the executive party
organ. In 1983, I quit the advisory-research group and was
elected as the party's secretary of research and education
(all of these are national-level positions). In this capacity, I
was in charge of the party's research and political education until 1984, when I became national financial secretary.
I quit this post in September 1985, when I became a federal deputy, or congressman. As such, I now only belong to
the PSUM's Central Committee and the Political Committee
within it.

CBG: How did you become a deputy? What is a plurinominal deputy?

JAV: Mexico's Chamber of Deputies is made up of four
hundred members. Three hundred of them are elected in
what we call uninominal districts, meaning regional units in
which a candidate wins by majority vote. One hundred
deputies are elected from regions known as plurinominal
districts, comprised of several states. In these districts, each
party puts up a list of twenty candidates (five regions carried five lists in 1985 to select one hundred deputies), and
the deputies are elected on the basis of the percentage vote
each party obtains in each region, up to twenty deputies per
district.

In my case, I was a candidate in Region 1 (my name
appeared second on the list), which includes Mexico City
and the states of Puebla and Tlaxcala. It's a formula which
is complicated to understand and carry out. The government
finds it hard to put it into practice.

CBG: These changes are the result of the reforms?

JAV: The 1979 reforms. Let's not forget that Communist
Party members did not enjoy political rights for about forty
years. The reforms of 1979 allowed them to recuperate these
rights and thus participate in elections. From another point
of view, we can say that the three most recent legislatures,
in which I've been a member, have opened a new chapter
as far as the participation of Mexico's independent Left is
concerned. This answers the second part of your question.
Let me now try to answer the first part—how I came to be a
legislator.

You'll recall that I said that I had already set a path
within the party which allowed me to get to know the party

and let the party get to know me, especially the party's rank and file. Our capacity to analyze a given issue was uncertain at the time because we didn't have many things we now have, so we were kept quite busy. My party position required travel to different parts of the country. This is explained by the fact that I used to advise not only our party's congressmen and the advisory staff members who worked with them but also our party members who had been elected into the various state legislatures.

In 1982, I was promoted to the Central Committee and then I became advisory head, as I've mentioned, from 1979 to 1983. I thus acquired valuable insights about a congressman's job, so it became quite natural for me to step into the actual job itself.

CBG: I happen to know that a legislator's need for a system to advise him on specific issues is quite important. I believe it is unusual to have such a system operating in the Mexican legislature.

JAV: It is unusual even now because we are the only party in the Chamber of Deputies that has had a legislative advisory system since 1979. The idea arose when our legislative team was elected that year. It was a very fortunate forward-looking decision taken by the party leadership at the time. There were eighteen deputies at the time, nine of which belonged to the Communist Party, and the other nine belonged to the leftist coalition, which eventually became known as the PSUM. Moreover, the legislative load is very heavy because the issues that are examined are quite varied. These may be legal, economic, political, and social, and they all require research.

The Communist Party leaders, I think correctly, decided that deputies were not specialists in the various issues they might have to face in the legislature. They weren't know-it-alls, and there was no reason why they had to be, nor did we have the capacity to give them special courses or workshops to prepare them in the various areas of concern. We had to recognize that they were politicians, and they could only know so much. But we also came to realize that our party could create teams of specialists that could offer the parliamentary support we needed. In other words, our idea was to help our deputies with whatever necessary data, analysis, and proposals they might need in order to help them do their job in congress, including the various committees, plenary sessions, et cetera. This is what we started to do, and this is what we continue to do.

Let me give you an example. Let's say we receive a bill from the president's office on a proposed federal budget. We then respond by forming a committee made up of deputies and advisers, who begin to study the bill as soon as possible. Both groups begin to examine specific sector data, expense targets, et cetera. Note that the advisers take on a responsibility at this point which is as heavy as the deputies'. In fact, the only thing the advisers don't do is speak on the floor. They are very trustworthy, and they are very strong in their specialty, and this allows our deputies to maximize their role as politicians. Our advisers may write bills we are interested in introducing or speeches for our deputies. When we ask one of our deputies to take the floor, he can do this by having an adviser back him up with a prepared speech, and we can thus take a stand on a given issue.

CBG: What informational resources do you use?

JAV: Our advisers enjoy access to all of the public information which the government publishes; they enjoy any informational source available.

CBG: But I mean, do you have a library, a resource center?

JAV: In the legislature? No. Our Chamber of Deputies lacks an information center. It lacks the most elementary technological aids. There are no computers anywhere in the chamber. In other words, what we do we do by using our own resources—what our own parliamentary group can dredge up.

CBG: I suppose you use libraries at the university?

JAV: We use public libraries and other resources external to the legislature. Look, we have had to resort to using computers belonging to our friends! We scratch our backs with our own fingernails!

CBG: In other words, the advisory system on which you rely is really put together informally, and it operates thanks to resources that become available at a given moment?

JAV: Yes.

CBG: Is the advisory system better off today than when you first organized it, or is it the same?

JAV: Let me respond by simply giving you my experience. I do not believe it is a comparative issue. The success of an advisory group like we now have depends on the deputies it serves. If they accept the fact that they need help, then it works fine. This may not be easy to do, however, because politicians can be afflicted with the pretensions of knowing it all and thus not needing anyone to advise them, much less write anything for them. A group of deputies like ours, I think, encourages the capabilities of our advisers, and these in turn can be strengthened by the deputies. By good fortune, our deputy group accepts being advised. I think our group is very mature, capable, and very experienced.

Let me tell you that a member of the PRI approached me in 1983 to ask me how to form an advisory group; they had assigned him to do so because they were interested in forming a PRI advisory team. In other words, when they decided they wanted such a team, they remarked: "It ought to be like what the PSUM has, but on a large scale."

CBG: This leads me to another question. How many other advisory teams exist, if we're talking about a party specific thing, and what is your assessment of them?

JAV: Other advisory teams? No. There are none in the chamber. Congressional committees have research personnel, but these people are really employees more than anything else. In other words, these people won't come to you and say: "This is what you need to do because our findings indicate it so." If it's an employee, I'll say instead: "Work out the data on this and produce a graph for me on it too." That's not a PSUM adviser; that's an employee. This is what I mean when I say that congressional committees have employees who are economists, lawyers, and so on. No one has a team like ours. The PRI probably doesn't have one because it has the entire state apparatus behind it. The PAN doesn't have one either; it probably leans on a network of professional offices (accountants or lawyers) whose members belong to the party. The rest of the parties—only God knows how they do it.

CBG: I've noticed that, during a floor session, deputies, especially those belonging to the PRI, handle a lot of what appears to be personal business in the chamber itself.

JAV: Yes, I think that's true, but it's natural too. On second thought, however, it may not be so natural, because the PRI has people in the chamber who have nothing else to do!

The PRI has 300 deputies, 40 of whom carry the burden of debating, analyzing the debate itself, and doing everything else that needs to be done in a place like this. This leaves 250 deputies who rarely take part in the debate; we can get to the end of a congressional session, and 150 to 200 PRI deputies won't have said a word before the chamber. What do they do? They have to be present in the chamber because there's got to be a quorum, so they attend to their business in the meantime. It is very difficult for us to do the same.

CBG: You don't do that?

JAV: We try not to. We're too few. We're twelve. We don't have that kind of flexibility.

For example, what were we doing in December [1985] when the legislative sessions were so long that they ran past midnight? Well, I had to get ready for budgetary debates (it's such a complex subject to begin with). The way we do it in the PSUM is as follows. When I see that they're debating a subject for which I'm not in charge, I leave the chamber. Three of my colleagues keep an eye on the floor activity. I tell them I'm going off the floor to prepare, but I do so for matters pertaining to our legislative tasks, not my personal business!

CBG: I suppose you respond to personal requests from ordinary citizens who may say: "Please do this for me." The PRI is faced with this, and I suppose you are too.

JAV: We attend to private citizens only with the flexibility that the congressional sessions permit. Requests of the kind you speak of usually come from workers, members of neighborhood groups, and peasants who come to complain about one thing or another, or they want something done for them. So we do it; we attend to them. It's necessary to point out that to do this while congress is meeting is a very complicated thing to do. However, we try to do it, and the advisers help us out on this matter too.

CBG: What happens between sessions?

JAV: When there are no sessions, I have a set of specific responsibilities. I am in charge of making sure that our party group is always ready to do what is needed. I have to make sure that the advisers are adequately engaged in worthy projects. I have to know what they are doing, coordinate what they do with Arnoldo Martínez, our general coordinator, and so on.

CBG: What are your relationships with your constituents?

JAV: I attend to them through the party networks, the regular party organs. For example, I spent this last weekend in Guadalajara attending a party meeting that was held there concerning election issues. My membership in the Political Committee requires this; I am responsible for the state of Jalisco; I am the contact, so to speak, between them and the national leadership. At other times, the party's electoral district officials organize tours for deputies to help them with their local campaigns. We go wherever we are needed, but we coordinate with the party to do this.

To be more specific about what I do at the local level, let me say that I was a candidate in the 24th electoral district in south Mexico City—in Tlalpan, where I live. What do I do [as a legislator]? I am in constant contact with the party committee there, which happens to be a zonal committee. I do a lot of things with them: We help neighborhood organizations with their problems, workers in our area who might be engaged in a dispute at the factory where they work, and so on. My party work is always connected with party needs, depending on what level I am operating.

My work routine is hard to predict, because anyone can call me and say to me: "Listen, we have to attend this meeting, so we are appointing you as our representative there. It has to do with this issue or that one." Of course, it ought to have to do with something I know about, right? It wouldn't be correct for them to assign me to things about which I know nothing! I know a few things, and I try to work in the areas I know.

When we're not in session here in the Chamber of Deputies, I belong to the Permanent Committee, where the work proceeds as usual. We meet tomorrow, for example, so today I have to prepare what I'm going to say tomorrow. In the committee we are discussing smog alerts (pollution may kill us all someday, here in Mexico City), electoral conflict connected with San Luis Potosí, internal committee problems, et cetera. I have to prepare all of this with the aid of our advisers with whom I am scheduled to meet; I have to meet with an expert on ecology who is drawing up some documents on smog. (I tell you, we're all going to die from the smog one of these days!) Then, I should add, I have to give time to foreign investigators who are out writing books!

CBG: Let's talk about the PSUM. What are its strengths and weaknesses? How do you see it within the framework of the Mexican Left?

JAV: The first thing I have to say is that the PSUM represents a fusion of several parties.[2] The most important and oldest of these was the Communist Party, founded in 1919. Because this is not the time to go into details, suffice it to say that it enjoyed its own existence with all of the corresponding ups and downs; it enjoyed sixty years of history which brought it a lot of weight. The PSUM also took in other parties: the Partido del Pueblo Mexicano, the Partido Socialista Revolucionario, the Movimiento de Acción Liberal Socialista, and the Movimiento de Acción Popular.

The challenge was to create a new party without denying the past; we needed to take advantage of positive experiences while being conscious, at the same time, not to simply change names. Internally, this consumed a lot of our personal effort: how to create a new party and avoid simply changing the name of the old one.

CBG: The PSUM, then, is not the Communist Party?

JAV: Ours is the United Socialist Mexican Party, and this has been our greatest challenge: to make a new party with its own profile, to make it different from the parties that gave life to it yet help it capture the advantages and virtues that each party brought to it. The party is five years old now; it has gone through a tense but interesting period of construction and reconstruction. The fact that permanent political activity is not one of the features of the Mexican people has guaranteed these changes. The Mexican people engage in politics only when critical moments arise, as in many other places naturally. In countries where the people engage themselves politically in a more continuous manner, however, fewer parties carry the brunt of the people's activities. In the absence of this condition, we act as organized party militants who supposedly engage in constant political activity. Finding organizational forms which best fit our circumstances here in Mexico has been one of our greatest challenges.

What do I see as a virtue within the party? I would say that the PSUM's principal virtue is its capacity for discussion, for finding adequate solutions to the problems of our time without getting trapped into inertia or dogmatism. In other words, we are trying to put together a party which fits the Mexico of today, even though what we do may not agree with textbook definitions. For example, we are not concerned with what Lenin said about parties. We want to create a party for today's Mexico, one that offers room for anyone who holds a socialist ideal for Mexico. We are not a Marxist-Leninist party. We refuse to define ourselves this way, because our party holds people who do not believe in Marxism-Leninism. Within the diversity, heterogeneity, and heterodoxy of the PSUM, we have people who can come in and say: "It's not necessary to read Marx. That's a waste of time! Let's read something else!" Others say: "It's not necessary to be Marxist, because definitions are fundamental in Marxism, [and] so who is going to do the defining?" What holds us together is a common socialist ideal, an ideal of transformation—the idea of a fatherland rather than doctrinal unity. This is the greatest advantage the PSUM holds. It is probably the reason why we have gone through a lot of conflict and splits, yet we remain alive and maintain our strength on the Left.

CBG: But what is a "socialist ideal"?

JAV: To put it in concrete terms, we have resolved to be willing to fight to bring an end to the exploitation of labor (which implies the existence of private property) and to achieve the socialization of political power. These represent the two big coordinates that guide our action. This is what we must face, and we must make this real in Mexico. We must be capable of upholding principles and programs based on those two grand definitions. This permits us to act here and now in a Mexico where a revolutionary crisis does not yet exist, because there is still enough time to peacefully resolve grave conflicts within an institutional framework. At the same time, we must be capable of keeping alive the ideal of revolutionary transformation not because it lives in books but because it lives in what we do. We want to change everything in this country. We want another society.

Facing this great objective of revolutionary transformation, how do we articulate our daily battle, how do we make it concrete on all fronts? These are important questions. We are a revolutionary party. We say we are, and that is how we stand, but we do constitute a new party, and we are very attractive to some and very repulsive to others.

CBG: So a lot of dialogue goes on in seeking this objective, a lot of views and opinions are examined? This is the strength of the party?

JAV: I think that the most enlivened discussions we have had within the party are not of an ideological character or doctrinaire. Instead, our best discussions have analyzed our country's present situation. These discussions are interesting because they reveal viewpoints held by those of us at middle leadership levels, those of us who are analysts, et al. So, rather than discussing how many camels can pass through the eye of a needle, we discuss Mexico's present situation, international affairs, and so on. The point is that we do not argue about ideology.

We've learned that the Left may be united if those of us who belong to it face issues which we hold in common: Mexico's unique problems, its workers, its peasants. If we don't do this, then we won't ever agree, and we'll fight over who is a true Marxist-Leninist or whether Lenin was right about this or that. We do discuss these things, but we try not to make them a matter of conflict. In the old days, when they became the basis of conflict, they helped disguise our inner struggles, and this led us into a mire.

CBG: I suppose that ideological conflict of the kind you're discussing splits the Left?

JAV: Yes, divisions are created, at least on the surface. Why are there so many parties on the Left? Is it because we can't agree, ideologically speaking? This may be part of the answer but not the whole answer. For example, the PPS defines itself as Marxist-Leninist. They will tell you, without a doubt, that they are more Stalinist than we are. Is that what separates us from the PPS? They would say so. I, on the other hand, would disagree. What separates us from the PPS is their praxis, which has nothing to do with Marxism-Leninism. They distinguish themselves by collaborating and supporting the Mexican government. I could say the same thing about the PST. Do we disagree with them about ideology, about different interpretations of Marx or Lenin or the classical writers of Marxism? No. What separates us is their outright collaborationism with the government, which often reaches a level of corruption and scandal.

What separates us from the PRT? Is it that they might be Trotskyists? No. Basically, their practices separate us; they are very inconsequential; they are ultraleftist at certain times; their posture is uneven. They probably say something similar about us, that our "reformism" and our willingness to "play around" with the Right separates us.

CBG: You haven't mentioned the PMT.

JAV: We must remember that the PMT is one of the parties that called for leftist unity the loudest. Its leaders helped us in our move toward unity by taking part in the writing of the founding documents of the PSUM. Yet the PMT stepped away from the fusion leading toward the creation of the PSUM only a week before it took place. So, if we're at odds with them, it's more over practices than ideology. We differ with them primarily because their vision of what a party does is too narrow. In my personal view (all of this represents my personal view), the PMT still needs to act like a party that can do something besides merely denouncing one thing or another. A national party needs to say something besides the fact that things aren't working right. It is necessary to offer a vision, to offer alternatives. The PMT's own pragmatism may trap it at critical moments. It's necessary to be punctual, to do everything that has to be done, but you need more. For example, they've never wanted to define themselves as Socialists personally nor as a Socialist Party collectively. What was their argument when they decided to avoid fusion with the PSUM? They didn't want to accept the hammer and sickle as a symbol because it was "foreign." They didn't join as a result. The truth had to be something else, right? They are strange. They say that the term "socialism" scares people off. We do not agree on these types of things, but, yes, we have fewer differences with the PMT than with any other leftist parties. Our skirmishes are over practical matters, mostly.

CBG: What of the new party, the PRS [Partido de la Revolución Socialista]?

JAV: The PRS is a group that broke away from the PSUM. Let me explain it this way. The PPM [Partido Popular Mexicano] represents one of the parties that split from the PPS in 1977 and then fused into the PSUM in 1981. They helped make up the coalition of the Left which later became the PSUM. An internal rift led by Alejandro Gascon Mercado in 1982 took place within the PSUM. He wanted the PSUM to declare its support for the dictatorship of the proletariat, that it consider itself an international party even though it wasn't the Communist Party any longer, and that the PSUM define itself vis-à-vis the Soviet Union. He and his friends were dyed-in-the-wool pro-Soviets, and this took him out of the PSUM.

What was behind all this? On the one hand, of course, there was a legitimate preoccupation with ideological purity. On the other, it triggered an internal struggle for the position of secretary-general of the PSUM. Alejandro Gascon wanted to become secretary-general under terms that the majority rejected. This began a period of conflict.

CBG: Barry Carr, an authority on contemporary Mexico, stated [at a conference at the UNAM in 1986] that the PSUM represents a "homecoming" of groups that had formerly split away from the Communist Party. What do you think?

JAV: This observation is partially true. It's hard to deny that, in the history of the Mexican Left, the Communist Party, which underwent many splits during its sixty-five years of existence, acted as a common source. Innumerable groups and individuals who had joined at one time or another fell away from it. I can cite Rafael Aguilar Talamantes, PST secretary-general, who was a leader in Juventud Comunista; Eduardo Valle, now a congressman and PMT leader, was also a Juventud Comunista member; and Demetrio Vallejo [d. 1986], who left the party and later returned to the PSUM. You will find many leaders who left the Communist Party at one time or another and now find themselves in the small groups that make up the rest of the Mexican Left.

So the idea that the PSUM represents a homecoming is true, but it is not entirely accurate. There is something that is missing in that statement: The PSUM holds groups that never belonged to the PSUM. These are leftist groups that held positions contrary to the Communist Party, like the *lombardista* movement that joined the PSUM via the Partido del Pueblo Mexicano directed by Alejandro Gascon Mercado. With the exception of some old-timers, these *lombardistas* never belonged to the Communist Party. The PPS supplied the PSUM with some people too. Finally, there is yet another movement that never belonged to the Communist party, although a few individuals in it did. This is the Movimiento de Acción Popular, where we find Rolando Cordera and Arnaldo Córdoba, among others, all of whom form an entire generation of Mexican intellectuals who firmly contribute to the nation's political life and to the PSUM itself.

Viewed in broad terms, I would say, then, that the PSUM embraces a current coming from the Communist

Party, a *lombardista* current from the PPS, and a stream that we could call a leftist-national current that came from the Movimiento de Acción Popular. So the idea that the PSUM represents a homecoming is a partial fact.

CBG: Licensiado, the PAN has undergone a resurgence recently. This resurgence seems to reflect the need for national policies favoring the middle classes in Mexico which are stronger now than thirty years ago.

JAV: The rise of *panismo* in the north represents a new phenomenon not seen in this country since the 1930s: forces on the Right capable of moving the masses, especially the middle classes but a lot of workers and peasants too. To stigmatize this phenomenon as rightist and unworthy does little good because it'll be there one way or another. It's important to know where it comes from, what spurs it, and how we might face it.

To put it briefly, the government decided to stop the *panistas* at whatever cost: by employing force, fraud, or whatever. Government officials consider it important not to let the *panistas* make any further advances, even if it means employing plainly antidemocratic techniques. What the government doesn't want to accept, even though I think it knows this quite well, is that this *panista* resurgence mirrors the discredit of the nation's political system and the exhaustion of the system's legitimacy among vast sectors of the population. This is a result of the government's conduct of national affairs. The government doesn't wish to accept that this phenomenon is connected to the most serious economic crisis Mexico has experienced and that this crisis is viewed widely as being the responsibility of the president who preceded Miguel de la Madrid [López Portillo].

Interestingly, the government has fashioned a conservative explanation of the economic crisis which it offers to the bar of national opinion. This explanation asserts that the crisis stems from the errors committed by the previous administration; this explanation has struck the populace deeply because the man in the street voices it; you hear it in the media, from church pulpits, from all of the institutions in this country that help shape popular opinion. We know, however, that it comes from the government. The PAN has decided to ride this wave of discontent and desperation. The people don't know what's going to happen next; they're insecure. Why do the people support the PAN? Several causes help explain why important sectors of the populace—middle classes, workers, peasants—are turning to the PAN.

First of all, the PAN enjoys more than forty years of electoral experience. In many elections it has only been the PRI versus the PAN. This is why the PAN has most impacted the conscience of the Mexican people. The Communist Party didn't exist continuously, nor the Left, in general, nor the PSUM. Moreover, certain segments of the Left succeeded only in bringing shame to the Mexican people. I'm talking about the PPS and other groups of the collaborationist Left.

Second, the PAN makes only one promise: to govern well and honestly. It is not a party that takes major risks before the people. The people don't view the PAN as a party that would provoke abrupt changes, for example. The revolutionary oppositionist Left, especially, still conveys the distorted imagery of violence and canceled freedoms which have been identified with socialist countries elsewhere. All of this weighs heavily in the minds of the people.

Let me add just one more thing. The advance of the Right in Mexico is real. It is not something which we have invented in the Left. It is a phenomenon which is present, and we're going to have it around for a good long while. This advance of the Right is manifested in several ways. One of these, perhaps not even the main one, is seen in the electoral victories the PAN has achieved. These victories should not be distorted, however. I have seen television reports in the United States that give the viewer a distorted reality of the PAN because they show it spreading across the entire width and breadth of Mexico. This is not true. The PAN's strength is concentrated in three northern states right now. The PAN is not a strong force in the southeast. It doesn't exist in the west (Nayarit) because we constitute the second strongest party there. The same may be said of the state of Guerrero as well.

CBG: Is it too simple to attribute the rise of the PAN to a new middle classness?

JAV: I believe it has something to do with the cultural traditions in the north (Mexico is very heterogenous; it has many different aspects to it). *Panismo* is a localized phenomenon. The strides the PAN has made are but one of the manifestations of a conservative upswing. Another example of it is seen in the media. The influence exerted by Televisa is sweeping. Televisa's Jacobo Zabludovsky, Mexico's most popular television personality, reaches out daily to more Mexican viewers than does the president of the republic. You can't overlook this.

CBG: Do you think U.S. influence is also responsible, "the American way of life"?

JAV: I think it is influential in certain regions of the country, in the north above all. The *panista* presence cannot be disassociated from U.S. influence nor from the objective conditions of the border. Let me use an anecdote that illustrates this. I have Francisco Barrios Terrazas in mind, the thirty-eight-year-old PAN candidate for the governorship of the state of Chihuahua; he formerly served as mayor of Ciudad Juárez. A few days before he accepted becoming a gubernatorial candidate, about a thousand people gathered in front of his house, including some women who tearfully asked him to lead the "civil rebellion" and thus take on the role as top *panista* leader in the state. His response was to go into seclusion and meditation. He fasted for three days, asking God to inspire him. A demonstration was organized when he finished his three-day fast, and only then did he accept the *panista* candidacy for Chihuahua. Up to now, I've seen this kind of politics only in the United States! It's very smooth, isn't it?

This gentleman belongs to an American religious sect made up of fundamentalists or something like it—people who read the Bible every day, et cetera. He represents something unique to the north. In the south, people would consider him a clown and throw stones at him! But not in the north.

CBG: Those are cultural influences from the United States.

JAV: And a scenario which is in keeping with American politics. You also have U.S. interests which are very strong in Mexico. For example, I don't think that the way the United States media presents the development of the Mexican political system or the PAN is a casual matter. I find it hard to believe that Americans simply don't know what is happening in Mexico. We believe, rather, that a distorted picture about us is nurtured within U.S. governmental circles, including the Department of State. In the end, this picture presents the PAN as an instrument.

The PAN, for example, has been accused of receiving monies from the Republican party's Foundation for

Democracy. We've never confirmed nor given much credence
to this, but this is a dangerous accusation. I don't know if it's
true; I suppose somebody has proof. We in the PSUM are
accused often of receiving "orders from Moscow," so we know
what this kind of accusation implies. This is why we can't be
a part of this type of slanderous campaign. One thing we do
say is that the PAN does benefit from U.S. politics.

Beyond this, I can only affirm that *panista* rhetoric has
little to do with Mexico's real problems. The PAN agrees
with the government's economic policy; they vote against it
only for tactical reasons. The PAN offers more of the same
economic ideas the government does. In politics all it wants
to do is govern honestly and without fraud. This is why its
rhetoric is a simplistic one; it vulgarizes national issues, yet
it's very attractive to a lot of folks.

CBG: What is the internal process once a bill is introduced?

JAV: Once introduced, the bill is presented to the plenary session or to the Permanent Committee if the legislature is in recess. In session the chamber president reads the
bill and has no choice but to turn it over to the pertinent
committee. The committee receiving it then distributes
copies of it to its members and prepares a report, for it or
against it.

CBG: Do these committees have their own advisers?

JAV: I already explained that to you. Each deputy has to
scratch himself with his own fingernails.

CBG: Committees don't have advisers.

JAV: Yes, yes.

CBG: In other words, the fashioning of this committee
report is entrusted to a handful of PRI deputies who are
supervised by the cabinet official linked closest to the substance of the bill.

JAV: The interjection of the executive office is permanent because it writes the bill, sends it to the legislature,
supervises the legislators who report on it, and, in some
cases, may even write the report itself. When no one is
available to do the appropriate job, the reports may come
from the cabinet offices themselves. In other words, when a
bill goes to a committee that does not have a *priista* with
sufficient ability to write a proper report, a fully written
report will be issued.

Once the report is written and approved by the committee, the bill returns to the plenary session. It's read once,

then twice, then it's discussed, and a vote is taken subsequently. The bill goes on to the senate. If it originated here in the Chamber of Deputies, then it goes to the executive for publication. That's the way it works.

CBG: Do all of the committees have a PRI majority?

JAV: All of them have an overwhelming majority, all of them.

CBG: Are all of the committees chaired by *priistas*?

JAV: All of them.

CBG: Has there ever been one chaired by—

JAV: Insofar as I can recall, never in the history of the Mexican congress, since the PRI has been PRI, has there ever been a committee chaired by a member of the opposition.

CBG: This brings us to another question. What you've done above is reveal one of the ways in which Mexican presidentialism operates.

JAV: I am not a political scientist, so I can't give you a well-finished explanation of what we, in Mexico, know as presidentialism. But I am a victim of presidentialism. In any case, how does it work in the Chamber of Deputies? To the great majority of the deputies, being part of the Chamber of Deputies represents an important step on the political ladder. In other words, serving as a PRI deputy or congressman means you can become something else later, you can keep on climbing. In order to keep on climbing within the political system, including the components that make up the PRI, you have to respond to certain interests.

The fundamental responsibility of all *priistas* does not lie with the people who elected them; it lies with the selectors. These may include the governor or whoever else played a role in their being nominated as candidates for the posts they hold. The three hundred PRI deputies in the chamber represent a pie of sorts that is divided up between the various groups that make up the ruling elite. For example, each government ministry enjoys a certain number of congressmen who act on its behalf.

The clearest examples of this may be seen in the chamber's economic committees. The chairman of the Committee on Budget and Programming and the chairman of the Treasury Committee are named by the corresponding cabinet officer, but this also works with the chairs of the Committees on Health, Patrimony, et cetera. [These officers are appointed by the president of the republic] so this whole system gyrates around one single figure: the president.

This interlacing of power diminishes the possibility of disagreement or public criticism. It may be all right to criticize internally, but please don't do it publicly. For example, if there is a PRI member who disagrees with a given bill sponsored by his party, and he does not want to vote in its favor, the only alternative he has is to abstain from voting even if he wants to vote against it. This does not mean that the president is all-powerful. It does mean, however, that the president has a controlling share in the decisions of the nation. When he decides something, everybody else has to line up. He has to recognize certain turfs, or power domains, which are not directly under his command, however. Practice may dictate their belonging to a certain secretary of state or a governor or person of influence, et al. The problem is that this kind of concentrated power creates a lot of obstacles in Mexico.

CBG: I understand that Pablo Gómez, [former] secretary-general of the PSUM, put forward the idea of a parliamentary system.

JAV: The party has discussed this idea. We are considering it as part of our party platform, as long as a parliamentary system can be adapted to the singularities and specificities that Mexican history and tradition require. We do believe nonetheless that stepping into a higher level of democratization, one that is more meaningful to the people, does require the reevaluation of the national legislature. In other words, we cannot continue to have a national congress that is relegated to approving initiatives coming from the president; let us not forget either that most of the legislature's own authority is delegated to the president at present! An independent legislature and a balance of power that really works are what we need.

CBG: Given the way things are going, this might become a reality someday.

JAV: Unfortunately, this cannot be achieved easily. The biggest problem we have in Mexico is how to dismantle this presidential system. We have to find a way to create a system of democratic institutions that will guarantee the force of law at the same time. In other words, within the parameters of our socialist vision, we must achieve institutional change yet permit the dismantling of the presidential system.

We can't dismantle it and then ask ourselves: "What now?" Rather, in a democratic operation we need to be putting together mechanisms which permit the channeling of popular participation so that the people can make decisions at different levels [at the same time]. The Chamber of Deputies is one of these mechanisms, but there are others as well, perhaps even more important than the Chamber of Deputies. I can think of labor unions, schools, *ejidos,* et cetera.

How do these people participate at present? Right now there's no way [they can do this]. The president has to decide everything, all the way from making sure that the victims of the 1985 earthquake receive homes to making certain that a school has enough classrooms. Everyone with a problem goes to the president. The way in which matters are decided has become so concentrated that the president has become essential to everything; power has become utterly concentrated. It is urgent to give real function to other institutions, to attribute authority to them in a way that is both genuine and democratic. But we can't do this tomorrow. Resistance to this kind of change by the power sources is infinite.

CBG: What is your opinion about the senate?

JAV: The senate is one of the most decrepit and flawed institutions in the Mexican political system. It is also the most useless. The Mexican senate has had a helter-skelter life; it's been quite uneven. It has been suppressed in certain periods—the nineteenth century, for example. People worked with a unicameral system during these periods. There have been great debates over the usefulness of the senate. In these debates, men as distinguished as Ignacio [Luis] Vallarta referred to the Mexican senate as a "cemetery for political nullities."

Later, the senate was reinstalled, and it acts as a counterweight to the Chamber of Deputies at the present time. It operates as a review chamber. In other words, the majority of bills which are important to the political, economic, and social life of the country are initiated in the chamber. They go from the chamber to the senate for review; it acts as a final filter. It is made up of PRI members exclusively.

In all of its recent history the Mexican senate has had only one member who did not belong to the PRI. This was Jorge Cruikshank Garcia of the PPS. His entry into the senate is connected to a big political scandal in which he exchanged a governorship (won by Alejandro Gascon Mercado) for a senate seat. He was supported by the PRI.

The senate has no importance today. If you attended any senate sessions, you know what I'm talking about. What kind of debates can you have if everybody belongs to the same party? It may be said, at the same time, that all of the senators are waiting either for retirement, a governorship, or a cabinet position. It serves as a "refrigerator" most of the time, where certain old politicians are preserved in hibernation, while others are cooling their heels waiting for better opportunities.

CBG: The press has said that the Left is losing strength. One of the reasons given is that perhaps the Left cannot offer more than what the Mexican state has already offered: bureaucratic statism and a publicly dominated economy. The Left can't offer anything else.

JAV: I think the criticism implied here holds together, in part. In other words, in Mexico and almost everywhere else in the world, including the socialist world, statism (the equivalent to socialism) has entered a moment of crisis. Said differently, we on the Left have to be capable of finding a new relationship between the state and society which clearly recognizes that statism (understood as the nondemocratic state ownership of the means of production) can only lead to situations worse than what we are presently fighting against.

This issue has been a particularly important one here because the Mexican state is so absorbing. The question of statism, as an option to resolving the problems of capitalism in Mexico, has been around a long time. In Mexico, statism took the form of nationalization with singularity. In other words, to nationalize actually meant to statize in Mexico. Mexican statism cannot be understood without nationalization, and to nationalize is to pass private property on to the public sector.

So what is the problem? The problem is converting private property to public without the democratic mechanisms of control which guarantee the social use of the expropriated goods. I believe that acts of nationalization in Mexico in the 1930s were supported by the masses. Here, I have in mind the nationalization of the railroads, the oil industry, and [certain] farmlands, especially when these were turned over to landless peasants. In its nationalizing aspects, Mexican statism represented a response to the [needs of the] masses [in the 1930s]. Later, nationalization became a mere bureaucratic and administrative act whose most pathetic reflection may be seen in the nationalization of the banking system [in 1982].

The nationalization of the banking system represents a nationalization act from the top, from an official's desk. It lacked a social movement that might have given it a reason for being. It was bereft of the popular pressures that might have demanded it, and, quite justly, it found its main weakness in that deficiency. This is why it became so easy for President Miguel de la Madrid, only three months later, to profoundly alter López Portillo's nationalizing decree by returning 34 percent of the shares to the original owners by stripping the new state banks of all the shares in nonbanking enterprises which they had held before and still maintain the functioning of the system without alteration.

The problem of the Left is not to deny nationalization nor to try to rewrite the history about such things. Rather, it is to fashion the option of a relationship between state and society that implies the democratization of both. I personally believe that no socialist project can do without nationalization or the conformation of state property, much less so in Mexico. Wherever you have the state administering goods, and society is controlling the administration of those goods free of patrimonialist practices, then you'll have something. In other words, without the profound democratization of society itself, there is no future for a statist project.

Even so, everybody wants to reduce the size of the state. Will the state be reduced to strengthen society? No, it'll be reduced to strengthen the bourgeoisie. Stated in different terms, what we've been facing for several years now is a world caught in a crisis; [we face] a struggle to distribute a diminishing economic surplus; this has reduced the bourgeoisie's breathing room, for which it now fights the state in an attempt to recuperate its position.

CBG: The PSUM's position on this, then, is to go forward with its statist posture but to continue to look for a special relationship between the public sector and the people who benefit from the state?

JAV: We do not renounce the idea that the process of nationalization can be positive in certain instances.

However, we do refuse to accept the idea that certain forms
of socialism insist that everything, all of the means of production, be converted into state property. No, I don't think
even Marx thought that, either. When Marx spoke of the
expropriation or the socialization of property, he thought of
it in terms of the basic means of production, not everything.
I believe that complete branches of production in Mexico
ought to continue in the grip of private property at this
time.

CBG: But there must be people on the Left who insist on
everything going to the state?

JAV: In the PSUM we know full well that there is a lot of
ground to cover in the area of nationalization: productive
sectors which are basic to the national interest and to the
satisfaction of social needs. I cite the case of the pharmaceutical industry: You can't leave the health of the Mexican
people in the hands of multinational corporations! That's
unthinkable!

Are there certain conditions which justify nationalization? Yes, I believe so. The public health sector today
already represents about half of the pharmaceutical market
in Mexico. This encourages a nationalized pharmaceutical
industry. Will that alone solve the problems? No, because
the other necessary ingredient is the democratic control of
that which is nationalized.

CBG: Yes, but what you're saying is that the PSUM is
searching for a better way to control things?

JAV: Why has statism lost all respect in Mexico? Because it is the synonym of corruption, inefficiency, wastage
of resources, and it is seen as not being useful for anything.
Go ahead and ask people on the street what they think of
PEMEX, how they have benefited from it, and they'll say
they haven't. They'll probably respond by complaining that
"they raised the price of gasoline at home while it's getting
cheaper abroad."

For most of the people the *paraestatal* sector appears far
removed from their life and their interests. It represents
something that belongs to the state, not to the nation; it
represents something in which they have nothing to say. In
other words, statism's discredit is real, and the Right, without a doubt, has organized a vile campaign against it,
against public enterprises. Even though it isn't entirely honest, this campaign is founded on solid ground: the [careless]

way in which Mexico has permitted its state-owned enterprises to operate within the economy.

CBG: Do you think it is possible, given the present circumstances, for the state to achieve this control now?

JAV: I think this is one of the basic conditions for state reform. The democratic reform of the state signifies a democratic rearrangement of what we could call the public economy, which includes *paraestatal* enterprises as most important.

CBG: Aren't steps being taken toward this end already? There is a lot of talk about this.

JAV: The necessary steps to achieve this are limited so far because the steps the government has taken are merely bureaucratic and administrative. The biggest step President de la Madrid took was in the creation of a federal comptroller which is part of the executive branch. Restated, this means that the executive controls the comptroller, and this is not control. It just can't be.

Today, the Left faces a very tough challenge. First of all, the challenge consists in persuading all of the Mexican people of the importance of these issues. Second, while being careful not to reject nationalization and the notion of state property, the Left faces the challenge of transforming the people's unhappiness with statism into a demand for control, participation, and democracy. If we don't face this challenge, the Right will win the race.

It's an easy matter for the Right. All they have to say is "down with the state-owned enterprises because they're bad; they're corrupt and inefficient." The Right doesn't offer a middle ground; it doesn't evaluate the good things which *paraestatales* have certainly bequeathed to Mexico. To demand their disappearance and their sale is enough for the Right.

CBG: The PSUM, then, clearly advocates controlling statism by advocating for honest and reasonable administrators?

JAV: In the PSUM we do not merely call for better and more reasonable bureaucrats. It's not really a problem of administrators. My argument strikes nearby, no doubt, but it isn't just a need for honest administrators, because it isn't solely a moral issue. Narciso Bassols, a very distinguished man of the Left during the [Lázaro] Cárdenas period, identified it most clearly when he stated that "in Mexico, the problem of corruption is not a moral problem; it is an economic problem."

Corruption represents a grease which oils the intrastate machinery serving the state and the private sector. By the way, the private sector in this country has never been free of corruption. If there is a sector that cannot wear the mask of honesty, it's the private sector, the bourgeoisie.

CBG: This means that, if you pay an administrator a fair salary, he is no longer going to be corrupt?

JAV: What is required is participation. Specific mechanisms fashioned by the intervention of the people are needed. How do unions take part in public enterprises [today]? They don't; they don't have a part in the councils of administration. They lack a way to make their opinion count. This is why I said earlier that the two conditions are to democratize the state and democratize society. Ideally, PEMEX unions could act as models of workers' watchfulness there; but, the way things exist right now, they can't do that. Right now the unions can only symbolize greater corruption. I'm saying that it is necessary to democratize social organizations and the state simultaneously. If not, then there's no way out no matter how efficient or honest your administrators might be, and they do exist in the Mexican public sector.

The image of a public sector that is rotten with corruption to the core is false; this is what I personally believe. I believe that a generation of honest officials who are concerned for the future of their country exists today. But you also have the other kind of official, the corrupt one who is genuinely concerned only for his personal destiny; getting a raise is all he cares about. How is this going to be resolved? Through punitive measures? Penal measures? No. It's a socioeconomic problem.

CBG: What should the Left's position be in foreign affairs?

JAV: I think the Left still has much to learn and develop, especially in this area. In other words, we have to begin by recognizing the determining, unmodifiable geography that compels us to coexist with the most aggressive world power humanity has ever known. The story of Mexico's construction is the story, to a great degree, of resistance against our northern neighbor. Said in different words, Mexico probably leads the world in the experience gained by developing itself in the face of permanent aggression from U.S. administrations.

The Mexican Left must also understand that, in foreign affairs, the North American government does not always represent the views of all the North Americans. It must know there are ample democratic sectors (not leftists necessarily but indeed democratic) willing to understand what a socialist and democratic struggle might be in Mexico. The problem of the Left is to rise above this skin-deep anti-North Americanism that fails to make distinctions of any kind, that makes a tabula rasa of the United States, confusing the North American people with their government. To confuse the actions of the North American people with the actions of their government is a great error. Within a framework of reciprocal respect, the Mexican Left must find the understanding and comprehension for its program in widely defined North American circles. This is the path we must follow.

CBG: Has the PSUM ever considered it important to relate to Mexicans living in the United States?

JAV: This is a very important question for us. Curiously, the Communist Party enjoyed greater experience in this area than we have so far. Toward the end of the 1970s and the beginning of the 1980s, the Communist Party established contact with diverse organizations of Mexicans living in the United States who still hold onto their citizenship even though they form a part of the social circles there and participate in its political system. Some organizations directly connected to the U.S. Communist party, composed of Mexicans, were formed there too. Even so, a majority of the Mexican population in the United States holds onto its Mexican nationality, and, as such, it represents a potential subject for our party activity. To work among these people is fundamental.

Closer to home, the PSUM has fought for something not yet attained: the Mexican's right to vote abroad. We haven't been able to agree with other leftist groups about applying pressure on the government on this. According to the constitution, Mexicans living abroad enjoy the right to vote in Mexican consulates and embassies. In the 1982 elections we proposed to the Federal Electoral Commission that voting booths be installed in the United States, if we could arrive at an agreement with the North American government to

permit our citizens to vote in presidential elections. The
Mexican government said no; it didn't even want to discuss
it. Many millions of Mexicans live in the United States. For
the Mexican government this represents an uncontrollable
factor, and this is the reason why the government does not
accept the idea of giving them the vote. [We want some-
thing] similar to the French system that allows the French
community residing here in Mexico to cast its vote [in
French elections], small as it might be. However, we have
decided to work hard at it; it will mean a lot of political education. [We have to keep in mind that] these are Mexicans
who have left their country against their will.

CBG: So you don't have branches?

JAV: No, not at the present time.

CBG: Other parties have done that.

JAV: The Communist Party did have cells at one time—
in Los Angeles, San Ysidro—in that general area.

CBG: Your comments involve actual Mexicans living in
the United States. What do you think the party could do
with Mexican-Americans having a certain appreciation of
their cultural origins plus an interest in Mexican affairs?

JAV: I would frame my response to your question within
my earlier remarks about certain popular movements in the
United States meriting our contact. They represent a potential support base for a democratic and socialist struggle in
Mexico. They constitute a potential counterweight against
aggressive policies fashioned by the U.S. government. I
think that people of Mexican descent represent one of these
sectors because they already recognize their own unique-
ness. They're constantly preoccupied with Mexico's destiny;
they hold a legitimate preoccupation with its democratic
development. I think this is basic for them. I think there is a
commonality of interests on their part.

I'll admit to you that what we're talking about is little
known in the PSUM. It has been explored very little. The
contacts are limited to certain individuals, Chicano organizations, and universities. We need to widen our knowledge.
We also need to spread the word in these sectors about what
the PSUM represents. All of this should become part of a
long-term strategy that might diversify the PSUM's base of
support abroad, a strategy that seeks support among U.S.
citizens who will demand respect for Mexico's democratic
processes.

CBG: What awaits a young, professional politician of the Left once he has served in congress?

JAV: The role of people like me in Congress is connected with our role in the party. One option I have is to return to a directive position within the party in an area to which the collective party leadership believes I might be able to contribute. My interest in serving in that area is important too. It's not a matter of self-sacrifice either; several factors enter into play. I have other more tempting possibilities. I have worked as a party professional for many years, so now I think it would be a good thing to look for new opportunities disconnected from the party.

It's good that we're not faced with mere existential issues. In other words, all a *priista* has to face is: What position will I be given next? Not us. Rather than just facing a mere existentialist question, we have the advantage of knowing that whatever we do is connected with a greater good.

Notes

1. This chapter is based on several interviews held during the months of January and February 1986 in the Palacio Legislativo del Congreso de la Unión, near San Lázaro, Mexico City.

2. In 1986 the PSUM indeed represented a new breed of Latin American Communist Party members willing to combine with non-Communist leftist parties. See Barry Carr, "Mexican Communism, 1968–1981: Eurocommunism in the Americas?" *Journal of Latin American Studies* 17 (May 1985): 201–28.

CHAPTER 9

Heberto Castillo Martínez

In the late 1980s many forces finally pressed the Mexican Left into one single, cohesive body, and Heberto Castillo Martínez was one of the driving factors. His political pragmatism and his penchant for independent thought and action contributed significantly to leftist unity in Mexico.

A northerner with a unique personal background, Castillo concluded that his own intellectual skills were like everybody else's except that most people could not develop them because of socioeconomic circumstances. He has spent his life trying to create a political environment that would enhance the possibility of full intellectual development for all Mexicans.

Castillo studied at the UNAM at the same time that he gave classes to fellow students, and he eventually graduated with a degree in civil engineering. He studied and researched avidly when he was not taking part in politics and became an innovator and inventor in his professional field, which he discusses here. He was jailed in the late 1960s for allegedly organizing the student movement leading to the massacre of Tlaltelolco. Once released from jail, he founded the Partido Mexicano de los Trabajadores (PMT) which he used as a vehicle to make leftist unity a reality in the late 1980s.

Gathered within the PMS, the Left chose Castillo as its presidential candidate for the 1988 elections. He stepped down in favor of Cuauhtémoc Cárdenas a few weeks before election day, but remained to serve as one of the top PRD leaders in mid-1991.

CBG: Tell us your name and today's date.
HCM: My name is Heberto Castillo; today is February 21, 1986.[1]

CBG: Please tell us something about your parents, your place of birth, date of birth, and your early formation.

HCM: I was born in Ixhuatlán de Madero, Veracruz, on August 23, 1928. I come from well-to-do peasants, what you might refer to in Mexico as landowners who had come on hard times (my parents owned very little land at this time).

CBG: Is this in the northern part of the state?

HCM: It is in the northern part of Veracruz in an area known as the Veracruzan Huasteca. I spent the first part of my childhood there, and, at the age of six and a half, I moved to the federal district. I started primary school there [Ixhuatlán] in 1936; I always attended what we call official schools. I entered first grade already knowing how to read (you have to be seven years old in order to go to school), since I had learned on my own. I was very interested in reading newspapers and magazines at an early age.

CBG: Tell us something about your father, *don* Heberto. I'm sure your family cast a certain stamp on you.

HCM: My father, who is still alive today, worked very hard all his life. I've said he was a landowner who had come on hard times. He worked as a mule driver transporting merchandise into mountainous communities like my own (it had eight hundred inhabitants). Both my mother and father attended only primary school, but my father practically did everything on his own. He became a primary and secondary schoolteacher without formal training. Later, he started to write and won a national prize for short stories around 1934. He also became a film scriptwriter, and he served as one of the first movie directors for María Félix. He was a self-made man, indeed.

My mother stayed at home. She enjoyed cooking well, and she liked to knit; she was very good at making sweaters. She had seven children (one of my sisters died very young; I never really knew her). I was the fifth child and the most rebellious. I learned to read on my own because my brothers wouldn't read the comic books to me that arrived in town every fifteen days. My mother tried to teach me about religion, but I would never mind her. One day I got mad at her, and she gave up trying. I've always considered myself incapable of understanding the mysteries of religion. On the other hand, I believe we came to this world with only one objective, that is to survive. I believe mankind has to survive. I have concluded that the struggle to survive precedes the class struggle.

My hometown was filled with killers. It's in one of the toughest regions in the state, where conflicts are resolved by shooting to kill, just like in the movies. On Saturdays, as a child, I used to watch to see who would be brought in dead on a stretcher because of gunshot or machete wounds. I even witnessed gun duels in my hometown. It was like Macondo, the town Gabriel García Márquez writes about.[2] I've told him he described my hometown pretty well. It didn't have electric lights yet, radios, nor telephones. Electricity was not introduced until 1974. I was there when the first Popsicle factory was installed. Similar to what García Márquez writes, I was one of the children who rushed to touch the ice on the Popsicles, before actually tasting one, because it looked like the manufacturer was making cold glass.

CBG: What kind of ethnic groups were in your community?

HCM: Mostly Otomí Indians and white folk. We were part of the white folk; racism was strong there. I learned to become indignant in regard to the unfair things that took place there. Even as a child, I rebelled against my own people because they always were hostile toward the Indians. I used to spend a lot of time with the Otomís and talked with them a lot. They must have indulged me because my parents did not mistreat them, yet I was a white child.

CBG: Did your family hold that point of view, as a whole, then?

HCM: Yes, they were special that way, despite the fact that they owned some land and descended from owners of large estates. The area where I came from had oil too; it was close to Chicontepec, which is an oil reserve today. My ancestors owned oil land, and oil companies used to send royalties to my mother's family. It amounted to very little, of course, when you compare it to what the companies sent out of the country! My folks didn't have to worry about having to work, though.

In any case, my family was against the kind of racial repression that went on there. My parents were not militant about it until an uncle of mine arrived on the scene (he was my mother's brother) and joined the Mexican Communist Party (years later he worked with Colonel Adalberto Tejada, one of the precursors of Mexican agrarian reform, and still later he helped me when I took part in the

Movimiento de Liberacion Nacional). As a result, he and my
father were obligated to leave the area because certain men
wanted to kill them. As a child, I thus discovered that it is
dangerous to fight for equality; I learned this from my
father.

One of my first acts of rebellion against constituted
authority took place after I started primary school. I was
admitted at five and a half years old even though I wasn't
old enough, but I could read and write already. This encouraged me to play around during the first week of school
instead of paying attention to my teacher. In my hometown,
in those early days, it was common practice to recognize not
only the most outstanding students at the end of the week
but also the worst students too. We were brought together
into a tiny auditorium, and the solemn ceremony began. I
took a seat near some of my classmates. The teacher, who
taught all of the grade levels, addressed the parents who
were in attendance and began reading the names of students who were doing poorly. Reading in alphabetical order,
he pronounced the name of a student named Bravo who was
sitting in front of me. The teacher called out: "Bravo
Aguirre, Ramon!" The boy marched to center stage, and the
teacher gave him the order to "put out your hands!" When
the boy extended his hands, the teacher immediately
smacked them three times with a willow rod, and the boy
burst into tears and thus returned to his seat.

The teacher then announced: "Castillo Martínez,
Heberto! Come forward!" I rose to my feet; and, as you know,
the biggest insult in Mexico is to refer profanely to one's
mother, so I cried out to him: "*Chinga tu madre!*" fled the
room, and hid in the town cemetery.[3] Later that evening,
my parents brought me down from my hiding place and lec-
tured me about being stubborn and so on. I told them that I
didn't accept anyone laying their hands on me. I didn't go to
school there anymore; and, whenever the teacher walked
nearby, I would throw rocks at him. Later, we reconciled,
but I continued to study at home. I say all this because I
became quite intolerant of injustice and violence against
people.

I was able to meet very distinguished teachers in the
humanities, mathematics, biology, and so on when I got to
junior high school in Mexico City. They were eminent people, in fact. The school I'm referring to was known as the

Secundaria Numero Cuatro. For example, Octavio Paz and Carlos Pellicer were students there. The teachers took a liking to me because I studied hard. The chemistry teacher wanted me to study chemistry; the math teacher said the same thing about mathematics; and yet another one wanted me to study medicine. As a boy, I was fascinated by all the sciences. I didn't know what to focus on. This may be the reason why I've never been able to do only one thing. Today I'm an engineer, a painter, a writer, a politician, and an economist, although I only got a degree in engineering. Nevertheless, I attended talks given by Diego Rivera and [David Alfaro] Siqueiros, for example. When I went into high school, I volunteered to serve as an office boy for a group of eminent scientists; they accepted me no doubt because they thought my interest and enthusiasm were touching. I remember men in this group who had received national awards in their fields, like Ignacio González Guzmán in biology, Nabor Carrillo in physical engineering, Enrique Cabrera in cardiovascular medicine, and Jorge L. Tamayo in geography. These were men fifteen or twenty years older than I, but I enjoyed listening to them talk. One day Dr. Emilio Arturo Rosenblueth, Mexico's precursor in robotics, asked me whether I liked mathematics, and I said yes, of course. He then began to give me advice which I appreciated very much.

CBG: I understand you taught at the high-school level.

HCM: Yes, I began teaching in high school, but I didn't have an official job, really. Friends of mine would seek me out, and I would explain things to them. That's what I've done all my life. People say that I have always had my "little schools."

As I studied science in high school, I slowly began to understand certain political problems. I began to realize that society's biggest problem is its inability to survive. In other words, we need to make the necessary effort to survive. And, as time has gone by, I've become more convinced of this point of view, and I now believe that political action is necessary. Survival is not a scientific problem; it is a political problem.

When I was a student, I used to ask myself why it was that many young people couldn't learn as I did. Of course, I understood that there were different levels of intelligence, but I came to the conclusion that all human beings had the

capability of achieving the same fullness, a certain median
in learning, and that it was really a small number of people
who could not learn very much and thus were forced to
do something manual. Even when I was very young, I
used to think everybody could become a scientist. I had
very brilliant classmates in junior high school. I remember
that one of them made me very sad because he told me one
day that he would have to go to work upon graduating. "I've
got to help support my family as soon as I finish with junior
high," he lamented. I remember insisting that he go on to
high school and study, and he would simply reply that he
had to work. "No, I simply can't," he would say. I then came
to realize that, if I didn't consider myself well off, I at least
had a father and a mother that fed me and housed me (I
was about thirteen years old at the time). It seemed very
cruel to me to see a young man like my friend, smart as he
might have been, have to work instead of study. I concluded
then that it was necessary to guarantee the people's education; otherwise, it was all such a big waste.

CBG: Tell us briefly something about your profession.
What do you do when you're not involved with politics?

HCM: I'm a civil engineer. However, I've specialized in
the study of structures, or structural engineering. I spent a
lot of time visiting engineering schools in South America
and Europe (France, Germany, Greece, and England especially). I am referring to spatial or tridimensional structures
which are very much in use, from what I can see, in the
American South. It's a structure I designed in 1963–64 to
use in bridges and buildings too. In Mexico it's been used in
the construction of buildings. The Hotel Mexico, for example, was built using a structure I invented which I call
Tridilosa.[4] Aside from this, I taught structures, mathematics, physics, and mechanics for twenty years at the UNAM
and the Politécnico. I've written twelve technical books, one
of which is used as a textbook in Mexico, Venezuela, Peru,
and other places in South America.

I was one of the first people to apply computers in construction design and thus produced what I call shells. The
best advance that has been made possible with my theories
is the construction of stereo-bridges, which have been used
in Cuba and Nicaragua, where I donated some designs.
They're using them there. They've been used in Mexico more
so than before because they require 80 percent less concrete

and about 50 percent less steel than usual. I can build bridges that cost one third of what traditional bridges cost, and they're quite beautiful too. You can see one of them, the Puente de las Flores, on the Pan American Highway between Villahermosa and Tuxtla Gutiérrez on the road to Guatemala. It's 250 meters in length. There is another one in Michoacán on the road to Lázaro Cárdenas. Another one is being planned in the oil region of Tabasco near Frontera. This one is going to cost one quarter of what a regular bridge would cost. That's my job, fundamentally speaking. I can earn my living by working a couple of hours per month, so it doesn't require great effort. My entire family devotes itself to construction; I've given my designs to my children. I advise them, and they do the work.

CBG: In addition to being an engineer, you are also the leader and founder of a party. When did you organize that party and why?

HCM: The Partido Mexicano de los Trabajadores (PMT) was founded on September 8, 1974. However, the idea to start it began after I traveled around the country, visiting many communities from 1971 to 1974. Why was it founded? Mostly because I believed the time had come to join our country's cultural roots with its national politics. For example, I found that we had forgotten the organic structure our forefathers, the México, used to have. I refer partly to the way the México used to organize the land, produce goods, et cetera. Mexico's political organization [today] is a copy of what you find in other countries.

I say it is just a copy because our political organization is not true to what was borrowed abroad; it is a mere caricature. Nominally speaking, the Mexican political system is a federated one, as in the United States; but it is very different in essence. Our system does not emerge from states seeking a federation; instead, it is a nation that is beginning to fall apart on account of its differences. We are forgetting the ideas that inspired Zapata and Villa; [we are emulating a] pattern of a petite bourgeoisie dominating the highest offices of the land (you see this more clearly in Europe and the United States than in Mexico). The man who is rich is seen as the person who can best address life's problems. He who enjoys the riches has succeeded in life. This applies to the individual as it does to society; a rich nation may have truly resolved its biggest problems.

However, it isn't enough for one country alone to resolve its problems in order to guarantee the survival of its own species. Either our species survives everywhere, or it disappears completely. We just don't enjoy the option of saying, for example, that the Americans will survive, or the Swedes, the Japanese, the Germans, or the inhabitants of the developed north and that, if they survive and have enough to live on, then the rest of the world will survive too. The historical tendency is for the underprivileged people to grow more rapidly in numbers than the rich. A future where the wealthy grow fewer and the poor grow more numerous does not bode well. We are acting against our own species this way, not just against the people of a specific country.

CBG: You say that the idea for your party grew in 1971–72, but I know you were jailed in 1968. Why were you jailed, and what does that have to do with the founding of the party in 1974?

HCM: When I was in my last year in engineering school, in 1951, I took part in student politics. I did so because I came to realize that students who didn't do well at the university, academically speaking, did so not because they were lazy. They failed because most of them had to study and work at the same time. In other words, I discovered very powerful social differences at the university level.

This is about the time I concluded that Mexico did not have a party that truly represented the interests of the poor. Parties that spoke about the poor existed already, like the Communist Party and the PPS. However, their members appeared to me more like members of religious sects than political fighters because they spoke on behalf of the poor much like the priests do sometimes; they speak on behalf of God even though God has not given them formal or informal representation. This is why priests and Marxists seemed all alike to me. They spoke about the poor, on behalf of the poor, but they didn't coexist with the poor. This is why I took part in the demonstrations of 1954.

CBG: What happened in 1954?

HCM: The fall of the Jacobo Arbenz government of Guatemala took place in 1954. I learned about the Arbenz situation through Guatemalan students enrolled at the UNAM (the School of Engineering had students from Guatemala, Honduras, and El Salvador). This is when I began to participate in political matters and became acquainted with different political groups, many of whom had strange names or classified themselves by using such words as liberals, anarchists, Communists, Trotskyists, et cetera. This was when I discovered the strange world of politics and how it all reminded me of churches and religions. There was a general disquietude, but there were many labels.

This is when I met Lázaro Cárdenas, the former general and ex-Mexican president who supported this kind of struggle. I had known him since 1951, but, in 1954, I began to deal much more closely with him. From 1954 to 1961, I traveled throughout the country alongside General Cárdenas. As a result, I was able to observe workers' and peasants' organizations, and I found they didn't know the mechanics of organization too well. The theory of the labor union was fine, but, practically speaking, it didn't operate. Theoretically speaking, the *ejido* was fine, but it wasn't really operating in practice. I came to understand that the problem faced by these workers, and their organizations, was their being manipulated from above. I came to understand that the ruling class manipulates the directive function of peasants' and workers' organizations, using corruption as a device.

In any case, I came to see how Guatemala had been likewise subverted by Carlos Castillo Armas, Nicaragua by the Somozas, Haiti by—well, it was just a widespread pattern! I came to see how the elite in Mexico governs by corruption; it continues to be the key to power.

CBG: So in 1954 these ideas crystalized, and you then launched into politics?

HCM: Ideas concerning organization began crystalizing in my mind in 1954. I first tried to see which political groups I could fit into; then, I gradually came to realize the extent to which atomization had taken place due to the wars of ideology. Ideological purity had become the key weapon. I am referring, of course, to the *puros*, or the people who don't tolerate a single fault to virtue, the ones who end up being isolated and divided up into ever-smaller sects. This is what I learned up to about 1961, but I never took part in any one single group. This coincided with my touring the countryside.

CBG: Did you travel on your own? Did you represent anyone else?

HCM: No one. At times, however, General Cárdenas would invite me to join him as he traveled. In 1961 he convened the Latin American Conference for National Sovereignty, Peace, and Economic Emancipation, and I took part in a national committee designed to foster Mexico's movement for national liberation. I was very enthusiastic in those days, many of which stretched into sleepless nights of political activity.

What I learned from all this is that a person cannot take part in a political struggle on a part-time basis; my intellectual friends were really unable to dedicate themselves to this kind of task. I began to see the obvious; real revolutionaries could never say: "Well, I'll lecture at the university in the morning, and, in the afternoon, I'll devote myself to making revolution." I came to understand that, while it was necessary to foster revolution in Mexico, it could not be done in my spare time. A leader must always work full-time. Party leaders must be supported by the party members; and, when they aren't, then the leaders have to switch over to become bureaucrats. All of this became a field study for me in Mexican politics up until 1966.

CBG: Were you working as an engineer already?

HCM: Yes, of course. All this time, I had been working as a professor, and, by good fortune, I was a professor who built things. I would find a new theory and put it to work. I was always a professor-engineer, never just a teaching professor. I would do research, and then I would build. In 1965, I constructed the first bridge with my theories, almost at the same time that I was attending the Latin American Conference that I mentioned earlier. A lot of my friends used to ask me about how I could do all of this at the same time. In 1966, I was close to quitting the university and my engineering work in order to dedicate myself completely to the political struggle and work professionally only in my spare time.

My dilemma was resolved when some private companies bought my patents in 1967. These firms began paying royalties which allowed me to quit my regular jobs. I then began to dedicate almost all of my time to traveling. This is also the time in which many of my friends were getting killed, and my own life was placed in grave danger too. Presumably, local government officials learned that I was dedicating more time to political activities and decided that they would have fewer problems if they eliminated me.

By 1968, I was connected with the movement. I used to travel to the provinces to talk publicly about the revolutionary struggle and the need for organization. As a teacher, young people received me enthusiastically. I used to appear on television, and my name began to be publicized widely. Some people did not think I was the same person, the engineer and the politician. Some important businessmen once told me: "There is a Communist with the same name as yours!" I never tried to clear things up.

The student movement of 1968 swept us into a whirlwind, but I never agreed to leave the country like a lot of my fellow intellectuals did after the movement was crushed. They used to ask me why not, and I used to tell them that I had to stay and fight. You have to be committed to the end. Luckily, I didn't lose my life, but it wasn't because certain individuals didn't want to kill me. I hid for eight months trying to organize, myself, but was unable to.

CBG: Were you a member of the Consejo Nacional de Huelga [or the National Student Strike Committee, which coordinated the student movement]?

HCM: I was not part of the Consejo Nacional de Huelga because it was made up of students only. However, I served as a representative of the Coalición Nacional de Profesores Pro-Libertades Democráticas [Teachers' Coalition for Democratic Liberties]. The coalition appointed three professors to work with the students. I represented the technical departments of the national university; Eli de Gortari represented the humanist ones, and Fausto Trejo represented the Instituto Politécnico. All three of us went to jail. This didn't separate me from the struggle, because it allowed me to think things through. It is the only time in my life I've been at peace.

CBG: What were you accused of?

HCM: I was accused of being the leader of the 1968 movement which sought to overthrow the government. It was also alleged that I had conspired with the students to become the prime minister of a new government and that Fidel Castro had given us money when I attended the Tricontinental Congress meeting in Havana in 1966 as the Mexican representative. It was also said that I was intellectually responsible for the death of the soldiers at Tlaltelolco and the demonstrators too, of course.

CBG: Those were the accusations?

HCM: Yes. Each one of the ten counts imputed against me carried up to forty years in prison. In other words, the idea was for me to die in prison. I went before a judge only once because I took the opportunity to make statements to the reporters present and denounce the system. The judge did not call me again, and I have never stood before a judge since.

One day, emissaries of President Luis Echeverría came to my cell to propose to me that I leave the country. They suggested I go to Chile since Salvador Allende was presiding over a revolutionary government there (I met him at the Tricontinental meeting in Havana, and he was a personal friend of mine). I told the emissaries that there were others besides me, to begin with, about 150 students and three or four peasants and workers, and that I would not discuss anything with the emissaries unless these other prisoners were released. I said that, when they were free, though still in Mexico (the government was sending them abroad, and some didn't know how to read and write), I would then agree to discuss the matter.

Fifteen days later the jailers told me to go because I was free. I then gave my cell mates the books that I had (except for the history book I was writing then). Upon leaving, the chief jailer told me I had to sign a request for gaining my freedom. I replied that I hadn't asked to be jailed, that they had jailed me without my permission, and for that reason I had to leave without signing such a request. At that point, he went over to my wife, who was waiting nearby, and told her: "Look, would you please tell your husband not to be so stubborn," to which she replied: "You talk to him. I know him well." So the jailer and I talked again, and finally I said to him: "Look, don't insist. I'm going to leave here without signing anything. If you really want me to sign something, you're going to have to put me back in jail and let someone else try to convince me. You're wasting my time. Otherwise, you'll have to let me go back to my cell, where I have a lot of work to do." The jailer got very angry at that point. A little later, he approached me again and yanked me out into the street. I was free. A couple of years later, President Echeverría announced an amnesty, but I never had contact with the president's office again.

In jail, in the company of my cell mates, I saw the need to form a new political party. What does a "new" party

mean, in this sense? I had concluded by this time that, if
Mexico could not control its own territory to benefit the
Mexican people, it could not plan its own future. Somebody
might say that it is obvious that Mexico already controls its
own territory. Unfortunately, this is neither obvious nor
true. A large part of its territory is occupied by multinational corporations. If Mexico does not control its energy
needs, it cannot develop. Even though the expropriation of
the petroleum industry had already taken place, Mexico was
using its petroleum to aid in the development of parasites
residing within its own organism. The nationalized enterprises have acted as nursemaids to U.S. imperialist firms
as well as to very large Japanese and German companies.
These countries brought their factories to Mexico, and
PEMEX subsidized their energy needs; the Federal Electric
Commission subsidized their electrical needs, federal railroads their transport needs, and the larger Mexican system
their labor needs.

I had concluded, therefore, that the national systems
aimed at controlling the cost of living (like subsidies on food,
et cetera) did not really represent a benefit to the nation. If
I sell cheap wheat, cheap beans, cheap corn to the workers, I
am encouraging their employers to pay them less wages.
This is why I say I had concluded that our national wealth
had to be distributed to the Mexican people alone, not to
foreigners.

My cell mates and I also concluded that the law of supply and demand would prevent Mexico and the Mexican people from obtaining the capital we need to buy and to maintain the machinery and factories required. The needed
capital does not reside in Mexico; it resides in the United
States, Japan, and Germany. This means that, if we sold
things freely, the machinery and factories our country needs
to get ahead, we would be bought up by foreigners. This
would make us a nation of *maquiladoras,* or assemblers of
foreign-made parts. In the end, we would be working for foreigners. Look at our meeting place this morning. It belongs
to a chain which, along with others, has brought about the
disappearance of Mexican restaurants typical of those existing in the 1950s.

CBG: This is a VIPS restaurant.

HCM: When I was a student in 1947, my classmates and
I used to go to small Mexican restaurants that were quite

good. The only Mexican aspect of restaurants like the one
we are in at the moment is the staff: the waitresses, the
assistant managers, et al. This is what you find in the
tourist areas and in the productive sector of the country too.
These are the kinds of conclusions my cell mates and I came
to in those days.

CBG: As you sat in jail?

HCM: Yes, and we set them out with a lot of clarity in
our party platform.

CBG: Who sat with you in jail while you debated these
issues?

HCM: Many of my cell mates were young Communists.
Most of them insisted that the way to resolve these problems was to hum the familiar tune that the whole world
hears all of the time, the one based on Marxist-Leninist
thought.

We discussed the ideas of Karl Marx, Lenin, Leon
Trotsky, and so on, and I would always raise the names of
Leonardo da Vinci and Galileo. "I prefer these two men," I
would say, because no revolution has thus far been completely successful. Any revolutionary individual today has
to be conscious of the fact that, if the social relations of production are not transformed globally, we will disappear as a
species. I think Marx was a great thinker and a great revolutionary, but he is dead. The same is true for da Vinci and
Michelangelo. The great thinkers of the world are all dead.
What lives are their ideas and their hypotheses because
they wrote them down, and it is our responsibility to double-
check them before trying to use them. I used to tell my cell
mates: "I will not follow any idea that I cannot verify. None!"
I can't be forever saying: "Marx said this or that!" I may
borrow Mr. Marx's ideas, but it is my responsibility as to
the way I handle them. Just as I say to my friends who are
engineers, I can borrow ideas from [Isaac] Newton to build a
bridge but I can't say that he built it. I can't say, "Thanks to
Newton, I built this bridge!" I have to accept that, although
I used his ideas, nonetheless here is *my* bridge. The bridge
is different from anything Newton would have built, because
I built it.

"Let us establish a party where we can verify the ideas
of the great thinkers," I said. Let's measure them against
reality! Let's apply Lenin's ideas about organization to a
Mexican political party! Let's see if they work. I have my

doubts. What shall the principles of the new party be? Mexico's land must be for the Mexican people. This does not mean that we will not accept foreigners, but first let us satisfy the needs of the Mexican people. Let us develop ourselves first. Let's make sure that the Mexican people work and develop their own means of production.

In order to do this we must place barriers on free enterprise because, if we don't, then our initial premise becomes undermined; Mexican territory must be for the enjoyment of the Mexican people only. Anything that goes counter to our sense of nationhood must be rejected. We can't accept others to govern our affairs. We can share what lies within our territory, but only if we command the integrity of our territory and if we enjoy complete respect for our sovereignty. We can't become an isolated island after all. However, the whole thing must be erected on a just foundation. It follows, then, that unlimited private property cannot be tolerated. It doesn't exist anywhere else. If you can't have unlimited private property, then what do you have?

We want a society where the means of communication belong to everybody. Rules about property must be laid down. Each to his own need; from each according to his own capacity. Who determines this? Freely elected officials. Right now, whoever is elected uses force to defend his privileges. With us there would be no privileges except for the children and the handicapped. Power must be temporal. In Mexico we cannot accept governors for life. Personal power corrupts, and absolute power corrupts absolutely.

The key idea is that we no longer consider it possible to copy somebody else's schemes. For example, we can't accept doing away with all types of private property, because even the great socialist countries have found it necessary to keep it going indefinitely. What do I mean by private property? Specifically, I am referring to auto repair shops, watch repair shops, stores for electronic goods, clothing shops, small restaurants, et cetera. On the contrary, when everything becomes state property, the quality of the distributed good falls. The presence of private distributors is seen as necessary.

Does this sound Marxist? Yes, I identify a lot with his ideas on political economy, but I am not a Marxist. But I do defend a man's rights and, as such, the rights of a Mexican to his habitat as long as his traditions and customs are respected.

CBG: What is the status of the party today?

HCM: We have just begun. We have six deputies in congress, and we have not yet run candidates in local elections. We are now preparing for this. We have also learned that our organizational approach, in practical matters, runs parallel in congress with the party that calls itself Marxist, the PSUM, and with the Trotskyist party, the PRT. This is why the Right says to me: "You guys are a bunch of closet Communists!" No. We defend ideas similar to those of the parties just mentioned, but not because the ideas belong to Marx, but because they represent our ideas, which we must defend.

As a political party we have six positions in congress. While we may represent less than 2 percent of the total number of deputies, we enjoy first place in attendance, way over the PRI. We are the third most important party on the basis of statements made before the entire chamber. In other words, with only six deputies, we participate almost on the same level as the PRI. I've been told that, during the recess period, when national affairs come to the attention of the legislature through its Permanent Committee, we are the most important party at the speaker's rostrum.

Our biggest problem is economics. The problem opposition parties have, like the PMT, is that our message is blocked on radio, television, and in newspapers. We get around it, for example, when some of us publish newspaper articles on a personal basis or speak on the radio. Unfortunately, the problem is a financial one; it is very hard to depend on popular donations. We are looking for ways to keep going.

CBG: I can vouch for your claim that the PMT has an impact on the written media. Can it be said that part of the PMT's political program is to unify the Left?

HCM: Our major concern right now is the unification of the Left. But we've learned that we don't need organic unity. Let me give you an example. There are peasant groups that tell us: "We don't want to have anything to do with congress!" I respond: "O.K.; you're fighting for land, but you don't want anything to do with a party in congress. Don't you even want a party in congress to demand in congress what you yourself demand? Are you opposed to that?" They reply: "No, I'm not opposed to that." Then I say: "We'll defend your ideas even if you're opposed to it. Why don't we come together? In the end, no one in congress will take away my right to defend your rights to land."

Some of the leaders of the socialist parties get angry with me because I criticize their holding onto elected posts too long or because I chide the bureaucratic nature of their organizations. Our relations aren't too good with them. When we do meet, I tell them: "Even though you may not ask us, we'll defend the rights of the Soviets, the Cubans, the Chinese, and the Vietnamese because we can't go around asking permission to defend our species, the human race." When we defend them, we are also defending ourselves. I don't care what the Chinese Communist Party may say. If the Chinese people are fighting for something fair, then we can support them too.

The same happens with the leftist groups that exist on the fringes. Yesterday, for example, a meeting of peasant organizations took place here in the city, and we took part in the biggest campesino ceremony that has taken place in recent years. We invited them, but not to a PMT activity per se. We told them: "This is a free forum, so that you can share your ideas with our party members about what ought to be done in the countryside. You're free to call for the taking up of arms, if that's what you believe, or to having us help you connect with government officials so that they may hear your petitions. Here's the microphone." As a result, eight organizations had their say. Afterward, we marched through the streets. The importance of this is to agree to do something together. Instead of having a tiny group take over three little towns, and another group another two, let's coordinate the effort for that purpose; and, if we can't agree, let's not fight. Let's just say we couldn't do it. As I say, we are beginning a new era of relationships among the Left.

The PMT enjoys a key virtue; it accepts everyone. We don't fight with one party or another because we belong to one line of thought and someone else to another. Instead, we gather the best of all of the revolutionary parties in the world, including ideas that may have come from either the West or the East.

We believe that, by 1988, the process of unification will be much farther along. We'll finally have a unified organization, even though we're not sure what form it will take, maybe a party, a front, or a coalition. We have to recognize the political rights belonging not only to existing national parties and to regional parties but also to neighborhood groups, peasants, students and so forth. We want to give space to everyone. I believe all of the groups except the PST will participate because it's very hard to resist what we are offering.[5]

CBG: I noticed that Pablo Gómez, the leader of the PSUM, the largest party on the Left, recently expressed a reluctance to join with you. Is he still reluctant?

HCM: No. This is what I'm saying to you. When they see us joining up with other groups, they'll come in too. I'm carrying a letter of acceptance at this moment. It was signed yesterday, and we'll announce it to the press soon. But why is it working?

First of all, there is no preeminent group right now. Also, we're not fighting for leadership positions, and this is where the organizational ways of our forefathers are important to keep alive. I recently published an article in *Proceso* discussing this by illustrating the way Emiliano Zapata was designated leader of the revolution. He was selected in the way the people of his hometown used to select a *calpuleque,* back in the days of the México. The *calpuleque* was considered the wisest and the most honorable among the members of the *calpulli.* This is the way Zapata was designated. If the *calpuleque* fell into dishonor, or he failed in his responsibilities, he was substituted by someone else. It was not rare to see a *calpuleque* enjoy a leadership position all his life; but the point is that the people enjoyed the right to remove him.

The Left has been plagued with *cacicazgos* and caudillismos. It isn't that we have proposed that there be no caudillos. Rather, we have proposed that the caudillos be selected by the members of the *calpullis.* When we finally walk into the great national assembly of all of these organizations, we need to make sure that the pretensions of the past (wanting to divide the leadership according to parties, for example) are behind us. Let the people of this country decide who the *calpuleques* are going to be.

Our PSUM friends agreed just yesterday to work together toward unity and toward a proposal. From now on, we will publicly discuss the persons who might run as candidates in 1988 for president, senators, and congress members. We don't want proposals coming from the party leaders alone. We want them to come from the ranks, as products of vigorous discussion weighing what the candidates have done in the past and what they're doing now.

CBG: Is there another political principle that the PMT raises, outside of the need for unity?

HCM: We know that we can't change Mexico's political and economic path if no one is able to participate democratically in the countryside, in the unions, and in middle-class organizations. I believe the most important struggle will take place within peasant leagues, workers' organizations, and in organizations made up of office employees, housewives, et al. At the present time, we can't even win at the municipal level because the government controls the townships through the organizations I just mentioned. Then you have the PAN as a factor because the middle classes agree with their principles. (I tell you that the PAN attracts people only because it doesn't talk about Marx.)

In seeking political victory, these government-controlled organizations represent the bulwark we have not been able to breach. We can't win if we don't change the system. The government and the class in power now control the working class by corrupt methods. It's an infernal power! The CTM only protects venal unions; it won't accept new ones. If it doesn't register them, it keeps them out. In the countryside the Ministry of Agrarian Reform, the CNC, and the CCI [Confederación Campesina Independiente] represent farm sector organizations that exist under the grip of corruption. They're controlled too.

The PMT's objective is to persuade our friends on the Left of the need to fight for the rights of the workers. We need to collectively help the workers organize within the unions they have put together and to help those who have not yet formed unions. This is the only way we can breach the wall. We believe the workers can be supported within their own unions when a strong leftist party can help them on the outside. Right now union members who try to organize themselves from within are quickly crushed.

Right now the voice of the Left is only a little voice. If we get into congress, however, people will begin to hear us more clearly. Instead of having six PMT deputies, six PRT deputies, and twelve PSUM deputies, we could have twenty-four deputies, all within one party. (Plus one more because we have someone from the PST working with us already.) We could be twenty-five as opposed to six.

CBG: What is your opinion of the PAN?

HCM: The PAN was born in opposition to Lázaro Cárdenas's land reform and the defense of the workers. It was born in defense of the interests of the bourgeoisie. The

PRI has outdone the PAN in this area, naturally, because
it has concentrated its economic power while in office. The
PRI is home for the greatest number of right-wing people.

The PAN has developed without a program or a platform. It doesn't really offer a new alternative; it merely
seeks to please the middle classes. "I am going to fight for
your rights so that you may take your family to eat at a
VIPS restaurant once a week." This may be one of their
party principles, when you come right down to it. Another
may be the need "to have the government handle your taxes
honestly," or that "mayors, governors, or the president be
elected democratically." They merely seek political democracy. Anything is attainable with this banner, especially economic well-being. They uphold private property, forgetting
that private property, in the pure sense of the word, cannot
exist in this country, as a rule. Different traditional forms of
property already exist here, including private property, communal property, *ejido* property, and so on. Still, a lot of
campesinos want their titles to their little farms; the middle
classes want their little house or a small firm. The PAN represents those wishes.

In other words, the PAN doesn't offer socialism of any
kind. It offers cooperatives instead. They don't want to
divide factory ownership but would opt to have the workers
buy up business shares. It doesn't oppose big companies
operating in strategic areas of the economy, but they'll urge
the VIPS chain or other restaurants to issue shares so that
the waiters can buy them, so that they'll be owners too.
Besides, the PAN knows that it can come to power with the
aid of the United States and it plays around with this alternative. It offers itself to the United States as a potential
ally, one that won't cause embarrassments. It is willing to
become an ideological ally, and this will enable the United
States to say someday: "Like us, Mexico wants private
enterprise and individual rights." The PAN seeks to protect
anybody's right to have three Cadillacs and fifteen houses. If
anyone wants land, let them have it, let it be the survival of
the fittest.

Old liberal philosophy is their thesis. We tell them that,
if we open up the border, the penetration of the Mexican
economy will be complete. They don't believe that the big
fish eats the little fish. To them it's just a matter of individual potential. They often say: "Mexico could compete with all

of the nations of the world if the government were simply honest." Their central argument is that the government is corrupt; it wins the greatest number of voters on this account because the corruption of the PRI administrations is plain as day.

CBG: Do you agree with the view that the PRI is in decline?

HCM: No, I don't believe so. The PRI has the ability to continue on as the official party, because it enjoys all the power in the world. It has all of the possibilities of becoming just like the PAN. If the PRI is pressed because it loses voters, it may change as I'm suggesting. Right now, for example, the difference between the PRI and the PAN is that the PRI does not yet accept the PAN's arguments about ending the *ejido* system. It doesn't accept this because the PRI is in power and the PAN is not. The PRI knows that, when it takes away *ejido* property from millions of campesinos, it will face a revolution. The PRI may be able to deny personal freedom, but it can't easily take away property. The PRI may nationalize the banks away from the five hundred families who own them, but it cannot easily take the land away from the three million *ejidatarios* who know how to handle farm machinery.

CBG: It's been announced that land will no longer be distributed.

HCM: But it's one thing to deny someone something, and it's quite another to take something away from someone. To take away is so much different from simply denying.

CBG: My understanding of what you're saying is that, if the PRI is hard-pressed, it will become less corrupt.

HCM: Not just less corrupt. The PRI can become more *panista,* more willing to serve the United States, more disposed toward pushing Mexico into becoming like the United States. The PAN wants us to become like a United States on Mexican territory. The United States wouldn't even have to invade, no sir. Look, you and I are already sitting here in the United States, in this VIPS restaurant. If you wish, we can go over to Perisur or Perinorte, the big shopping malls which already represent the United States on Mexican soil. The only ones who don't quite fit in the malls are the buyers and the employees. We're Mexican. An ideal of the United States is to convert us into *maquiladores,* a nation of *maquiladora* workers.

CBG: Have you omitted something from your party's platform?

HCM: Let me just say this before we go on to another subject. To believe that the PRI is somehow in decline is to forget that it has enjoyed the ability to adjust to all circumstances. The country is facing the possibility of a social explosion. Perhaps, at the beginning, an occurrence of this sort would force the PRI to become a PAN. By this I mean that the PRI would be forced to move to the Right, be amenable to the International Monetary Fund, to international banks, to the monetary theory of free commerce, et cetera. If this happened, Mexico would be like Argentina, Uruguay, or Brazil. I would say that the economy would collapse within five years.

If the military were in power, the officers would say: "We don't want any more of this; let democracy return." You may recall that, when economic chaos began to reign in these countries, the officers changed their minds and then said: "Let democracy continue; they've learned their lesson!" Democracy has the advantage that the final responsibility rests with the people who select the governors. If someone doesn't work out, then you get somebody else. In a government by law, if someone breaks the law, everybody knows whom to complain to. That's what's happening to the PRI today. Having a democracy simply won't change things right away. The big economic problems will still persist; but that's democracy! The force of democracy resides with the workers and the peasants, and they can make things change. We think the country is at a crossroads of the kind I describe above.

The Mexican government will continue to be surrounded by chaos. You can already see this by reading the newspapers. For example, Jesús Silva Herzog, economic minister [in the de la Madrid administration], says that we are going to have to lower the price of oil so that the United States can buy it. In other words, it seems that it doesn't matter how much money we get. What does matter is that we meet the oil quota. It's fine to sell a million barrels even though they pay us for less than eight hundred thousand. We can't pay what we owe, but we're giving the oil away.

If I'm not mistaken, we will receive $5 million for our oil this year, but we will have to pay $12 million in interest in 1986. They also say that 1987 will be worse. How can we get better, as the government insists we will, when we're so sick? We're losing blood. It's like someone saying to me: "This gentleman is quite sick; he suffers from uncontrolled hemorrhaging, but he's getting better!" The Mexican economy is in the same situation, but the PRI and the government continue to borrow money from the United States. If a man says to me: "Look, things are not going well for you. Let's be friends or allies. Tell me what you need." I respond: "Look, I need more credit to pay my bureaucrats and to pay for a new port facility. In the meantime, you can just keep PEMEX, or keep this industry or that one. In fact, I'll sell everything!" He says: "Fine!" This is what we're already doing.

CBG: Given the circumstances at this time, how can corruption be eliminated from the Mexican political system?

HCM: The only thing we can do is to be vigilant. Let me give you an example. The government just appointed me as a political commissar in an earthquake reconstruction committee in Tlaltelolco (an urban district in Mexico City), where damage was most intense. Since I'm a technician and an engineer (a specialist in structural problems) and I'm respected by Mexican engineers, the government decided to give me that appointment. When the people see me, they will ask: "What is he doing here?" Someone will answer: "He's here because everyone recognizes his professional prestige."

Why do I serve the government there? I serve because the government told the people of Tlaltelolco: "If Heberto Castillo, the engineer, forms part of the committee, we know there won't be any corruption." But, if the *tlaltelolcas* can't see any changes for the better, they'll think that the government bought out the engineer. The bottom line is that, if things aren't done right, I have to say immediately that there's fraud involved and resign.

Why did the government agree to behave honestly and not give in to corruption involving the reconstruction of Tlaltelolco? Probably because there is a lot of political pressure. The government must give in. My presence is not enough to guarantee that no one will steal anymore. I have to *do* something. I propose that each apartment dweller whose home is going to be repaired on account of the earthquake serve as the supervisor. I'll tell each person to make sure that the contractor is paid only for what he did. This

way a supervisor is present wherever the contractor's work
is done, and he will have to make sure that they're not
charged unfairly. This means that the people will be
vigilant.

CBG: Would you please address the economic crisis
which is afflicting Mexico at the present time? Please
describe it and tell us why it came about and what ought to
be done about it.

HCM: I believe the origin of the Mexican crisis is similar
to that of the crises affecting the countries of Latin America
and other dependent countries in the Third World. The economic domination by multinational corporations based in
the United States, Japan, Germany, or England is the common foe. The United States leads this group in economic
domination and exploitation.

The crisis arises naturally when the resources of the
poor countries are sacked. The idea that an industrial
nation can sack a nonindustrial one may or may not be
accepted by the industrialized countries. Euphemistically,
this process may be referred to as "industrialization," sometimes even "civilization." In this process the big multinational corporations come to the less developed countries to
look for gold, diamonds, oil, and sulphur; on other occasions
they look for agricultural raw materials and foodstuffs. All
of them arrive with the idea of extracting materials. The
United Fruit Company is a typical example of this process.

Today these enterprises exist all over Mexico. Over 90
percent of the commercialization or the distribution of foodstuffs produced in the countryside is controlled by multinationals. A visit to a supermarket reveals the presence of
multinational corporations; this is demonstrated by almost
any jar or canned good on the shelf whose labels reveal the
presence of multinational corporations. Some may say this
represents a step forward. They note that we have canned
goods and that this way we don't let pineapples, strawber-
ries, or apples get spoiled. Everything is taken advantage of!
But who benefits from this? For a long time, foreign
investors came to our country to increase their capital accumulation here. This era opened up officially in 1946 with
the administration of Miguel Alemán. The date varies in
other countries.

How does this capital accumulation work? In most cases,
fiscal incentives are given to foreign investors. Labor incen-

tives are also extended, such as government control of labor unions so that the workers won't strike for higher wages. Other opportunities are offered in the area of social security by providing low benefit levels. Energy products, like oil and electricity, are practically given away to foreign firms. Since railroads are state owned, fees stay cheap, but no new lines are built. Instead, highways are built, raising both the cost of transportation and the distribution of goods. This opens the way for big firms to manufacture vehicles, trailers, and large trucks, especially. Transportation thrives on gasoline, oil, rubber, synthetic rubber, tires, and related products.

The neocolonization of the world is based on generating profits for the countries that do the penetrating, but little care is given to bringing solutions to the countries that are penetrated. That's the problem! If you take a look at the development of the United States, you find that profits are important, but you also find that businesses do something to raise the standard of living of the people, so that they can then turn around and buy from the very businesses they work for. In other words, the idea is to create a market as well as to create a consumer purchasing power. Then the market can thrive.

In our countries, they have sought to develop the ability to exploit. "This tribe controls a lot of lumber, let's open up some roads to take it out!" Raising the tribe's standard of living is not the aim. "This country has a lot of gold, let's build some mines and some roads to take it out." The quality of life of the local people is another matter. If you examine some statistics, you'll find that, for every dollar entering Mexico in the last twenty-five years or so, $2.60 have gone back out in profit.[6] If this is true, how can development theories discuss the "development" or "riches" to be produced or the "benefits" that will accrue? I'm not even considering the goods themselves that left our borders, the silver, gold, oil, which will never come back! The business advantage is great this way.

Look at what's been happening in Mexico. In the last twenty-five years, foreign capital has poured into Mexico. Where has it gone? A good portion of Canadian money went into the electrical sector, and, during the López Mateos administration, Mexico nationalized it. During this period, investments in primary industries were rechanneled into

manufacturing, agriculture, and cattle raising. Now, investments pour into the electrical goods industries; Mexico has a
lot of subsidiaries belonging to electrical goods companies
based in the United States, Germany, and Japan. This kind
of investment is one of the most profitable. Investments
have also gone into pharmaceuticals and chemical pharmaceuticals. Ford, Chrysler, and General Motors established
automobile plants here too. Tractor manufacturers were followed by construction equipment firms and toolmakers.
(Tourism too, of course.)

CBG: In answering my question, you've offered an outline of the kind of development problems seen in Mexico and
elsewhere in the Third World. But I too have noticed that
those products you have just identified are now made in
Mexico. In Central America, by contrast, almost everything
is imported. Nicaraguans are using tires, today, imported
from Russia and Bulgaria. One could say that Mexico enjoys
quite an advantage in certain areas, and one could also say
that such advantages differ within the Third World.

HCM: Yes, but I have to point out simple but relevant
ideas. It is true that there is certain wealth in Mexico. We
have certain factories and plants here. But whose are they?
What the multinational companies have done is to trans-
plant their technology and their firms abroad, and, in doing
so, they have only installed *maquiladoras,* or assembly
plants. These plants represent companies that serve only
the interests of the foreigners. In the end, Mexico becomes a
dependent country whose industry, commerce, and tourist
facilities lie in foreign hands. Mexico is simply becoming a
giant *maquiladora,* a mere assembler. As such, it will now
sell goods to countries like those in Central America.
Industrial expansion in the United States, Germany, and
Japan follows this pattern of installing assembly factories in
Mexico, Taiwan, and South Korea. The problem is that the
natives of these countries don't own these factories.

CBG: How is this relevant to the economic crisis?

HCM: It is directly relevant! However, the problem
doesn't belong to the multinational corporations; the problem belongs to Mexico. This is where the rub lies. The
maquiladoras enjoy clear advantages because they set up
their factories on Mexican territory; they bring in their capital goods and the components for assembly. Mexican workers then do the job of assembling the components and get

their wages paid. Taxes are collected by the government too, but is there anything else?

All of this takes place because a certain order and arrangement have been provided by the Mexicans, collectively speaking. This means that someone has to build the roads, string up electric cables to back-country towns, build the ports, and so on. Unemployment payments, if they existed, would be paid by the Mexicans. What does this mean to the foreigners? It means they get more for their money!

As I stated earlier, for every dollar that comes in, $2.60 go out. What kind of business gives you that margin? White slavery [prostitution] and drug trafficking are the only ones I can think of. This kind of arrangement is most unfair! There is no single business in the United States that gives you that kind of profit margin. You don't find it in Germany, Japan, nor England! This explains their tendency to produce goods outside their borders; it makes for a good profit.

However, this advantage depends upon the unmerciful exploitation of the workers. Whose responsibility is it that salaries in Mexico are so low in comparison to the United States? It may be said that it belongs to the government of Mexico because it has failed to defend the interests of its own citizens. It also belongs to the foreign businesses who pay those salaries and reap the profits. A day's labor in Mexico is equivalent to an hour's pay in the United States; all you have to do is just cross the border. It's more profitable to manufacture goods in a country where wages are much lower.

CBG: So you're saying that the economic crisis comes from the problems connected with all these corporations?

HCM: Where do you think we're going to get the extra dollar or so to pay corporate profits? I've asked economists where they think Mexico can squeeze out the $1.60 needed to make ends meet. The answer is that Mexico borrows abroad. We borrow to pay the multinationals the interest we owe them, regardless of the fact that they have already stripped our silver, gold, and other riches. To make matters worse, we still have to pay them interest and then turn right around and borrow more from them!

Because more money goes out than comes in, the debt grows every year. This means that international bankers have speculated with us for the last twelve years or so. They charge Mexico 8 percent of its gross domestic product just in interest alone. Out of an investment of about $100 billion, the banks take a squeaky-clean 8 percent, or about $12 billion per year. Based on what we've paid, we could have paid off the principal in a mere six years! I insist the debt situation represents a ferocious form of exploitation.

While this overall pattern of unfair fiscal relations already existed, Mexico actually made things worse for itself. It increased oil sales beginning in 1976, but, in order to sell more, it became necessary to borrow more in order to have PEMEX produce more. The numbers on this are quite clear. Since 1976, Mexico tripled its external debt from $25 billion to $75 billion. And Mexico also paid $75 billion in interest during this time. The bottom line is that Mexico paid what it continued to owe, and it also transferred three billion barrels of oil which it doesn't have now. It's given everything away!

The situation I've outlined above is due to torpid government policies (I would even say antinational) that place us in the service of foreign interests. But my key argument is that we do this in the belief, for example, that we need foreign companies to make tires for us so that we don't have to import them.

It's fitting to say too that all of this has created a consumption pattern that exceeds our economic capacity in Mexico. A lot of my colleagues and I (university professors), for instance, live in a style typical of the middle class in the United States. I would say that about five to six million Mexicans live in a relatively high standard while about seventy-four or seventy-five million live in deplorable substandard conditions. This way of doing things is simply not right.

There's something else that is seldom accounted for; in Mexico we have a labor surplus. We have about twenty-five million Mexicans who are capable of working. Although it is difficult to quantify, we also have at least three million people who are unemployed. Underemployment must be at about twelve million too. Still, the industrialized countries feel they have to use labor-saving devices and modern techniques that employ fewer people each day. This occurs in the industrialized nations like the United States, Japan, Germany, England, Italy, et cetera. Because we're dependent on them, they send us their technology, which requires fewer workers.

CBG: We can use the example of Teléfonos de Mexico, the Mexican national telephone company, that wants to "go digital."

HCM: Yes, it is increasing labor-saving technology in order to automate itself. This will leave many workers out on the street. It is an irrational solution in a country requiring more jobs.

CBG: Given the economic situation you've identified, what does the PMT want to do about it?

HCM: The PMT wants to do everything contrary to what is being done now. In other words, Mexico cannot continue to pay its debt and survive at the same time, because it doesn't have the money to do both. Someone said recently that it would be dangerous not to pay the debt. I believe it would be just as dangerous for someone who has been losing blood for two hours to lose more. "Help! I'm bleeding! What can you do for me? Bring me a tourniquet, do something, I'm having a hemorrhage!" "It's not a convenient situation to be in," I would tell that person. "No, you're right, it's not convenient." I would reply: "Well, why don't you stop it?" It's a silly question, isn't it? They say it's too dangerous for Mexico not to pay? Yes, but payment will end when Mexico runs out of money, like the man with the hemorrhage. It will stop when he runs out of blood.

Government officials don't understand the simple calculations we do in congress daily. It appears that international bankers and officials from the monetary fund don't understand them either. For example, Mexico is selling oil this year [1986] at $11 per barrel instead of the $28 per barrel it was getting just recently. Also, instead of selling 1.5 million barrels daily, Mexico is selling only 1.1 million. In other words, Mexico is selling about $12.1 million worth of oil daily (1.1 million barrels times $11). This means that Mexico will earn $4.3 billion this year and, if things go well, perhaps $5 billion. Last year, however, we sold $14 billion worth, which means we lost $9 billion this year alone due to a price drop.

Let's add up our other export earnings. With difficulty, we will earn $7 billion with manufacturing exports. This means we'll have $7 billion from manufacturing exports plus $5 billion from oil sales, which totals $12 billion in export earnings. But we have to pay $12 billion in interest. If international bankers feel generous this year, we might have to pay only $10 billion, which would leave us $2 billion. How can we live on this? I tell you we can't afford to pay our debt! Someone might say: "Well, at least you're paying off the interest." I would have to respond: "Yes, but now I have only $2 billion left, and I still have to pay $10 billion for imports" (in 1981 we imported $21 billion worth; right now we are at half the imports we received five years ago).

This lays bare what any economist can see; Mexican industrialists face a grave situation because, in order to manufacture their products, they require goods from abroad that must be paid in dollars, not pesos. We thus have a gap of about $8 to $9 billion this year alone. Who is going to lend to us if we can't pay it back? In this economic crisis, we're coming to the point where we have to say that we can't pay anything else! What will the international banks do? They'll respond by saying: "No, you've got to pay me!" We have to respond: "But the country has no money!" They'll respond in exasperation: "This is all absurd!" Then we say: "What do you suggest?" They'll say: "Since you can't pay what you owe, let us come into your territory so we can set up some factories, exploit your resources, including your labor, but don't charge us taxes." In other words, Mexico again becomes conquest territory like in the American West. It looks to me like this is the alternative facing a government that doesn't understand, one that can't sit down and reason with its creditors and make them see the impossibility of what they demand.

The PMT's alternative is the product of the following reasoning. What can we do if we're handing over oil to pay debt interest, and, in addition, foreigners are only paying us practically what it costs us to produce it? They already forced us to stop exploring because we had no money to continue exploring on our own. If it costs $17 to produce a given item, and I am forced to sell it at $11, it's not convenient to produce it. I am obliged to tell the government: "If you're taking oil out of the ground to hand it over to foreigners, on top of your investing to search for more oil without due compensation, then it's better you don't produce any more. Don't sell any oil. Use it at home." This is why the PMT says: "Don't pay the debt, and don't sell oil."

CBG: Are you saying that the debt shouldn't be paid for the sake of simply not paying or to force negotiation?

HCM: We're saying, Don't pay! But the PMT could also

say: "Let's sit down with our creditors and ask them how they think we might be able to pay." They could respond by saying to us: "Look, because there is a lot of time ahead of us, don't pay me now. The danger of a civil war hangs over you because the people cannot go hungry indefinitely. There's also the danger that the political structure of the country will soon come apart. Chaos threatens. This dangerous atmosphere creates a risk for Volkswagen, General Motors, Chrysler, IBM, et cetera. The risk you're facing is having to abandon factories and investments, because violence can become uncontrollable." Our creditors could say these things to us because they already know that trouble is brewing. We're not making this up.

CBG: What would happen if the government did what you asked?

HCM: I think the international banks would agree on economic incentives. They'd say: "If these people can't pay, then it's better for me that they not die off. If they owe us, let them live." (In Mexico we say humorously: "How could he die if he still owed me?") I'm assuming the bankers would say: "I fear my debtor is in bad shape; and, if he dies, I've lost everything. If I help him get better, he'll pay me off because he'll be able to work." I believe they would respond by saying: "Let's work on some support plans for these people and let everybody know, at the same time, that we won't syphon off everything."

CBG: Why doesn't the government say this openly?

HCM: I think it's because it would give the opposition an opportunity to win some elections. I consider it an error for the government to monopolize the search for debt solutions, because it is committing this country's future without consulting with the people. In other words, we're dealing with the egotism of those in power, who don't want to share their power.

CBG: Given these conditions, how does your party feel about the oft-mentioned *paraestatales*?

HCM: I believe that our economic problems have a lot to do with *paraestatales*. If the government could only understand that it needs to charge fair prices to multinational corporations for the use of electricity, oil, gas, and services, a lot of problems would be eliminated.

CBG: It wouldn't be necessary to cut them out?

HCM: Gosh, no! They have helped keep us afloat, especially PEMEX and the Federal Commission on Electricity!

What has happened is that we have transferred their profits and earnings over to the multinational corporations by subsidizing these multinationals with cheap energy produced by the *paraestatales*. People ignore how much oil the multinationals consume. They're the ones that use up the energy resources of this country. Industry consumes the most energy in any country!

CBG: It's been said that there are many *paraestatales* that should not have been absorbed by the government.

HCM: The PAN and the rest of the Right are the ones who have been saying this. With some exceptions, I believe that the government must control basic industries like pharmaceuticals, food industries, transportation, electricity, water, drainage, et cetera. The problem has been that, in the flurry of subsidizing some businesses, all of them became subsidized.

Look, if you compare the cost of a liter of mineral water with that of a liter of oil, you'll find that the oil is cheaper. People ordinarily don't make these comparisons; they don't pay attention to the terrible imbalance involved. They might find it a blessing and say: "Well, if oil is cheaper than mineral water, then we must be the ones who are benefiting from this situation." This is not so. If Mexican workers use up any gasoline, they do so only on the buses they ride. The people who use gasoline are the businesspeople or middle-class people who own automobiles; Mexican workers don't own automobiles. The biggest share of gasoline goes to businesspeople with cars. They are the ones who really use oil and gasoline, and they are the ones who are being subsidized by low prices!

The PMT urges that subsidies be discriminatory. Let the public transportation and the electricity the average citizen uses be subsidized, but not personal transportation. There ought to be a right way to charge for electricity, oil, gas, transportation by rail, et cetera. The *paraestatales* ought to be charged what is fair, and this alone would be a boon to our economy.

CBG: Are *paraestatales* run efficiently?

HCM: I'd say not in PEMEX's case. If I sell you oil at half the cost, I'll lose, but not because of inefficiency. It could be because I took the product out of the market. We find ourselves in a strong buyer's market, yet we take our product out of the market. We practically gave away our oil for

years. Whom did we give it to? Did we give it to the poor
folk of this country? No; peasants don't even use it. A
donkey doesn't drink gasoline, and many people use wood
stoves that don't burn gas. Country folk consume wood and
charcoal mostly, and transportation is on donkey or on foot.

CBG: If you and your party came to power, what would
be your position on foreign capital?

HCM: We would welcome businesses that produce something we don't. Good examples of these are seen in the high-
tech field, like computers and industrial engines. We would
also support small- and medium-sized industries. In many
ways it can be said that high-tech industry is incompatible
with the level of our development. What we need are light
industries that provide employment for our people. For
example, if I had to choose between starting a tortilla factory that is operated by machinery and one which relies on
hand labor, I would have to consider not only the cost of tortillas but also the amount of labor it would produce. If we
have to construct a dam, I would say: "Let's see what is best,
lots of earth-moving machinery or lots of laborers?" I'd look
for a balance between creating jobs with labor that is slow
and going ahead with efficient technology that does the job
rapidly. Let's not forget that unemployed people usually get
into trouble, because, if they're hungry, they may steal or
kill someone. It is preferable to give a man a job for his sake
and for the sake of society as well. Our efficiency may not
compare with the "efficiency" of big industry in other countries, but ours solves a lot of our problems for us.

Modernity for the United States cannot be the same
thing for Mexico. In Mexico we can afford to build a lot of
houses by joining partition walls because we create jobs for
the partition-wall builders. In the United States, on the
other hand, the custom is to build houses without partition
walls; we'd have to be careful about this. Ideally, we would
support small business and industry. We'd give everyone a
chance, but we'd avoid big consortiums with the exception of
those areas that require it, like steel, aluminum, window
glass, and bathroom fixtures. There are many products that
have to be made by complex industries.

CBG: What do you think of private enterprise in
Mexico's economic development?

HCM: My view is that Mexico has been fashioned both
by working-class people and by small- and medium-sized

industrialists and merchants. These are the people who
helped create the oil and electrical industries, automobile
manufacturing, electronics, et cetera. The people from the
private sector created these industries, not the government.
The government has defended the national interest on certain occasions by maintaining that basic industries should
not be privately owned. I'll tell you that I'm a mortal enemy
of the idea that the oil industry should be privately owned. I
say the same about electricity, railroads, public transportation in the city, and the food industry. I'm not saying that
there shouldn't be private businesses. I am an enemy of
monopolies and of the concentration of economic power. I
am opposed to radio and television monopolies. I don't think
that television should be private precisely because it isn't
easy for a small-business person to do well in it.

I am a supporter of industry, however. I am in favor of
private contractors, for example, who make and repair
houses. But I don't think anyone can compete with the state
in the construction of mass housing, roads, railroads, or
ports. Large entities are needed to do this kind of work. The
same with medical practice. I support socialized medicine
because a hospital requires very expensive equipment, like
cobalt machines, laser ray machines, and the rest; all of
which would be very expensive for a single doctor.

CBG: Do you think the private sector failed to handle
responsibly the resources given to it for the benefit of the
country?

HCM: One could say that this is true, but I don't think it
is because they lack ability. I think it's because the private
sector has not cared to handle these resources responsibly.
The private sector has always been penetrated by outside
interests. If I arrive as a foreign businessperson, I will want
to make my earnings without delay because I will always be
an outsider and will have to move on. But, if I'm a Mexican
businessman, I'm building my own future here and that of
my children and grandchildren. My investments will be for
the future, not for quick profit. The fact that private business does exist clearly shows a willingness on the part of
certain individuals to invest with the country's future in
mind. Sidral Mundet, a beverage company, comes to mind. It
was started by a Spaniard who took up the challenge of
investing for the future here.

CBG: Can you think of somebody else?

HCM: Another example is Jacobo Zaidenweber, a Jewish man who heads a very big textile company. He too set his roots down in Mexico. I am opposed to the big foreign investor who takes without giving. I am not opposed to the small- and medium-sized businessman who creates jobs, produces, and defends the country too.

CBG: You must be very opposed to Mexico's entry into GATT.

HCM: If Mexico becomes part of GATT, all of the small- and medium-sized industries I mentioned above will die because the big multinationals will flood the country with their goods and thus take over. Becoming part of GATT is part of the process of economic integration.

CBG: My understanding is that doing so will help get rid of "inefficient" business.

HCM: I see this more as a pretext, not an argument. What is an inefficient industry? This is where the dilemma lies. In order to become efficient, must we produce like the Japanese? Do we really want to keep the human hand away from production the way some bread items, cookies, and other such products advertise? When we enter a hospital as a patient, one of these days, do we want a robot to take us to an operating room and have a computer operate on us using laser rays? Is that the future to which we aspire in Mexico? It might be for Japan or the United States, but it isn't for Mexico. In Mexico, to mechanize things in such a way that you take jobs away from people who need them means the eventual destruction of the human species. It is one thing to let machines do a man's heavy work, but it is quite another to put him out of a job. We are against Mexico's entering GATT the same way we are against Mexico's ending up in the hands of big multinational corporations. We must recognize the conditions in which we live and not pretend to live the way people do in the United States.

CBG: If my recollection is right, *ingeniero,* the last decision leading Mexico toward GATT was made without consulting congress. Am I wrong?

HCM: No, but, even if it had been consulted, it wouldn't have made a difference. That's a feature of the Mexican congress. Our congress is run by a PRI majority, and this majority does only what the president tells it to do. There's no way to modify legislation. The decision to enter GATT belongs to the president, and no one can stop this.

The repercussions of Mexico's entry into GATT may be the only way to cancel Mexico's membership. These will include the disappearance of the small- and medium-sized industries. Many of these firms will go broke; they'll sell. Some Jewish textile manufacturers were saying to me just the other day: "If Taiwan comes here, we'll sell our businesses to them. Even now we would sell!" They want to get out of the market. They'd rather invest their dollars in short-term accounts.[7]

CBG: What will the effect be on the labor unions?

HCM: The creation of revolutionary conditions. When? It's hard to say, but the process is going in that direction. The unions will have to break their links. Right now the workers are tied to their union bosses, who are in turned tied to the employers and the government. The ties will be broken, and the rupture will be violent

CBG: What position does your party take in the area of foreign relations?

HCM: In the area of foreign relations, our party coincides with the government in most areas. This is so with respect to the Contadora process, its support of Nicaragua, El Salvador, the Chilean people, and *juarista* policy, which is traditionally Mexican.

CBG: So you're in agreement?

HCM: We're in agreement, basically speaking. There aren't any discrepancies.

CBG: Do you think Mexican foreign policy contradicts internal politics?

HCM: I wouldn't say it contradicts it; I would say it contrasts it. Since independence, Mexican foreign policy has helped the government maintain its internal hegemony to some extent, because it generates a certain international prestige. Consequently, many people outside the country look at those of us who struggle from within and say: "Mexico follows admirable international policies; I wonder why these people fight with the government!"

CBG: I know that Rosario Ibarra de Piedra has stated much of what you're saying regarding human rights, that Mexico supports human rights abroad but not at home.

HCM: I wouldn't make that claim. I think it's a bit exaggerated. Because of its prestige abroad, Mexico can appear as a socialist country to a lot of observers. Some years ago, I attended some international congresses in Africa and Asia, and I heard people say: "Goodness, I didn't know that Mexico was a socialist country." They had heard about Mexico's position regarding the rights of nations, which is viewed as a progressive position.

With regard to Mexico's internal politics, I believe torture is practiced and authority is abused. I also have to add, however, that it has diminished considerably in the last ten years. This is why I don't agree with Rosario Ibarra, who maintains that there has been no change in this area at all. How long has she been insisting that about five hundred people are among the "disappeared"? About ten years. An intelligent observer will quickly notice that the number doesn't change over time, so he might say: "Gosh, the number doesn't increase, they must appear and disappear! Perhaps they renew themselves!" The truth is that we've been able to reduce the repression level since 1968, but not eliminate it, unfortunately. It's still around. One of our comrades who was kidnapped some time back was finally released just yesterday. Being repressed is part of the occupational hazards, right? It's been thirteen years since I was last beaten up. In fact, I used to get a yearly beating for about five or six years in a row!

CBG: You mean a physical beating? They would hurt you?

HCM: They would beat me to a pulp! They used to apprehend me, insult me, and beat me, leaving me laid out completely! It got to a point where I used to try to figure out how long it had been since the last beating in order to find out when they would begin looking for me again. The last time it happened was August 5, 1976.

CBG: As far as you know, government agents or police would appear from nowhere and beat you up?

HCM: They would apprehend me, insult me, and beat me! Then the president would make excuses about it. In fact, two presidents made excuses to me about it by explaining that the whole thing had been an error!

CBG: How does your party view Reagan's policy on Central America?

HCM: We consider Reagan's policy on Central America demented! He's as arrogant as he is powerful. He considers himself to be enlightened enough to say: "This is good, this is bad!" He represents a total disrespect to international law; he's the one who sees the mote in his brother's eye but considers not the beam in his own; he's the biggest terrorist alive right now. Yet he is a person of sympathy and charisma. It's lamentable that a people as industrious and hard-working as the Americans have been won over by Reagan's bellicose alternatives. We consider this a problem. The vice president, who hovers nearby, belongs to the same school and shares the same viewpoint.

A world war threatens! We are concerned about the need to wake up everybody in the United States, about making them see the need to respect the way other people live their lives. They have no right to stick their noses in other people's affairs. They have no right to condemn a social and economic system on the other side of the border which may be different from theirs.

CBG: Do you think Soviet policy toward Latin America has changed much in the last ten years?

HCM: I don't think it has changed fundamentally. The USSR has always maintained an observer's position in Latin America with the exception of Cuba. Cultural missions, including exhibits of various sorts, have been the only things that the USSR has sent to Latin America. The Red Circus and the Russian Ballet come to mind. There is a handful of Soviet products in Mexico too, but there's no Russian presence; we don't even know any Russians personally!

Notes

1. This was the first of several interview dates. Heberto Castillo was interviewed in his home in southern Mexico City, the temporary PMT headquarters following the 1985 earthquake, and in several VIPS restaurants of the capital city.

2. Gabriel García Márquez, *One Hundred Years of Solitude* (New York: Avon, 1971).

3. In this context, *chinga tu madre* may be translated as "go fuck yourself." See Octavio Paz's discussion of the various forms of the verb *chingar* in his *Labyrinth of Solitude: Life and Thought in Mexico* (New York: Grove, 1961), 73–80.

4. The giant Hotel Mexico was undamaged in the earthquake of September 1985.

5. Heberto Castillo played a vital role in helping to achieve the political unification of Mexico's leftist opposition. As discussed in Chap. 2, Castillo's PMT joined the PSUM, and other smaller political groups, soon after this interview took place, in order to

form the PMS. In the meantime, Cuauhtémoc Cárdenas emerged as a national leader and he and his supporters allied themselves with the PMS for the 1988 elections. The alliance was later transformed into the PRD which embodies Mexico's unified Left, albeit a moderate one.

6. Cockcroft, *Mexico: Class Formation*, 256.

7. Short-term investments do better in high-inflation economies than long-term investments.

Appendixes

APPENDIX 1

Cuauhtémoc Cárdenas and the Rise of Transborder Politics

Did the appearance of a strong political opposition in Mexico capable of vying effectively with the official party, which has monopolized politics since 1929, have any effect on Mexican-Americans in the United States?[1] This essay will use preliminary information to show that the appearance of such an opposition in 1988, led by Cuauhtémoc Cárdenas, brought new life to the political consciousness of both Mexican citizens residing in the United States and Mexican-Americans.[2] This consciousness appears to have been raised by direct actions taken by Cárdenas and other leaders of the *cardenista* party known as the Partido de la Revolución Democrática (PRD). Evidence shows that political leaders in Mexico who had dismissed the political interests of Mexicanos in the United States prior to 1988 also felt the impact of Cárdenas's actions in favor of political communication across the U.S.-Mexico border.

When Jesús González Schmal, a conservative party leader,[3] was asked in 1986 whether his organization enjoyed any relations with the thousands of Mexican-American communities, he replied, "No, we haven't done [political] work there, even though many of the Mexicans [living in the United States] write to us constantly." The party leader and former congressman added that many Mexicans in the United States donated money to the PAN, but, nonetheless, "the PAN does not actively work over there, nor do I see the possibility [of doing so] either."[4]

When Jorge Alcocer was asked a similar question, he responded in a slightly different way.[5] A leftist party leader supporting the candidacy of Cuauhtémoc Cárdenas in 1988 and a former congressman as well, Alcocer answered by noting that his party had established certain contacts "with diverse organizations of Mexicans living in the United States" in the late 1970s and early 1980s, but it was not engaged in this effort in 1986. A frequent contributor to the well-known weekly *Proceso*, Alcocer acknowledged the potential significance of political communication across the border:

> [*Mexicanos* in the United States] represent a potential support base for a democratic and socialist struggle in Mexico. They constitute a potential counterweight against aggressive policies fashioned by the U.S. government. I think that people of Mexican descent [in the United States] represent [a support base] because they already recognize their own uniqueness. They're constantly preoccupied with Mexico's destiny; they hold a legitimate preoccupation with its democratic development. I think this is basic for them. I think there is a commonality of interests on their part.[6]

Early Instances of U.S. Interest in Mexican Politics

A commonality of interests in the political arena has long existed between *mexicanos* in the United States and the citizens of Mexico. However, the expression of these interests in the form of organized activity appears to be underrecorded in Mexican-American studies. Nevertheless, activity by U.S. *mexicanos* connected to politics in their homeland surfaces in the literature from time to time.

We can begin with the so-called Plan de San Diego of 1915. It is a bizarre example of the commonality of interests between U.S. *mexicanos* and politics in Mexico, but some Mexican-American historians include it in their work nonetheless. They often interpret it as an Anglo-concocted scare that was employed by U.S. authorities to increase their domination, in Texas especially, and to add to the tension existing between Anglos and *mexicanos* during the Mexican Revolution. Rudy Acuña, for example, writes that

Anglo authorities used it "as an excuse to step up an unprecedented reign of terror along the border."[7] The plan allegedly called for a general uprising and the massacre by Mexicans of all white males over the age of sixteen on a given date, followed by the creation of "a Chicano nation" in the southwest. However, Mexico specialists Don M. Coerver and Linda B. Hall attribute the bloody plan to a zealot who supported an ousted Mexican leader, Victoriano Huerta. Presumably, he tried to create trouble on U.S. soil for Huerta's opponent in Mexico City, Venustiano Carranza, by propagating a terrifying scheme such as the Plan de San Diego.[8] For the purposes of this discussion, the plan remains wrapped in conjecture to some extent. Nonetheless, it dramatically illustrates one way in which Mexican politics spilled across the border and caused ugly ripples on the northern side.

Historians of U.S.-Mexico border communities have begun to point to other political ripples traveling across the border. They unveil patterns of political communication between the two countries in a manner that is more real historically than the Plan de San Diego. Oscar J. Martínez, for example, identifies a plethora of activity between El Paso and Ciudad Juárez at different periods, especially during the revolutionary years from 1910 to 1920.[9] This activity could take a passive form; El Pasoans gathered on the northern bank of the Río Grande to watch numerous revolutionary happenings in Juárez, including the arrival of Pancho Villa's troops. On another occasion, passivity was disregarded in favor of hostility, when Anglo demonstrations were held in the Mexican district of El Paso after Villa massacred fifteen American engineers in Santa Ysabel, Chihuahua, in 1916. The demonstrations were intended to throw troublesome Mexican aliens back across the border.[10] In researching his book about El Paso, Mario T. García found that American authorities went to special pains to detain Mexicans in the area who plotted against the government of Porfirio Díaz. One of these many plotters was Victor L. Ochoa, who was apprehended in 1893 for organizing insurgents "and sending them into Mexico to fight government forces."[11]

Although East Los Angeles is not a border community technically speaking, it has also been heavily influenced by events in Mexico, and it too may be included here. Ricardo

Romo shows that Mexican immigrants who streamed into the city in the first decades of the twentieth century "made every effort to keep up with the political affairs in their former homeland."[12] His study includes a discussion of the revolutionary activities of Ricardo Flores Magón, a political refugee from Mexico who arrived in East Los Angeles in 1907. With the help of political activists connected with the International Workers of the World (IWW) and local residents, Flores Magón opened the headquarters of the Partido Liberal Mexicano (PLM) at 519 1/2 East Fourth Street. Here he published and distributed *Regeneración*, a newspaper he had started in Mexico City that attacked the Porfirio Díaz regime and called for a revolutionary uprising in Mexico. A revolution eventually materialized, but not in the way Flores Magón envisioned. Romo believes that the East Los Angeles-based PLM was the most active anti-Díaz organization.[13] Specialists of the period generally agree that the PLM was one of the most important revolutionary organizations at the time.[14] It was active enough to promote the invasion of a portion of Baja California in an attempt to establish a socialist bastion against the Díaz government, and, in so doing, it whipped up furious controversy among Angelenos.[15]

Political communication unrelated to Mexico's tumultuous revolution exists as well, but it has largely escaped the eye of investigators so far. For example, as a child in the 1940s, I accompanied my parents to many meetings organized by the Unión Nacional Sinarquista in San Fernando, California. The meetings, led by José Macías, were attended almost exclusively by Mexican immigrants living in the northeastern section of the San Fernando Valley, including the communities of San Fernando and Pacoima. Those attending included Macías, Tomás Gasca, my *padrino* Rodolfo Ortega, my parents Bernabé and Guadalupe Gil, and others. Members of this group, known as *sinarquistas,* were mostly small-town people from Jalisco and Michoacán who had inherited the rambunctious independence of the Cristeros, rebels against the Mexican government in the late 1920s. That uprising, known as *la Cristiada*, was a religious, agrarian, antigovernment response to the modernist, socialist definition of the Mexican Revolution.[16] High-level *sinarquista* leaders in Mexico City are said to have been linked to officials of the German embassy in the late 1930s. However, Salvador Abascal, a *sinarquista* leader with a following in southern California, is supposed to have declared Adolf Hitler "an enemy of God."[17] My parents also supported *sinarquismo* by attending rallies in East Los Angeles and purchasing *El Sinarquista*, and later *Orden*, the publicity organs of the Unión Sinarquista that were sold at the door of Santa Rosa Catholic Church, where *sinarquistas* and other *mexicanos* worshiped. The activities of *sinarquistas* or any other political group of Mexicans in the United States remain to be examined.

Any visitor to Santa Rosa Church, in San Fernando, California, in the early 1990s would note, by virtue of the parish's cultural-religious activity, that Mexican immigrant parishioners outnumber Mexican-Americans more than in the 1940s. If the visitor inquired of those parishioners what, if any, political views they might have regarding contemporary Mexico, he or she would discover a gold mine of information. As García and Martínez learned for El Paso and Ciudad Juarez, respectively, and Romo for East Los Angeles regarding the early 1900s, the inquisitive visitor would uncover in the 1990s the fact that most parishioners of Santa Rosa Catholic Church, like *mexicanos* residing elsewhere in the United States, enjoy a keen awareness of Mexican politics.

Recent Increases in Mexican-American Political Involvement

U.S. *mexicanos'* awareness of political events in Mexico grew considerably in the late 1980s, especially when Cuauhtémoc Cárdenas emerged as a strong contender against the PRI in 1987. Three explanations may help us understand this phenomenon. One is the link between Cárdenas and the people of Michoacán. He is the son of the most revolutionary president in Mexican history, Lázaro Cárdenas, who was born and raised in Michoacán. Cuauhtémoc Cárdenas seems to have inherited the special link connecting his father and the small-town people and peasants of the central west region of Mexico that includes Michoacán. Small farmers and peasants of this area viewed Lázaro Cárdenas as an embodiment of their own aspirations and their mistrust of prior government leaders. As one Mexican-born political organizer in the city of Los Angeles phrased it, Cuauhtémoc Cárdenas carried a name that was incorruptible (*el nombre ha sido insobornable*), and this merited his support.[18]

The antigovernment Cristero revolt was strongest in the late 1920s in the west central region of Mexico, as was *sinarquismo* in the 1930s and 1940s. The Tarascan Indian empire dominated Michoacán prior to the arrival of the Spanish in the 1500s, and many *michoacanos* believe that Tarascan blood flows through the veins of the Cárdenas clan. Consequently, they feel close to Cuauhtémoc in a charismatic fashion, since Tarascan Indians formed the base of Michoacán peasantry in the 1700s. The fact that his first name is Aztec, unusual among most Mexicans, probably adds to this personalist phenomenon. *Michoacano* support for the younger Cárdenas is probably connected as well to the fact that his father paid special attention to *michoacano* peasants when land was distributed to them under the revolutionary agrarian reform laws fortified by his administration. The roads and other communication systems that have added to the prosperity of the state since the 1940s also helped the ties between *tata* Lázaro and the ordinary citizen of this area.

When the number of Mexicans immigrating to the United States increased dramatically in the 1920s, *michoacanos* made up a sizable portion. Manuel Gamio, who traced the destinations of money orders mailed to Mexico from U.S. post offices in the mid-1920s, discovered in 1926 that the state of Michoacán was the largest recipient.[19] In other words, by 1926, Michoacán had become the most important sender of immigrants, followed by Guanajuato and Jalisco, its neighbors. This important clue also may help us understand why Cárdenas struck a political chord among Mexicans living in the United States in a manner which no other Mexican politician has equaled.

A second explanation for the growth interest in recent Mexican politics is the sheer increase in the number of Mexicans and Mexican-Americans living in the United States in the late 1980s. In 1973 there were about 6.5 million in the country.[20] By 1989 the number had grown to nearly 20 million. The Los Angeles area alone had 3 million, the largest concentration of people of Mexican descent anywhere outside Mexico City.[21] Knowledge of this demographic pattern impelled Cárdenas to break existing molds, among Mexican politicians, by visiting participants in the diaspora to the north and raising their political awareness. His trips to the United States began before the critical election of 1988, and they have continued since.

A longtime friend and aide of Cuauhtémoc Cárdenas has conjectured that the candidate's visits to California and Washington beginning in 1985 may have been organized with an eye to the future.[22] Since then, Cárdenas had visited interested groups in Boston (Harvard University), Washington, DC, Texas, Washington state, and California (not to mention his visits to Argentina and Cuba). In November 1989 he barnstormed the Los Angeles area, where he met with editorial writers, held radio interviews, and attended numerous receptions held in his honor, including those organized by the Mexican American Political Association and the University of Southern California. He also hobnobbed with well-known Mexican-American leaders, such as Bert Corona and Abel Maya, and important political leaders in the California south, including actress Jane Fonda, wealthy liberal patron Stanley K. Sheinbaum, and former Governor Edmund G. Brown, Jr.[23] He then traveled to Seattle and delivered a lecture on Mexican politics at the University of Washington. The loquacious Porfirio Muñoz Ledo, second most important member of the Cárdenas organization and a 1990 candidate for the governorship of Guanajuato, visited the American Southwest as frequently as Cárdenas had done, if not more, for the purpose of establishing links between the *cardenista* leaders and community organizations.[24]

When Cárdenas was asked to comment on the support he was receiving in the United States, he answered:

> We think that our relations with Mexicans residing in the United States and with Americans of Mexican origin need to be strengthened. We think the Mexican government has practically abandoned the Mexicans living there. It could have employed the Mexican consulates to defend the human rights of the Mexicans or simply their rights as workers there. This could have been done vigorously. Some consulates have done this; many have not. . . . The support of social, educational, and cultural organizations for the benefit of the bilingual immigrant population could have been an important activity for the Mexican government.[25]

A third explanation for renewed political interest on the part of *mexicanos* in the United States is the increase in

awareness and education among their ranks. The number of
Hispanic students enrolled in college grew from approximately 242,000 in 1972 to 654,000 in 1988,[26] or from 2 percent of the total U.S. college population in 1970 to 10 percent in 1988.[27] Chicano studies curricula, new in American
universities since 1970, often include the study of Mexico in
one fashion or another. Furthermore, a greater understanding among U.S. academics and college students of what
authoritarian governments in Latin America may be, and
how these may actually function, probably contributed to an
increased sensitivity among Mexican-Americans toward
modern Mexico. This greater awareness has probably helped
disseminate ideas on how the PRI regime has repressed and
otherwise controlled opposition groups since 1929.

What is the cumulative effect of this novel exposure of
Mexican politicians like Cuauhtémoc Cárdenas and Porfirio
Muñoz Ledo to Mexican Hispanics in the Southwest? The
clearest answer is connected with the support groups organized in the United States on behalf of Mexican opposition
leaders in the late 1980s. Some of the earliest were the pro-
Castillo committees assembled in 1987 to give a helping
hand to Heberto Castillo, a presidential candidate of the
unified Left in the 1988 campaign who stepped down in
favor of Cárdenas. Castillo visited the Los Angeles area
many times in 1987.[28]

One result of the novel transborder organizing may be
appreciated in the statement of a pro-Castillo committee
member who wrote a letter to a newspaper editor and
signed it with the initials JRP. He (she?) exhorted fellow
Mexicans in the United States to persuade their friends and
relatives living in Mexico to vote and oppose firmly PRI corruption and threats. Offering convincing evidence of political
awareness among *mexicanos*, JRP also wrote: "We demand
of the Mexican government to do all it can to let us exercise
our right to vote by absentee ballot in the election for president." In addition to stressing that the PRI government has
refused to extend to Mexicans living outside the country the
right to vote in any election by using absentee ballots, the
letter vowed that the pro-Castillo organization would nevertheless carry out "symbolic elections" in the heart of Los
Angeles, La Placita. This would be a token of their commitment for political change in their home country.[29] Melesio
Mejía, a printer from Ciudad Guzmán, Jalisco, explained

that he and several others participated actively in Los Angeles PRD committees because they had come to repudiate the authoritarianism of the PRI long before. Believing that the PRI system in Mexico was approaching its final end, Mejía stated that he worked on behalf of Cuauhtémoc Cárdenas because the candidate "had a historical obligation by virtue of his incorruptible surname; we were all supporters of his father too."[30] Mejía helped organize anti-PRI demonstrations in front of the Los Angeles consulate general's office, which were going on daily up to the time of this writing.

Cárdenas's popularity beyond the American Southwest, in communities far removed from the border, also helps us appreciate the political awareness of Mexicans in the United States. This became evident in the Pacific Northwest in 1985, as already mentioned, two years before Cárdenas became Mexico's best-known opposition leader. While serving as governor of Michoacán, he was invited by *michoacanos* living in the Yakima Valley to visit with them. When he finally came, in May 1985, their response was jubilant. A large number of Mexican and Mexican-American workers and their families turned out to hear his words of encouragement and best wishes. Members of Seattle's Mexican-American organizations, celebrating Cinco de Mayo, feted him at Seattle Central Community College and warmly received his praise for their efforts in maintaining their cultural roots. After Cárdenas broke with the PRI in late 1987 and thus became an independent presidential candidate, he received support from as far away as Alaska. A *michoacano* living in Kodiak traveled to Mexico City in the first days of 1987 to convey his support and that of "about 300 Mexicans in that region" and to express their urgent desire to be able to vote by absentee ballots.[31]

Not only has Cuauhtémoc Cárdenas broken the mold by which Mexican politicians and government officials generally disregarded the *mexicanos* of the United States, but it also appears that he may have fashioned a new one. Whereas González Schmal felt assured in 1986 that there were no plans for the PAN to pay attention to Mexican-American communities, Cárdenas's courting of these groups probably forced Manuel Clouthier, the PAN presidential candidate in 1988, to take a cue. He toured Mexican communities in Los Angeles in early 1989 as well. No other PAN

leader had done this. Moreover, in December 1989 the new
Mexican foreign minister, Fernando Solana, made contact
with Mexican-American leaders at a black-tie award dinner
in which he expressed his belief that their community was
"an ideal vehicle" for better communication between the
United States and Mexico.[32] After Mexican President Carlos
Salinas de Gortari announced his determination to revolu-
tionize his country's economic policy by seeking a free-trade
agreement with Washington, he dispatched three top government representatives to Los Angeles in late October
1990. These officials carried Salinas's message concerning
his controversial proposal to the Mexican communities via
La Opinión, Los Angeles's Spanish-language newspaper.
The officials assigned to this trip were Miguel Alemán
Velasco, special Mexican ambassador; Claudio X. González,
President Salinas's special adviser on foreign investment;
and Jaime Zabludovsky, coordinator of the president's team
for free-trade negotiations.[33]

President Salinas appears to have met Cuauhtémoc
Cárdenas hand to hand in seeking the sympathy of *mexicanos* in the United States. On November 12, 1990, Salinas
invited three of the most highly reputed Mexican-Americans
to Mexico City and decorated them with the nation's most
distinguished medal of honor.[34] He presented the Order of
the Aztec Eagle, the prized recognition given to foreigners,
to César Chávez,[35] the aging labor leader who had succeeded in organizing America's farm workers in the 1970s;
Julián Samora,[36] a Mexican-American historian who placed
undocumented immigrants within a historical framework;
and Américo Paredes,[37] an innovator in border ethno-
musicology. No Mexican-American had received anything
similar.

The event may have been the handiwork of an office cre-
ated within the Mexican Foreign Ministry at the behest of
President Salinas, reportedly charged with overseeing
Mexican-American affairs exclusively. The award process
appears to reflect organizational efficiency on the part of the
Salinas administration as well as a particular expediency.
The PRI government's relations with the *mexicanos* of the
United States before 1988 were hardly consequential, if not
nonexistent, but they suddenly proved to be important during the 1988 presidential campaign, as the discussion below
suggests. The honoring of the Mexican-Americans and the

creation of the foreign affairs office nevertheless substantiate the argument that Cuauhtémoc Cárdenas's efforts to spur interest within the United States during a time of political transformation in Mexico has been so effective that even the president has felt obligated to take part in transborder communication.[38]

The Question of Mexican-American Involvement

The raised consciousness among *mexicanos* living in the United States seems to have contributed to an international controversy a few weeks before Mexico's 1988 presidential election. At issue was a proposed amendment to the 1988 California Democratic platform offered in preparation for the national party convention, which later nominated Michael Dukakis for president. Members of the California Democratic party Chicano caucus proposed that the platform recognize the violation of human rights in Mexico. Moreover, the amendment also requested that "the U.S. government demand that the Mexican government respect existing laws and give Mexican citizens living abroad the right to vote."[39]

Opposition leaders in Mexico City welcomed the spirit and letter of the Democratic party proposal when its text was reprinted there. Alberto Loyola, official PAN spokesman, expressed satisfaction with the proposal when he stated to the press: "It is true that human rights are violated here in election time," and he immediately proceeded to offer a recent example. Heberto Castillo, a PRD leader, likewise agreed with the proposal because "human rights are [indeed] violated in Mexico."[40]

The PRI, however, condemned the Democratic party proposal. Juan Enríquez, director of PRI Foreign Press Office and a close associate of President Salinas, declared that "the amendment writers do not have the right to affirm that human rights are violated in Mexico at election time." When reporters inquired about absentee ballots for Mexicans in the United States, he responded by affirming that such ballots were against the law. Furthermore, he explained, "there is no money to organize the logistics of an event of that kind; in any case we would have to entertain a petition from the interested parties."[41] A Los Angeles reporter working for *La Opinión* later interviewed an unidentified but influential member of the Salinas de Gortari foreign policy planning team who pronounced the California Democratic party proposal a "dangerous development." He predicted that, once elected, Salinas would form a special government policy toward Chicanos and initiate a finely tuned lobbying effort in the U.S. Congress. He admitted that "Mexico has kept the Chicano problem on a back burner" and implied that this would have to be corrected somehow.[42] The Salinas team's ability to follow up on novel policy proposals appears to be praiseworthy because a special office in charge of Mexican-American affairs was reportedly installed by the president after the fraud-filled election, as discussed above.

The strongest attack on the Democratic party proposal was penned by Jorge Bustamante, president of the Colegio de la Frontera Norte, a small but influential research center in Tijuana. A sociologist and expert on border issues, Bustamante deplored the proposal as "interventionist and filled with stereotypical generalities and false assertions." He suggested that one might have expected this posture from anti-Mexican politicians like Jesse Helms, but to have it come from Chicanos "was all the more surprising." Some might think it proves an old adage, he added, that wood from the same tree makes the best wedge. This, however, is not the case, he noted.

Brushing aside human rights abuses, whose number had risen in Mexico, Bustamante cut quickly to the core of the controversy by unveiling the risk involved in proposing U.S. intervention to right a wrong on the basis of an ethnic concern. He observed that "Chicanos forget they are still citizens of a country that historically has launched the greatest assaults against our sovereignty."[43] Regardless of whether the do-gooder is named Sánchez or some other Spanish surname, it is still interventionism, he added. Although he did not mention anyone specifically, he also chided leaders of the opposition for seeking Chicano support, because "the typical gringo response is that if someone donates money in support of a project, then he or she is entitled to openly cast an opinion about that project." Citing a locally known Mexican businessman in Los Angeles who condemned the PRI and supported the Democratic party proposal in order to bring change to Mexico from the outside, Bustamante

likened him and others to the people who supported
Manifest Destiny as an excuse to grab land from Mexico in
the 1840s.

Raul Ruiz, a Los Angeles professor and longtime Chicano activist, rejected the interventionist argument. "Advocating clean elections is a universal desire," he explained.
"We think it is reasonable for the Mexican government to
recognize the rights of Mexicans inside and out of the country." Phil Richt, copresident of the Democratic Platform
Committee, defended the proposal because "we have asked
the U.S. government to advocate for the rights of Soviet citizens to leave [the Soviet Union] if they wish to do so." If
Americans can do this with the Soviet Union, why can't they
ask Mexico something similar?[44]

If the Democratic platform proposal was ill advised,
Bustamante was forced to recognize nonetheless that the
entire episode served to underscore an important lesson.
"For good or bad," he admitted, "Chicanos will play a more
important role in U.S.-Mexican relations in the future." This
role, he added, will be connected to the importance that U.S.
political parties give to the Mexican-American population,
even though a bloc vote may still lie in the future. An article
written by Alejandro Rosas, a former Mexican journalist living in Los Angeles, served to expand Bustamante's conclusions. By concentrating his gaze on Mexican citizens residing in the United States, Rosas happily detected a "renewed
civic spirit" among them whenever they raised their voice in
support or condemnation of political trends in Mexico. This
renewed spirit revealed not only "their desire to stay united
and linked to Mexico's destiny despite the distance separating them from their birthplace" but also their "extraordi-
nary political maturity and organizational capacity."[45] In
other words, Rosas recognized that Mexicans in the United
States enjoy the capacity to make themselves heard no matter what their status or economic condition might be.
Whether Mexican-Americans receive proper political recognition from U.S. parties or not, the force of their expression
would continue to be felt.

Both Mexican-Americans, as U.S. citizens, and Mexican
aliens residing in the United States as guests or protociti-
zens, will probably continue to join forces in voicing their
views about politics in Mexico and generating support for
one Mexican political group or another. As one Cárdenas

supporter exclaimed to a reporter, "We are following what the Jews do for Israel."[46] Indeed, the analogy may be helpful. In times of crisis in the Middle East, the activity of U.S. Jews may be seen to increase; when the crisis is resolved, the activity decreases. A parallel can be found in Cuban-American political activity, which heats and cools in accordance with Fidel Castro's latest success or failure.

The foregoing discussion is offered, then, to demonstrate that an awareness of Mexican politics by *mexicanos* in the United States is not new. It is underrecorded by Mexican-American studies. Furthermore, this awareness has blossomed in a manner not seen before. The role that Cuauhtémoc Cárdenas and other PRD leaders have taken in cultivating this phenomenon of political communication is fresh and fundamental at the same time. The statements gathered from Jesús González Schmal and Jorge Alcocer in 1986 merely serve as a convenient standard against which the words and actions of PRD leaders may be measured. Their statements also serve to show how quickly things have changed. Four years later, even the president of Mexico appeared to be courting the sympathy of *mexicanos* in the United States.

The political awareness of *mexicanos*, and the transborder communication that accompanies it, are also connected to the fundamental transformation that the Mexican body politic is undergoing in the late 1980s and in the 1990s. Like the constituent members of any other modern state, the Mexican people have further matured as a nation and have demonstrated their wish to change or replace political forms imposed upon them sixty years earlier. It is noteworthy in this respect that Mexicans living in the United States do not appear to support the PRI. In any case, changing the political forms will be a slow and painful process, and it will not be free of crises.

What might the role of U.S. *mexicanos* be during this slow and difficult period of transformation? The three factors outlined above suggest that they will continue to be connected, in one way or another, to friends and relatives in their homeland. Will their genuine concern take the form observed in the California Democratic platform meetings? Only time will tell. Nonetheless, it appears that U.S. citizens, especially *mexicanos*, will be inexorably tied to Mexico's political changes. It is also clear that the definition of those ties will be directly affected by the degree of knowledge observant Americans have about their neighbor. The sophistication of their knowledge and its political result remain to be seen and recorded for posterity.

Notes

1. The Partido Revolucionario Institucional (PRI), Mexico's official party, won all presidential and gubernatorial elections between 1929 and 1989. Its victories usually have been the result of machine politics combined with fraud.

2. In this essay the word "*mexicano*" means any person of Mexican descent residing in the United States. This may include a person born in Mexico or a Mexican-American born in the United States. "Chicano" is a synonym for "Mexican-American."

3. González Schmal was the PAN secretary of foreign affairs. He was interviewed on February 27, 1986, in Mexico City. See pp. 99–119, esp. p. 118.

4. PAN is the acronym for Partido de Acción Nacional. See Donald J. Mabry, *Mexico's Acción Nacional: A Catholic Alternative to Revolution* (Syracuse, NY: Syracuse University Press, 1973).

5. Jorge Alcocer joined the Mexican Communist Party (PCM) and later became a member of the Partido Socialista Unificado Mexicano (PSUM). He was interviewed on several dates in January and February 1986 in Mexico City. See pp. 215–43.

6. See p. 242.

7. Rudy Acuña, *Occupied America: A History of Chicanos,* 3d ed. (New York: Harper and Row, 1988), 161-62.

8. The third edition of Acuña's *Occupied America* includes a footnote listing Don M. Coerver and Linda B. Hall, *Texas and the Mexican Revolution: A Study in State and National Border Policy, 1910–1920* (San Antonio: Trinity University Press, 1984). See a modified version of the Plan de San Diego in Oscar J. Martínez, *Fragments of the Mexican Revolution: Personal Accounts from the Border* (Albuquerque: University of New Mexico Press, 1983), 145–48.

9. Oscar J. Martínez, *Border Boom Town: Ciudad Juárez since 1848* (Austin: University of Texas Press, 1975).

10. Ibid., 39. See also Martínez's "Excitement along the Border, Early 1910s," in his *Fragments of the Mexican Revolution,* 65–133.

11. Mario T. García, *Desert Immigrants: The Mexicans of El Paso, 1880–1920* (New Haven: Yale University Press, 1981), 173.

12. Ricardo Romo, *East Los Angeles: History of a Barrio* (Austin: University of Texas Press, 1983), 95.

13. Ibid., 92.

14. See Cockcroft, *Intellectual Precursors.*

15. Romo, *East Los Angeles,* 93. See also Lowell L. Blaisdell, *Desert Revolution: Baja California, 1911* (Madison: University of Wisconsin Press, 1962).

16. See Jean A. Meyer, *The Cristero Rebellion: The Mexican People between Church and State, 1926–1929* (New York: Cambridge University Press, 1976).

17. "Unión Nacional Sinarquista," *Diccionario enciclopédico de México. Ilustrado. Humberto Musacchio* (Mexico City: Andrés León Editor, 1989), 2091–93; Guadalupe B. Gil, interview, San Fernando, California, October 21, 1990.

18. Melesio Mejía, telephone interview, November 13, 1990.

19. Manuel Gamio, *Mexican Immigration to the United States: A Study of Human Migration and Adjustment* (1930; reprint, New York: Dover Publications, 1971), 13.

20. Joan W. Moore, *Mexican Americans,* 2d ed. (New York: Prentice-Hall, 1976), 54–55.

21. *New York Times,* December 8, 1989.

22. Roberto Barnard, telephone interview, November 9, 1990.

23. *New York Times,* December 8, 1989.

24. Barnard, telephone interview.

25. Cuauhtémoc Cárdenas, interview, Mexico City, January 10, 1988. See p. 170.

26. U.S. Bureau of the Census, *Current Population Report. P-20, No. 443. School Enrollment. Social and Economic Characteristics of Students. 1987 and 1988* (Washington, DC: Government Printing Office, 1990), 177.

27. U.S. Department of Commerce, Bureau of the Census, *Statistical Abstract of the U.S.* (Washington, DC: Government Printing Office, 1990), 132.

28. Mejía, telephone interview.

29. *La Opinión,* May 27, 1988.

30. Mejía, telephone interview.

31. *La Jornada,* December 6, 1987.

32. *New York Times,* December 8, 1989.

33. *La Opinión,* October 30, 1990.

34. Ibid., November 13, 1990.

35. A considerable amount of literature may be consulted concerning César Chávez and the farm workers' movement. See, for example, Jacques Levy, *César Chávez: Autobiography of La Causa* (New York: Norton, 1975).

36. Julian Samora's best-known work is *Los Mojados: The Wetback Story* (Notre Dame, IN: University of Notre Dame Press, 1971).

37. Américo Paredes's best-known work is *With His Pistol in His Hand: A Borderland Ballad and Its Hero* (Austin: University of Texas Press, 1958).

38. *La Opinión*, November 13, 1990.
39. Ibid., May 27, 1988.
40. Ibid., May 29, 1988.
41. Ibid., June 1, 1988.
42. Ibid.
43. *Excelsior*, May 31, 1988.
44. *La Opinión*, May 27, 1988.
45. Ibid., June 3, 1988.
46. *New York Times*, December 8, 1989.

APPENDIX 2

Bio-glossary

Alemán Valdés, Miguel (1902–1983)
> President of Mexico, 1946–1952, and leader of the PRI right wing during the 1940s and 1950s.

Alfa Group
> One of the holding companies controlled by the Monterrey Group, Alfa includes such companies as Hylsa, S.A., and Nylon de México, S.A. See listing in Abraham Nuncio, *El grupo Monterrey* (Mexico City: Editorial Nueva Imagen, 1982); Appendix B. The Monterrey Group, one of the most powerful business groups in Mexico in the late 1980s, controlled four holding companies in 1982: Alfa, Visa, Vitro, and Cydsa.

Allende Gossens, Salvador (1908–1973)
> President of Chile, 1970–1973, he sought to introduce socialism peacefully but was overthrown by the military with the support of the United States.

Almazán, Juan Andreu (1891–1965)
> Although wealthy, in the 1910 revolution he fought for both Francisco I. Madero and Emiliano Zapata, considered liberal revolutionary leaders. He turned his back on them by joining the person deemed responsible for Madero's assassination, General Victoriano Huerta. Almazán rose to brigadier general, joined the liberal Alvaro Obregón, and in 1939 took up the conservative cause again by heading his own party, called the Partido Revolucionario de Unificación Nacional (PRUN). He was forced into exile later that year.

apertura
> Literally an "opening," it refers to the political reform policies fashioned by President Echeverría in the 1970s to mollify young leftists alienated by the government's role in the 1968 massacre at Tlaltelolco. The policies opened the body politic by encouraging opposition groups, leftist ones especially, to compete in congressional elections.

Arbenz Guzmán, Jacobo (1913–1971)
His reformist Guatemalan government was overthrown by
Carlos Castillo Armas, whose troops were organized and
financed by the U.S. Central Intelligence Agency. See Stephen
Schlesinger and Stephen Kinzer, *Bitter Fruit: The Untold
Story of the American Coup in Guatemala* (Garden City, NY:
Anchor Books, 1983).

Article 27
Article 27 of the Mexican constitution reads in part:

The Nation shall at all times have the right to impose on private
property such limitations as the public interest may demand, as well
as regulate the utilization of natural resources which are susceptible
to appropriation . . . in the nation is vested the direct ownership of all
natural resources . . . all minerals or substances . . . petroleum . . .
ownership by the Nation is inalienable and the exploitation, use, or
appropriation . . . may not be undertaken except through concessions
granted by the Federal Executive.

Constitution of the United Mexican States, 1917 (Washington,
DC: Pan American Union, 1961), 8–9.

Avila Camacho, Manuel (1897–1955)
Military general who served as president, 1940–1946. His
administration served as a transition between the liberalism
of his predecessor, Lázaro Cárdenas, and the conservativism
of his successor, Miguel Alemán Valdes.

Baker Plan
Fearing a reluctance of commercial banks to lend additional
money to hard-pressed Third World countries, given the
downturn in world trade and commodity prices in the mid-
1980s, the U.S. government proposed at the Seoul meeting of
the IMF what is known as the Baker Plan: the IMF was to
lend an additional $20 billion to these countries between 1986
and 1989 through commercial banks, and the bulk of
repayments due the IMF was to be relent to particularly poor
countries with serious external payment difficulties. These
monies would be forthcoming if public expenditures were
reduced and other stringent fiscal measures were taken. The
Baker Plan has been criticized as a mere postponement of the
problem. See *1986, Britannica Book of the Year* (Chicago:
Encyclopaedia Britannica, 1986), 220.

bank nationalization
President José López Portillo decreed on September 1, 1982,
the cancellation of banking concessions previously given by

the Mexican federal government to the various businesses engaged in providing banking services. The decree sought to end a speculative spiral and a critical capital flight, both of which were exacerbating the condition of the Mexican economy. The decree affected many banks, including the six largest: Bancomer, Banamex, Banca Serfin, Banco Mexicano Somes, Multibanco Comermex, and Banco Internacional. See David Colmenares et al., *La nacionalización de la banca* (Mexico City: Terra Nova, 1982), 49. The decree was reversed by President Carlos Salinas de Gortari in 1989.

Bassols, Narciso (1897–1959)
Major Marxist author and statesman who served as minister of education, government secretary, and treasurer during the 1930s.

bonds for debt, or debt equity swap
A complicated attempt to encourage the government of Mexico to convert its foreign debt into bonds that it would emit for purchase by foreign investors employing discounted Mexican debt instruments.

Cabañas, Lucio (1939–1975)
Schoolteacher from Guerrero and former Communist Party member who led a rebellion in his home state against the government in 1974. The Mexican army crushed the rebellion, and Cabañas was killed as a result. Valentín Campa discusses him at length in *Mi testimonio: Memorias de un comunista en México* (Mexico City: Editores Cultura Popular, 1978).

cacique
A local strong man in Spanish America. The term is Arawak in origin, and it is nearly synonymous with caudillo.

caciquismo
The political dimensions of cacique-led society.

Calles, Plutarco Elias (1877–1945)
As president, 1924–1928, he was best known for implementing constitutional provisions that reduced the power of the Catholic church and for founding the official party. He acted as the power behind the throne between 1928 and 1936, although his power began to diminish as early as 1934.

calpulli
An Aztec territorial unit occupied by a group of families presumably related. It also became known as a barrio, and

calpulleque (or *calpuleque*) elders were politically responsible for members of the unit. Heberto Castillo favors reviving the concept as part of his answer to a need to redefine Mexico and its culture.

Campa, Valentín (1904–)
A railroad worker in the early 1920s, he became a prominent Communist union leader in the 1930s and a national political leader in the 1950s. He wrote his memoirs (see Bibliography).

campesino
A peasant or small farmer.

CANACINTRA (Cámara Nacional de la Industria de Transformación)
Founded in 1942, it is a national organization of industrialists that lobbies on behalf of Mexican industrialization.

Cárdenas del Río, Lázaro (1895–1970)
Often compared with Franklin Delano Roosevelt, he is considered Mexico's most revolutionary president (1934–1940) because of his willingness to employ the power of the state to promote change on behalf of workers and peasants.

Carranza, Venustiano (1859–1920)
Landowner turned revolutionary leader in 1913 and president of Mexico (1917–1920). Considered a conservative, he did not oppose ratification of the left-leaning constitution of 1917.

Carrillo, Nabor (1911–1967)
Distinguished author and engineer specializing in soil mechanics and foundation engineering.

caudillismo
The phenomenon of caudillo politics. *See also* cacique.

caudillo
A man who leads others by dint of his personal appearance and strength. This type of individual filled the political vacuum created by ineffective government in certain regions, especially in the nineteenth and early twentieth centuries. Also, a natural leader, a strong man, or dictator. The term may be applied to women, although rarely.

CCI (Confederación Campesina Independiente)
An independent national confederation of peasant leagues organized to counteract the government-controlled CNC.

charrismo
The *charro* phenomenon, usually in a political sense.

charro
Enjoying more than one meaning, culturally the word refers to a gentleman-cowboy type of eighteenth-century Mexico whose colorful garb (tight-fitting pants, short jacket, and wide-brimmed hat) was adopted by musicians from Jalisco in the twentieth century. Politically, the word became an adjective in the 1960s to refer to unions and individuals co-opted by the government.

Clouthier, Manuel J. (1934–1989)
Popular businessman who emerged as a presidential candidate representing the PAN in 1988.

CNC (Confederación Nacional Campesina)
Originally formed as the Confederación Campesina Mexicana to give peasant support to the candidacy of Lázaro Cárdenas, it was reorganized in 1938 with the present name. It eventually became the government-controlled national federation of peasant leagues.

CNOP (Confederación Nacional de Organizaciones Populares)
Founded in 1943 to institutionalize the participation of citizens not directly favored by Lázaro Cárdenas's revolutionary policies, it includes largely middle-class interest groups made up of lawyers, bureaucrats, civic associations, and student and women's organizations. A minority influence in national politics when it first appeared, under the direction of professional politicians it has become a crucial force in the 1980s.

Comintern (Communist International, or Third International)
An association of national Communist parties founded in 1919. Although it was supposed to promote world revolution, it functioned as a Soviet leash on the Communist movement around the world. The Communist International zigzagged in accordance with Soviet policy shifts and was officially dissolved in 1943.

contras
Nicaraguan rebels who were organized and financed by the U.S. Central Intelligence Agency as part of the Reagan administration's anti-Communist policy for Central America

Corriente Democrática
Name given to the reform wing of the PRI in the period before the 1988 election. Its leaders, Porfirio Muñoz Ledo and Cuauhtémoc Cárdenas, eventually cut their ties with the PRI and formed Mexico's most important opposition party, the PRD.

Cristero Rebellion, *la Cristiada,* or Cristero Revolt
Peasants led by conservative landowners and rebel priests against the government in 1927 for its anticlerical posture; the rebellion fizzled after 1929.

CTM (Confederación de Trabajadores Mexicanos)
Founded in 1935 by Vicente Lombardo Toledano as a national labor federation sympathetic to President Lázaro Cárdenas, it originally included agricultural and industrial workers and promoted higher wages. Under Fidel Velásquez, it became pro-government in the 1950s; and, while it promoted health and other benefits for workers, it gradually turned into the most important *charro* institution, restraining industrial wage increases and otherwise supporting PRI administrations.

cupulismo
The practice of allowing the *cúpula,* or top-level people, of an organization to make all of the important decisions. Meaning top-down decision making, it is synonymous with *verticalismo.*

dedazo
A popular term given to the simple but effective way in which leaders of the PRI and the president's office unilaterally decide who will be selected as candidates to run in elections in which the PRI always wins. The term comes from *dedo,* finger; it means the fingering of an elected official-to-be.

de la Madrid, Miguel (1935–)
Economist who became president, 1982–1988, and guided the country through difficult economic times.

desaparecidos
The term means the "disappeared ones" and refers to mostly young participants in leftist organizations who disappeared during a period of strong governmental repression in the late 1960s and early 1970s. Though their numbers are fewer than in Argentina and Chile, where a similar phenomenon took place during the same period, there is no agreement on how many there might have been. The government's response has been equivocal at best.

Díaz, Porfirio (1830–1915)
A military general, he controlled Mexico between 1876 and 1911. He introduced modern industry to the nation, but regulated its politics singlehandedly. He was forced into exile by the 1910 revolution. He was one of Latin America's most famous dictators.

Díaz Ordaz, Gustavo (1911–1979)
As president, 1964–1970, he served during the massacre of Tlaltelolco; he is considered one of the most conservative executives in recent times.

Echeverría Alvarez, Luis (1922–)
The most powerful cabinet member of the time of the 1968 massacre (see Tlaltelolco), he subsequently served as president, 1970–1976. His administration pursued policies that sought to mollify young intellectuals alienated by the events of 1968.

ejido
Parcels distributed by the government to landless farmers as part of an official revolutionary agrarian reform program. The plots may be worked individually or collectively. The *ejido* holder is known as an *ejidatario*.

Estrada Doctrine
The belief that the recognition of a government should be granted automatically, regardless of its origin. This doctrine was issued by Genaro Estrada, Mexican foreign minister in 1930.

FDN (Frente Democrático Nacional)
An alliance of political groups whose leader, Cuauhtémoc Cárdenas, ran as an opposition candidate in the presidential elections of 1988 and obtained the greatest number of opposition votes ever. Most of the groups in the FDN fused into the PRD after the elections.

Félix, María (1914–)
During Mexico's classic movie-making period, from the 1940s to the 1950s, she was one of the most distinguished stars.

GATT (General Agreement on Tariffs and Trade)
The product of a movement begun in 1948 to sponsor and promote free trade among nations through commercial treaties and the reduction of subsidies. Mexico agreed to enter GATT in 1985.

Gobernación, Secretaría de (Government Secretariat)
The most powerful cabinet-level agency in Mexico. Its functions are similar to those of the U.S. Office of the Attorney
General but exceed it. The *secretaría* monitors and controls
the political and administrative functions of all governmental
agencies in the country, including investigative and enforcement aspects. It controls elections and regulates the states to
the extent of making their power disappear, constitutionally
speaking, when an unresolvable federal-state conflict arises.

Gómez, Pablo (1946–)
A leftist student leader in 1968, he became secretary-general
of the PSUM and later a PRD leader.

Gómez Morín, Manuel (1897–1972)
Lawyer and member of a National Preparatory School
graduating class of brilliant students, he served his country as
a professor and later dean of the UNAM School of Law, as a
rector of the UNAM, as the founder and first chairman of the
board of the Banco de México, and in many other top government positions. He was also founder of the PAN and is
considered its legendary ideologue.

González Guevara, Rodolfo (1918–)
Distinguished member of the PRI and former Mexican am-
bassador to Spain, he helped form the Corriente Democrática.
He eventually quit the official party and joined the PRD.

González Guzmán, Ignacio (1898–1972)
Distinguished medical surgeon who specialized in hematology.
Among the many professional posts he held were presidencies
of the National Academy of Medicine and the International
Society of Hematology.

Guevara, Ernesto ("Che") (1928–1967)
Argentine-born medical doctor turned revolutionary leader and
theorist, he witnessed the U.S. overthrow of Jacobo Arbenz
Guzmán and later joined Fidel Castro in the overthrow of
Fulgencio Batista in Cuba in 1959. In revolutionary Cuba he
served as Castro's adviser and, briefly, as head of the National
Bank and Minister of Industry. U.S.-trained troops killed him
in Bolivia as he attempted to start a revolution. To many Latin
Americans he symbolizes the region's need for sovereignty.

hectare
A metric unit for measuring land; one hectare equals 2.47
acres.

Henríquez Guzmán, Miguel (1898–1972)
General who was proposed as a PRI presidential candidate in 1951 by old-guard *cardenistas* alienated by President Miguel Alemán's conservative administration. Dissident *priistas* and others formed a Federación de Partidos del Pueblo (FPP) under whose ticket the general competed in the elections of 1952. Cuauhtémoc Cárdenas is said to have participated in FPP activities as a young man, along with his mother. When the 1952 balloting produced a less-than-expected result, and the PRI government sought to ban the FPP later, a small group of Henríquez supporters organized a local revolt in González Schmal's hometown that was put down immediately. This understudied episode contains many parallels with neo-*cardenismo* of the late 1980s. See chapter 3 in Olga Pellicer de Brody and José Luis Reyna, *Período 1952–1960: El afianzamiento de la estabilidad política*, vol. 22 of *Historia de la revolución mexicana* (Mexico City: El Colegio de México, 1978).

henriquista movement
See Henríquez Guzmán, Miguel.

Ibarra de Piedra, Rosario (1928–)
A housewife and mother, her son became a *desaparecido* in the early 1970s. In her efforts to locate him, she formed a national organization of mothers of *desaparecidos* and gained national prominence as an opposition leader. She ran for president in 1988 on the PRT ticket, although she claimed no membership in the party.

IMF (International Monetary Fund)
Based in Washington, DC, the IMF is a specialized agency of the United Nations founded in 1944 to secure international monetary cooperation, stabilize exchange rates, and expand international liquidity. It has become not only a convenient instrument of consultative cooperation and a research center on monetary issues but also a fiscal watchdog. It serves in this role in relation to those member nations that borrow from its special standby credit reserves normally used to resolve balance-of-payments difficulties. This function has brought it considerable criticism, especially from people who believe the agency is dominated by U.S. interests since the United States is a major creditor. See *The New Encyclopaedia Britannica* (Chicago: Encyclopaedia Britannica, 1986), 6:351.

JCM (Juventud Comunista Mexicana)
An affiliate for the young of the now-extinct Mexican Communist Party.

Juárez, Benito (1806–1872)
The only Indian (a Zapotec) to serve as president, he kept the idea of an independent republic alive in the 1860s when the French invaded Mexico. Compared to Abraham Lincoln by many people, he towers over other political figures of his time in his emphasis on Mexican independence and nationalism.

Kalecki, Michal (1899–1970)
Eclipsed by the shadow of the British economist John Maynard Keynes, Kalecki began publishing major and more useful components of what came to be known as Keynesian economic theory before Keynes himself did.

lombardista
A follower of Vicente Lombardo Toledano.

Lombardo Toledano, Vicente (1894–1968)
Marxist intellectual and activist, although never a Communist in a regular way, who organized the Confederación General de Obreros y Campesinos Mexicanos (CGOCM), which was later converted into the Confederación de Trabajadores Mexicanos (CTM). He supported the administration of Lázaro Cárdenas but was expelled from the CTM in 1948, whereupon he founded the Partido Popular, later known as the Partido Popular Socialista (PPS).

López Mateos, Adolfo (1910–1969)
President of Mexico, 1958–1964. A firm exponent of the semisocialist ideology associated with the Mexican revolution, he repressed the Communist-led railroad workers strikes of 1958–59 nevertheless.

López Portillo, José (1920–)
As president, 1976–1982, he presided over the oil boom and the nation's excessive borrowing, which laid the basis for the economic crisis that began in 1981.

Madero, Francisco I. (1873–1912)
Played one of the most important roles in initiating the revolution of 1910 against Porfirio Díaz. He was Pablo Emilio Madero's uncle.

maquiladoras
The name given to the assembly plants located on the southern side of the U.S.-Mexican border that import American components. The finished products return to the U.S. market. Special fiscal arrangements are established for this process,

which is also known as in-bond manufacturing. A *maquilador* is a person or a group holding the job of *maquilar*.

Martínez Verdugo, Arnoldo (1925–)
Paper mill worker who became a major figure in the Mexican Communist Party in the 1950s and 1960s. He strove to reduce its old Leninist mold and, in so doing, served as one of the first Communist deputies in the national legislature in the post-Cárdenas era, 1979–1982. He was cofounder of the PSUM and has authored various works on Mexican politics.

Mexican Miracle
The unusual economic growth between 1945 and 1970. Aided by the early phase of industrialization and authoritarian practices, including *charrismo*, the Mexican economy expanded by an average of more than 6 percent annually during these years.

MRM (Movimiento Revolucionario del Magisterio)
Formed by schoolteachers in 1956, it was one of the first labor movements organized to resist government control.

national front
Also known as a popular front, it represents one of the many policies taken up by the Communist International. Instead of pursuing revolution, as they had done previously, the Communist parties around the world were obligated to create popular fronts in 1935 in an effort to defeat rising fascism. These fronts included Socialists and liberals, and they were instructed to make "transitional demands" on existing regimes, instead of fighting against them. See "The Third International," *The New Encyclopaedia Britannica* (Chicago: Encyclopaedia Britannica, 1975), 5:384.

National Strike Committee, National Student Strike Committee, or Student Strike Committee
Made up exclusively of students, it was the organizing body of the 1968 movement that fought for reform. Its initiatives led to the government's massacre of hundreds of people at the Plaza of Three Cultures in Tlaltelolco, Mexico City.

Obregón, Alvaro (1880–1928)
Schoolteacher turned revolutionary who became a general and later a popular president, 1920–1924. He was reelected in 1928 but assassinated soon thereafter.

OPEC (Organization of Petroleum Exporting Countries)
OPEC was formed in 1960 by the states of the Middle East in an effort to exercise leverage over oil production and prices,

hitherto the province of oil companies. Its members control about four fifths of non-Communist oil production; Mexico is not a member but heeds its general policies.

Opus Dei (God's work)
An international organization with headquarters in Spain, composed mostly of laypersons who seek private Christian perfection and strive to implement Christian ideals in their chosen professions. Founded in 1928 and approved by the Holy See in 1950, it became an influential and elitist organization during the 1960s in Spain. It operates numerous schools and training institutions. See *The New Encyclopaedia Britannica* (Chicago: Encyclopaedia Britannica, 1975), 7:557.

PAN (Partido de Acción Nacional)
The first major party in Mexico that was organized to compete with the official party. Founded in 1939, its objectives were to counteract the anticlerical measures imposed by the revolutionary administrations. It is considered Mexico's conservative party, although it has evolved through various ideological stages since its founding.

panista
A member or supporter of the PAN.

paraestatales (parastate industry)
A state-owned industry; PEMEX is the most widely recognized example.

PARM (Partido Auténtico de la Revolución Mexicana)
Organized initially by General Jacinto B. Treviño during the administration of Adolfo Ruiz Cortínes (1952–1958), it is said to have been made up of Treviño's fellow ex-combatants with little or no purpose as a political party. A minuscule organization whose ideology paralleled that of the official party, it functioned as a satellite party of the PRI until 1987.

partidos paleros (satellite parties)
A pejorative but nonetheless popular name applied to certain political parties, especially from the 1960s through the mid-1980s. Members of satellite parties were allowed and encouraged by the PRI to maintain their organizations, small as they might be, by seeking constituents in order to gain congressional seats and the relevant benefits that accrue from elected posts. The PRI used these organizations, for all practical purposes, to enhance the impression that opposition parties functioned openly in Mexico.

Paz, Octavio (1914–)
A leading Mexican intellectual of the twentieth century, he is a poet, essayist, historian, and statesman. He received a Nobel Prize in 1990.

PCM (Partido Comunista Mexicano)
One of the most dynamic of the Latin American Communist parties, it was founded in 1919 and, despite many internal divisions, played an important political role in Mexico in the first half of the twentieth century. It elected a strong legislative corps in the late 1970s as a result of the political *apertura* until fusing with other parties to form the PSUM in 1981.

PDM (Partido Democrático Mexicano)
Organized in the early 1970s and registered in 1979 for the first time, it considered itself a party that "ran parallel" to the Unión Nacional Sinarquista. The PDM may be considered a modern "cousin" of the *sinarquistas*, but, reflective of its agrarian-oriented constituency, it failed to reach the legal minimum number of votes in 1988.

pedemista
A member or supporter of the PDM.

Pellicer, Carlos (1897?–1977)
Internationally known Mexican poet and essayist.

PEMEX (Petróleos de México)
Mexico's largest and most powerful *paraestatal* in charge of developing, processing, and marketing petroleum and petroleum products in Mexico and abroad.

perredista
A member or supporter of the PRD.

pesumista
A member or supporter of the PSUM.

PMS (Partido Mexicano Socialista)
A fusion of several leftist parties, including the PSUM, it was organized in 1987 in an effort to gather the Mexican Left in preparation for the 1988 presidential election. The PSUM was the largest organization to join the coalition, but the PMT, among others, was included as well. The PMS was superseded by the PRD.

PMT (Partido Mexicano de los Trabajadores)
Founded in 1974 mostly through the efforts of Heberto Castillo, it is a minority organization that has not

functioned as a satellite party. Castillo's interview outlines its history.

PNR (Partido Nacional Revolucionario)
The first phase (1928–1938) of the official party now known as the PRI.

POCM (Partido Obrero Campesino Mexicano)
Organized in 1940, it represents one of the various organizations that splintered away from the PCM. It rejoined the PCM in 1959.

popular front
See national front.

Portes Gil, Emilio (1891–1978)
Served as provisional president of Mexico in 1929 and in many governmental posts afterward.

PPM (Partido Popular Mexicano)
Made up of activists who broke away from the PPS for doctrinal and personal reasons in the late 1970s, it never played a significant political role. Its members subsequently chose to join the PSUM, although many did not remain in it for long.

PPS (Partido Popular Socialista)
Founded as the Partido Popular in 1948 by Vicente Lombardo Toledano, it attracted many leftists, including dissidents from both the Communist Party and the official party. Up to the early 1970s, the PPS and the Communist Party held most of the Mexican Left. With the passing of Lombardo Toledano, the PPS lost its strength and played the role of a satellite party until 1987.

PRD (Partido de la Revolución Democrática)
The most recent stage of the reconstituted Left in Mexico was created by the various elements that made up neo-*cardenismo* immediately following the 1988 presidential election. Its purpose is to marshal the forces of the Center-Left for 1994 and all of the interim local elections. It held its first congress in late 1990.

PRI (Partido Revolucionario Institucional)
The most recent and, thus far, longest-lasting phase (1946–present) of the official party that has ruled Mexico since 1929.

priista
A member or supporter of the PRI.

PRM (Partido Revolucionario Mexicano)
The second phase (1938–1946) of the official party that later became the PRI.

PRS (Partido de la Revolución Socialista)
Organized in about 1982, it is one of several miniparties of the Left organized at one time or another by Alejandro Gascón Mercado, a long-time Stalinist. Its members bolted from the PSUM and have played no important role thus far.

PRT (Partido Revolucionario de los Trabajadores)
Registered in 1986, it was the ultra-left party in Mexico by virtue of its orientation toward Trotskyism. Its 1988 presidential candidate, Rosario Ibarra de Piedra, publicly stated she was not a Trotskyist, but the PRT failed to attract the minimum number of votes to stay in operation legally.

PSD (Partido Socialista Democrático)
Taking advantage of the political reforms of the 1970s, it obtained official registry in 1981. Its political ideology is reflected in its title, and its membership is reputedly middle class, including many businessmen. It has failed to play an important role thus far.

PST (Partido Socialista de los Trabajadores)
Viewed by some as a *partido palero*, the PST was organized in the 1970s by Rafael Aguilar Talamantes. It heeds peasant demands that were brushed off by the PRI and consequently retains enough voter support to enjoy a minor presence in the legislature.

PSUM (Partido Socialista Unificado Mexicano)
Representing the first major stage in the moderation and reunification of the Left, it was organized in 1981 from various leftist parties, including the Communist Party. The PSUM is described in considerable detail by Jorge Alcocer. It merged with the PMS in 1987.

reforma política, la
Mexican legislation begun in the 1960s and enhanced in the 1970s that opened the political system to opposition parties through carefully calibrated legal mechanisms.

revolutionary family
A concept developed by Frank B. Brandenburg in his book *The Making of Modern Mexico* (Englewood Cliffs, NJ: Prentice-Hall, 1964) in an effort to answer the question: Who rules Mexico? The revolutionary family consists of a national elite

led by a paternal president who manipulates three layers of high government officials and thus rules the country. Although it has long been regarded as obsolete, the term lingers.

Rosenblueth, Emilio Arturo (1926-)
Distinguished engineer born in Chihuahua who initially studied at the UNAM and later earned his Ph.D. at the University of Illinois. He served as professor of seismic engineering at the UNAM and received Mexico's National Science Award in 1974 and international awards in later years. He also served as president of the Mexican Academy of Science Research.

Sada Zambrano, Rogelio
Former director general of Vitro, one of the Monterrey Group holding companies. He was dismissed in November 1985 reportedly because he took part in a PAN demonstration.

Salinas de Gortari, Carlos (1948-)
In the most hotly contested presidential election in modern Mexican history, he became president, 1988–1994. He graduated with an economics degree from the UNAM in 1969 and obtained a Ph.D. in economics from Harvard in 1978. He taught economics and public administration at the UNAM (1971–1976), and his many government jobs almost always involved economic planning and decision making. He was secretary of budget and planning for President de la Madrid, and he has authored several works in his field.

SIDERMEX
Siderúrgica de México, a state-owned steel corporation.

Simpson-Mazolli Law
Known also as Public Law 99-603, it was passed on November 6, 1986, in an effort to reduce illegal immigration to the United States. It revised and amended immigration policies by establishing penalties for knowingly employing undocumented aliens, and it granted amnesty for specific groups of undocumented aliens.

sinarquismo
A rural conservative movement that rose in the late 1930s in west-central Mexico against the government's anticlerical and pro-Socialist policies. Many peasants who did not benefit from land reform programs supported it. Some of its national leaders were connected with Nazi diplomats.

Siqueiros, David Alfaro (1896–1974)
Member of the Mexican Communist Party, he was one of the world's most prominent muralists. He employed artistic imagery that effectively conveyed Marxist and Leninist ideals. He was jailed many times by the Mexican government for his militancy and was implicated in an attempt against Leon Trotsky's life.

SNTE (Sindicato Nacional de Trabajadores de la Educación)
A dynamic national teachers federation that acted on behalf of its members through the 1950s. It was tightly controlled by *charro* leaders until the late 1980s.

Tamayo, Jorge L. (1912–)
Distinguished Mexican geographer and author.

Televisa
A privately owned television network enjoying nearly monopolistic privileges by virtue of its close working relationship with the PRI administration.

Tello, Carlos (1938–)
Economist and author of many studies who served as President López Portillo's director of the Banco de México, the nation's central bank.

Tlaltelolco massacre, October massacre, or Massacre of 1968
Plaza de Tlaltelolco, or Plaza de las Tres Culturas, is a square in Mexico City where at least three hundred demonstrators were killed by soldiers on October 2, 1968.

Tlaltelolco Treaty
Also known as the Treaty for the Prohibition of Nuclear Weapons in Latin America, this treaty represents a concerted effort by Latin American countries to achieve the military denuclearization of the region. Supported by the United Nations, the treaty was signed in 1976.

UNAM (Universidad Nacional Autónoma de México)
Also referred to in this volume as the national university, it has functioned since the colonial period. It became a huge institution located in southern Mexico City, with more than one hundred thousand students registered in its multiple programs and decentralized schools.

Unión Nacional Sinarquista (Sinarquista Party)
The political organization formed by *sinarquismo* in 1938.

university autonomy
Relative freedom enjoyed by Latin American universities to conduct their own affairs without interference from authoritarian governments. This topic has received little attention from serious writers.

Vallarta, Ignacio Luis (1830–1893)
As one of Benito Juárez's supporters, he served as governor of the state of Jalisco, federal government secretary, and head of the supreme court.

Vasconcelos, José (1889–1954)
Secretary of education from 1920 to 1924, he led a movement against the official party in 1929. One of his books, *La raza cósmica*, gave rise to the popular idea, lionized after his death, of equating the Mexican people to the "cosmic race," the first of many racial blends that would "dominate" the world.

Velázquez, Fidel (1900–)
A milkman and union leader who entered politics on the side of the government. Under controversial circumstances, he became the secretary-general of the CTM in 1940 and has occupied that post since. He is referred to as Mexico's labor czar.

verticalismo
Decision making that is largely top-down. The term is another way of referring to nondemocratic actions.

Villa, Francisco ("Pancho") (1878–1923)
Considered a bandit by many people before the onset of the uprising in 1910, he emerged as one of the most powerful revolutionary leaders in the north. He remains a controversial figure because he played an important role in overthrowing prerevolutionary elites but lacked a clear ideology and committed unsavory atrocities.

VIPS
A restaurant chain in Mexico in the 1980s. It belongs to the Grupo Aurrerá, headed by Gerónimo Arango Arias, and enjoys significant foreign investment. It is favored by middle-class clients or otherwise upwardly mobile Mexicans.

Visa
One of several holding companies held by the Monterrey Group of powerful businessmen. *See* Alfa Group.

Vitro
One of several holding companies held by the Monterrey Group of powerful businessmen. *See* Alfa Group.

Zapata, Emiliano (1879–1919)
Provincial leader turned revolutionary in 1911, he fought against the ravages of early industrialization in his home state of Morelos and for a return to preindustrial values, including communally owned land. He also attacked political cronyism and the oppression of peasants. He is a symbol of the revolution of Mexico.

Bibliography

Books and Articles

Acuña, Rudy. *Occupied America: A History of Chicanos.* 3d ed. New York: Harper and Row, 1988.

Alexander, Robert J. *Communism in Latin America.* New Brunswick, NJ: Rutgers University Press, 1967.

Alvarez, Alejandro. "Crisis in Mexico: Impacts on the Working Class and the Labor Movement." In Barry Carr and Ricardo Anzaldúa Montoya, eds., *The Mexican Left, the Popular Movements, and the Politics of Austerity,* 47–58. Monograph Series, no. 18. San Diego: Center for U.S.-Mexican Studies, University of California at San Diego, 1986.

America's Watch. "Human Rights in Mexico: A Policy of Impunity." N.p. Typewritten manuscripts with "Embargo Date A.M. Papers on June 13, 1990."

Amnesty International Report 1988. London: Amnesty International Publications, 1988.

Amnesty International Report 1990. London: Amnesty International Publications, 1990.

Asamblea de barrios de la ciudad. Cronología y documentos. N.p., n.d.

Asamblea de barrios de la ciudad. Tres años de lucha. Declaraciones. N.p., n.d.

Bailey, David C. *Viva Cristo Rey: The Cristero Rebellion and the Church-State Conflict in Mexico.* Austin: University of Texas Press, 1974.

Bailey, John J. *Governing Mexico: The Statecraft of Crisis Management.* New York: St. Martin's, 1988.

Bailey, Norman A., and Richard Cohen. *The Mexican Time Bomb.* Twentieth Century Fund Paper. New York: Priority Press, 1987.

Basáñez, Miguel, and Enrique Alducín, eds. "Valores, actitudes y opiniones." *Nexos* 11:129 (September 1988): 63–65.

Bernstein, Marvin D. *The Mexican Mining Industry, 1890–1950.* Albany: State University of New York Press, 1964.

Blaisdell, Lowell L. *Desert Revolution: Baja California, 1911.* Madison: University of Wisconsin Press, 1962.

Boils, Guillermo. *Los militares y la política en México, 1915–1974.* Mexico City: Ediciones "El Caballito," 1975.

Bolivar E., Augusto. "La sociedad civil es burguesa." *El cotidiano: Revista de la realidad mexicana actual* 2:8 (November-December 1985): 27–30.

Bortz, Jeffrey. "The Dilemma of Mexican Labor." *Current History: A World Affairs Journal* 86 (March 1987): 105–9.

Brandenburg, Frank B. *The Making of Modern Mexico.* Englewood Cliffs, NJ: Prentice-Hall, 1964.

Brownstein, Ronald, and Nina Easton, eds. *Reagan's Ruling Class: Portraits of the President's Top 100 Officials.* Washington, DC: Presidential Accountability Group, 1982.

Buendía, Manuel. *La CIA en México.* Mexico City: Ediciones Oceano, 1983.

———. *Los petroleros.* Mexico City: Ediciones Oceano, 1985.

———. *La ultraderecha en México.* Mexico City: Ediciones Oceano, 1984.

Bulnes, Francisco. *El verdadero Díaz y la revolución.* Mexico City: Editora Nacional, 1952.

Burgoa Orihuela, Ignacio. *Acusamos! Que no queden impunes los culpables de la crisis!* Mexico City: Edamex, 1983.

Cadena Roa, Jorge. "Las demandas de la sociedad civil, los partidos políticos y las respuestas del sistema." In Pablo González Casanova and Jorge Cadena Roa, coords., *Primer informe sobre la democracia: México 1988,* 285–327. Mexico City: Siglo XXI, 1988.

Camp, Roderic Ai. "The Cabinet and the *Técnico* in Mexico and the United States." *Journal of Comparative Administration* 3:2 (August 1971): 188–214.

———. "Camarillas in Mexican Politics: The Case of the Salinas Cabinet." *Mexican Studies* 6:1 (Winter 1990): 85–107.

———. *Entrepreneurs and Politicians in Twentieth Century Mexico.* New York: Oxford University Press, 1989.

———. *Mexican Political Biographies, 1935–1981.* Tucson: University of Arizona Press, 1982.

———. *Mexico's Leaders, Their Education and Recruitment.* Tucson: University of Arizona Press, 1980.

———. *Who's Who in Mexico Today.* Boulder: Westview Press, 1988.

Campa, Valentín. *Mi testimonio: Memorias de un comunista Mexicano,* 3d ed. Mexico City: Editores Cultura Popular, 1985.

Cárdenas, Cuauhtémoc. *Cuauhtémoc Cárdenas: Nuestra lucha apenas comienza.* Mexico City: Editorial Nuestro Tiempo, 1988.

Carr, Barry. *Mexican Communism, 1968–1983 (Eurocommunism in the Americas?)* San Diego: Center for U.S.-Mexican Studies, University of California at San Diego, 1985.

———. "Mexican Communism, 1968–1981: Eurocommunism in

the Americas?" *Journal of Latin American Studies* 17 (May 1985): 201–28.

———. "The PSUM: The Unification Process on the Mexican Left, 1981–1985." In Judith Gentleman, ed., *Mexican Politics in Transition*, 281–304. Boulder: Westview Press, 1987.

Carr, Barry, and Ricardo Anzaldúa Montoya, eds. *The Mexican Left, the Popular Movements, and the Politics of Austerity.* Monograph Series, no. 18. San Diego: Center for U.S.-Mexican Studies, University of California at San Diego, 1987.

Castañeda, Jorge. "Salinas's International Relations Gamble." *Journal of International Affairs* 43:2 (Winter 1990): 407–22.

Clendenen, Clarence C. *Blood on the Border: The United States Army and the Mexican Irregulars.* London: Macmillan, 1969.

Cline, Howard F. *The United States and Mexico.* New York: Atheneum, 1963.

Cockcroft, James D. *Intellectual Precursors of the Mexican Revolution, 1900–1913.* Austin: University of Texas Press, 1976.

———. *Mexico: Class Formation, Capital Accumulation and the State.* New York: Monthly Review Press, 1983.

Coerver, Don M., and Linda B. Hall. *Texas and the Mexican Revolution: A Study in State and National Border Policy, 1910–1920.* San Antonio: Trinity University Press, 1984.

Colburn, Forrest D. "Mexico's Financial Crisis." *Latin American Research Review* 19:2 (1984): 220–24.

Colmenares, David, Luis Angeles, and Carlos Ramírez. *La devaluación de 1982.* Mexico City: Tierra Nova, 1982.

———. *La nacionalización de la banca.* Mexico City: Tierra Nova, 1982.

Concheiro B., Juan Luis. "En la lucha por la democracia y la unidad de la izquierda." In Arnoldo Martínez Verdugo, ed., *Historia del comunismo en México.* Mexico City: Editorial Grijalbo, 1985.

Constitution of the United Mexican States, 1917. Washington, DC: Pan American Union, 1961.

Cornelius, Wayne A., and Ann L. Craig. "Comments on Roderic Camp, 'Comparing Political Generations in Mexico: The Last One Hundred Years.' " Paper presented at 7th Conference of Mexican and North American Historians, San Diego, October 19, 1990.

———. "Mexico: Salinas and the PRI at the Crossroads." *Journal of Democracy* 1:3 (Summer 1990): 61–70.

———. "Politics in Mexico." In Gabriel A. Almond and G. Bingham Powell, Jr., eds., *Comparative Politics Today*, 411–65. Boston: Little, Brown, 1984.

Craig, Richard B. "Illicit Drug Traffic: Implications for South American Source Countries." *Journal of Inter-American Studies and World Affairs* 29:2 (Summer 1987): 1–34.

Cumberland, Charles C. *Mexican Revolution: Genesis under Madero*. Austin: University of Texas Press, 1952.

De Sheinbaum, Bertha Lerner. "El estado mexicano y el 6 de julio de 1988." *Revista mexicana de sociología* 51:4 (October-December 1989): 199–237.

Diccionario enciclopédico de México. Ilustrado. Humberto Musacchio. Mexico City: Andrés León Editor, 1989.

"Electoral Reform." Fourteen pages of faxed materials provided by the Mexican embassy in Washington, DC, on October 13, 1990.

Enciclopedia de México. Mexico City: Enciclopedia de México, 1970.

Estévez, Jaime. "Crisis mundial y proyecto nacional." In Pablo González Casanova and Hector Aguilar Camín, coords., *México ante la crisis: El contexto internacional y la crisis económica*, 1:45–53. 2 vols. Mexico City: Siglo Veintiuno Editores, 1985.

Falcón, Romana. *Revolución y caciquismo. San Luis Potosí, 1910–1938*. Mexico City: Colegio de México, 1984.

Friedrich, Paul. *Agrarian Revolt in a Mexican Village*. Chicago: University of Chicago Press, 1977.

Galarza, Ernesto. *Merchants of Labor: The Bracero Story*. Santa Barbara: McNally and Loftin, 1964.

Gamio, Manuel. *Mexican Immigration to the United States: A Study of Human Migration and Adjustment*. 1930. Reprint. New York: Dover Publications, 1971.

García, Mario T. *Desert Immigrants: The Mexicans of El Paso, 1880–1920*. New Haven: Yale University Press, 1981.

García Márquez, Gabriel. *One Hundred Years of Solitude*. New York: Avon, 1971.

Gentleman, Judith. *Mexican Oil and Dependent Development*. New York: P. Lang, 1984.

Gentleman, Judith, ed. *Mexican Politics in Transition*. Boulder: Westview Press, 1987.

Gil, Carlos B., ed. *The Age of Porfirio Díaz: Selected Readings*. Albuquerque: University of New Mexico Press, 1977.

———. "Massacre at Tlaltelolco: Historical Perspectives and Bibliographic Notes." Unpublished manuscript, version A (1986).

———. "Massacre at Tlaltelolco: Its Complexities and Its Literature." Unpublished manuscript, version B (1986).

Gilly, Adolfo. "The Mexican Regime in Its Dilemma." *Journal of International Affairs* 43 (1990): 273–90.

González Casanova, Pablo. "México ante la crisis mundial." In González Casanova and Hector Aguilar Camín, coords., *México ante la crisis: El contexto internacional y la crisis económica*, 1:13–28. 2 vols. Mexico City: Siglo Veintiuno Editores, 1985.

González Casanova, Pablo, and Hector Aguilar Camín, coords. *México ante la crisis: El contexto internacional y la crisis económica.* 2 vols. Mexico City: Siglo Veintiuno Editores, 1985.

González Casanova, Pablo, and Jorge Cadena Roa, coords. *Primer informe sobre la democracia: México 1988.* Mexico City: Siglo XXI, 1988.

González González, José. *Lo negro del negro Durazo.* Mexico City: Editorial Posada, 1983.

González Schmal, Jesús. *A la democracia sin violencia.* Mexico City: Epessa, 1986.

Graham, Richard, ed. *The Idea of Race in Latin America, 1870–1940.* Austin: University of Texas Press, 1990.

Grayson, George W. "An Overdose of Corruption: The Domestic Politics of Mexican Oil." *Caribbean Review* 13:3 (Summer 1984): 23–24.

————. *The Politics of Mexican Oil.* Pittsburgh: University of Pittsburgh Press, 1980.

Guillén Romo, Héctor. *Orígenes de la crisis en México, inflación, y endeudamiento externo, 1940–1982.* Colección Problemas de México. Mexico City: Ediciones Era, 1984.

Haces, Cosme. *Crisis! MMH ante la herencia de JLP. Crónica de un trimestre negro.* Mexico City: Edamex, 1983.

Haddox, John H. *Vasconcelos of Mexico: Philosopher and Prophet.* Austin: University of Texas Press, 1967.

Hall, Linda. *Alvaro Obregón: Power and Revolution in Mexico, 1911–1920.* College Station: Texas A & M University Press, 1981.

Hansen, Roger D. *The Politics of Mexican Development.* Baltimore: Johns Hopkins University Press, 1974.

Immerman, Richard H. *The CIA in Guatemala: The Foreign Policy of Intervention.* Austin: University of Texas Press, 1982.

Jacobo M., Edmundo, and Luis Méndez. "Bueno . . . y después de todo, cual sociedad civil?" *El cotidiano: Revista de la realidad actual mexicana* 2:8 (November-December 1985): 23–26.

Jancar, Barbara Wolfe. *Czechoslovakia and the Absolute Monopoly of Power: A Study of Political Power in a Communist System.* New York: Praeger, 1971.

Johnson, John J. *The Emergence of the Middle Sectors.* Stanford, CA: Stanford University Press, 1958.

Johnson, Kenneth F. *Mexican Democracy: A Critical View.* New York: Praeger, 1984.

Kay, Cristóbal. *Latin American Theories of Development and Underdevelopment.* London: Routledge, 1989.

Khindaria, Brij. "Foundation for Survival: The Desperate Need for Cooperation between North and South Nations." In *1981,*

Britannica Book of the Year, 65–69. Chicago: Encyclopaedia Britannica, 1981.

Knight, Alan. *The Mexican Revolution*. 2 vols. Cambridge: Cambridge University Press, 1986.

———. "Racism, Revolution, and *Indigenismo*: Mexico, 1910–1940." In Richard Graham, ed., *The Idea of Race in Latin America, 1870–1940*, 71–113. Austin: University of Texas Press, 1990.

La Raza Cósmica/The Cosmic Race. 1925. Reprint. Series Pensamiento Mexicano, no. 1. Los Angeles: California State University at Los Angeles, 1979.

León, Samuel, and Ignacio Marván. "Movimientos sociales en México (1968–1983). Panorama general y perspectivas." *Estudios políticos* 3:2 (April-June 1984): 5–18.

Levy, Daniel C. *University and Government in Mexico: Autonomy in an Authoritarian System*. New York: Praeger, 1980.

Levy, Daniel C., and Gabriel Székely. *Mexico, Paradox of Stability and Change*. Boulder: Westview Press, 1983.

Levy, Jacques. *César Chávez: Autobiography of La Causa*. New York: Norton, 1975.

Lieuwin, Edwin. *Mexican Militarism: The Political Rise and Fall of the Revolutionary Army*. Albuquerque: University of New Mexico Press, 1968.

Linz, Juan J. "An Authoritarian Regime: Spain." In Erik Allardt and Yrjö Littumen, eds., *Cleavages, Ideologies and Party Systems: Contributions to Comparative Political Sociology*, 291–341. Helsinki: Transactions of the Westermarck Society, 1964.

Loaeza, Soledad. "El estudio de las clases medias mexicanas después de 1940." *Estudios políticos* 3:2 (April-June 1984): 52–62.

Mabry, Donald J. *Mexico's Acción Nacional: A Catholic Alternative to Revolution*. Syracuse, NY: Syracuse University Press, 1973.

Madero, Pablo Emilio. *500 horas de hielo*. Mexico City: n.p., 1985.

Marcos, Patricio E. "Paradojas de la corrupción." *Revista mexicana de ciencias políticas y sociales* 28:110 (October-December 1982): 123–38.

Martínez, Oscar J. *Border Boom Town: Ciudad Juárez since 1848*. Austin: University of Texas Press, 1975.

———. *Fragments of the Mexican Revolution: Personal Accounts from the Border*. Albuquerque: University of New Mexico Press, 1983.

Martínez Verdugo, Arnoldo, ed. *Historia del comunismo en México*. Mexico City: Editorial Grijalba, 1985.

Medin, Tzvi. *Ideología y praxis política de Lázaro Cárdenas*. 4th ed. Mexico City: Siglo Veintiuno Editores, 1976.

Medina, Luis, and Blanca Torres, eds. *Del cardenismo al avilaca-machismo, 1940–1952*. Vol. 18 of *Historia de la revolución mexicana*. Mexico City: Colegio de México, 1978.

Meyer, Jean A. *The Cristero Rebellion: The Mexican People between Church and State, 1926–1929*. New York: Cambridge University Press, 1976.

Meyer, Lorenzo, and Héctor Aguilar Camín. *A la sombra de la revolución mexicana*. Mexico City: Cal y Arena, 1990.

Meyer, Lorenzo, Rafael Segovia, and Alejandra Lajous. *Los inicios de la institucionalización, 1928–1934*. Vol. 12 of *Historia de la revolución mexicana*. Mexico City: Colegio de México, 1978.

Meyer, Michael C., and William L. Sherman. *The Course of Mexican History*. 3d ed. New York: Oxford University Press, 1987.

Michaels, Albert L. "Fascism to Sinarquismo: Popular Nationalism against the Mexican Revolution." *Journal of Church and State* 8 (1966): 234–50.

———. "The Mexican Election of 1940." Special Studies, no. 5. Buffalo: Council on International Studies, State University of New York, 1971.

Michels, Robert. *Political Parties: A Sociological Study of the Oligarchical Tendencies of Modern Democracy*. Glencoe, IL: Free Press, 1949.

Middlebrook, Kenneth J. "Political Reform and Political Change in Mexico." *Latin America and Caribbean Contemporary Record* 1 (1983): 149–61.

Millon, Robert P. *The Ideology of a Peasant Revolutionary, Zapata*. New York: International Publishers, 1959.

———. *Mexican Marxist: Vicente Lombardo Toledano*. Chapel Hill: University of North Carolina Press, 1966.

Molina Enríquez, Andrés. *Los grandes problemas nacionales*. Mexico City: Imprenta de A. Carranza e hijos, 1909.

Molinar, Juan, and Jeff Weldon. "Elecciones de 1988 en México." Unpublished manuscript. Center for U.S.-Mexican Studies, University of California at San Diego.

Montes de Oca, Rosa Elena. "State and Peasant." In José Luis Reyna and Richard S. Weinert, eds., *Authoritarianism in Mexico*, 47–63. Philadelphia: Institute for the Study of Human Issues, 1977.

Moore, Joan W. *Mexican Americans*. 2d ed. New York: Prentice Hall, 1976.

Moreno, Daniel. *Los partidos políticos del México contemporáneo, 1916–1985*. 10th ed. Mexico City: Pax-Mexico, 1985.

Morris, Stephen D. *Los presindenciables: Mexico's Next Jefe, 1988*. Tempe, AZ: Incamex, 1987.

Mosk, Sanford. *Industrial Revolution in Mexico*. Berkeley: University of California Press, 1950.

Muñoz Ledo, Porfirio. *Compromisos.* Mexico City: Editorial Pozada, 1989.

———. *La construcción del futuro de América Latina.* N.p.: UNESCO, 1988.

Myrdal, Gunnar. *Beyond the Welfare State: Economic Planning and Its International Implications.* New Haven: Yale University Press, 1960.

Nacional Financiera, S.A. *La economía en cifras.* Mexico City: Nacional Financiera, 1978.

The New Encyclopaedia Britannica. Chicago: Encyclopaedia Britannica, 1975.

Niemeyer, E. V., Jr. *Revolution at Querétaro: The Mexican Constitutional Convention of 1916–1917.* Austin: University of Texas Press, 1974.

1968: El principio del poder. Mexico City: Proceso, 1980.

1986, Britannica Book of the Year. Chicago: Encyclopaedia Britannica, 1986.

Nuncio, Abraham. *El grupo Monterrey.* Mexico City: Editorial Nueva Imagen, 1982.

Ortiz, Orlando, comp. *Genaro Vásquez.* Mexico City: Editorial Diógenes, 1972.

Ovalle Favela, José. "Aspectos sociales y políticos de la Constitución mexicana de 1917." *Pensamiento Político* 20 (October 1975): 195–210.

Padgett, Vincent L. *The Mexican Political System.* Boston: Houghton Mifflin, 1966.

Paredes, Américo. *With His Pistol in His Hand: A Borderland Ballad and Its Hero.* Austin: University of Texas Press, 1958.

Paz, Octavio. *Labyrinth of Solitude: Life and Thought in Mexico.* Translated by Lysander Kemp. New York: Grove, 1961.

———. *The Other Mexico: Critique of the Pyramid.* Translated by Lysander Kemp. New York: Grove, 1972.

Pazos, Luis. *La estatización de la banca. Hacia un capitalismo de estado?* Mexico City: Editorial Diana, 1982.

Pellicer de Brody, Olga, and José Luis Reyna. *Período 1952–1960: El afianzamiento de la estabilidad política.* Vol. 22 of *Historia de la revolución mexicana.* Mexico City: Colegio de México, 1978.

Poniatowska, Elena. "Los hospitales jamás deberían caerse." *La Jornada,* October-November 1985.

———. *Massacre in Mexico.* Translated by Helen R. Lane. New York: Viking, 1971.

———. *La noche de Tlaltelolco: Testimonios de historia oral.* Mexico City: Ediciones Era, 1978.

Portes Gil, Emilio. *Quince años de política mexicana.* Mexico City: Ediciones Botas, 1954.

Price, Glen W. *Origins of the War with Mexico: The Polk-Stockton Intrigue.* Austin: University of Texas Press, 1967.

Propuesta democrática. N.p., 1987.

Quintana López, Enrique. "El terremoto: Efectos económicos y perspectivas de la reconstrucción." *El cotidiano: Revista de la realidad mexicana actual* 2:8 (November-December 1985): 85–90.

Quirk, Robert E. *An Affair of Honor: Woodrow Wilson and the Occupation of Veracruz.* New York: Norton, 1962.

Reding, Andrew. "The Democratic Current: A New Era in Mexican Politics." *World Policy Journal* 5:2 (Spring 1988): 323–66.

———. "Mexico at a Crossroads: The 1988 Election and Beyond." *World Policy Journal* 5:4 (Fall 1988): 615–49.

———. "Mexico under Salinas: A Facade of Reform." *World Policy Journal* 6:4 (Fall 1989): 685–729.

Reyna, José Luis. "La negociación controlada con el movimiento obrero." In Olga Pellicer de Brody and José Luis Reyna, *Período 1952–1960: El afianzamiento de la estabilidad política,* 73–106. Vol. 22 of *Historia de la revolución mexicana.* Mexico City: Colegio de México, 1978.

———. "Redefining the Authoritarian Regime." In José Luis Reyna and Richard S. Weinert, eds., *Authoritarianism in Mexico,* 155–71. Inter-American Politics Series. Philadelphia: Institute for the Study of Human Issues, 1977.

Reyna, José Luis, and Richard S. Weinert, eds. *Authoritarianism in Mexico.* Inter-American Politics Series. Philadelphia: Institute for the Study of Human Issues, 1977.

Reynolds, Clark W. "Beyond the Mexican Crisis: Implications for Business and the U.S. Government." In House of Representatives, Committee on Foreign Affairs, 98th Cong., 2d Sess., *The Mexican Economic Crisis: Policy Implications for the United States,* 131–55. Washington, DC: Government Printing Office, 1984.

Richmond, Douglas W. "Venustiano Carranza." In George Wolfskill and Richmond, eds., *Essays on the Mexican Revolution: Revisionist Views of the Leaders,* 48–80. Walter Prescott Webb Memorial Lectures. Austin: University of Texas Press, 1979.

Riding, Alan. *Distant Neighbors.* New York: Vintage Books, 1986.

Romo, Ricardo. *East Los Angeles; History of a Barrio.* Austin: University of Texas Press, 1983.

Ross, Stanley R. *Francisco I. Madero: Apostle of Mexican Democracy.* New York: Columbia University Press, 1955.

Rossiter, Clinton. "Conservatism." In David Sills, ed., *International Encyclopedia of the Social Sciences,* 3:290–95. London: Free Press, 1979.

Ruiz, Ramón E. *The Great Rebellion, 1905–1924*. New York: Norton, 1980.

Salazar C., Luis. "Sismo, política y gobierno." *El cotidiano: Revista de la realidad mexicana actual* 2:8 (November-December 1985): 19–22.

Samora, Julian. *Los Mojados: The Wetback Story*. Notre Dame, IN: University of Notre Dame Press, 1971.

Sanderson, Susan Walsh, and Robert H. Hayes. "Mexico—Opening ahead of Eastern Europe." *Harvard Business Review* 68:5 (September-October 1990): 32–42.

Sauer, Franz A. von. *The Alienated "Loyal" Opposition: Mexico's Partido Acción Nacional*. Albuquerque: University of New Mexico Press, 1974.

Schlesinger, Stephen, and Stephen Kinzer. *Bitter Fruit: The Untold Story of the American Coup in Guatemala*. Garden City, NY: Anchor Books, 1983.

Scott, Robert E. *Government in Transition*. 2d ed. Urbana: University of Illinois Press, 1964.

Sedwitz, Walter J. "Mexico's 1954 Devaluation in Retrospect." *Inter-American Economic Affairs* 10:2 (Autumn 1956): 22–44.

Segovia, Rafael, and Alejandra Lajous. "La consolidación del poder." In Lorenzo Meyer et al., *Los inicios de la institucionalización, 1928–1934*, 5–84. Vol. 12 of *Historia de la revolución mexicana*. Mexico City: Colegio de México, 1978.

Semo, Enrique. "The Mexican Left and the Economic Crisis." In Barry Carr and Ricardo Anzaldúa Montoya, eds., *The Mexican Left, the Popular Movements, and the Politics of Austerity*, 19–32 Monograph Series, no. 18. San Diego: Center for U.S.-Mexican Studies, University of California at San Diego, 1987.

Shannon, Elaine. *Desperados: Latin Drug Lords, U.S. Lawmen, and the War America Can't Win*. New York: Viking Penguin, 1988.

Sills, David, ed. *International Encyclopedia of the Social Sciences*. 16 vols. Vol. 18, *Biographical Supplement*. London: Free Press, 1979.

Smith, David G. "Liberalism." In David Sills, ed., *International Encyclopedia of the Social Sciences*, 9:276–82. London: Free Press, 1979.

Smith, Peter H. *Labyrinths of Power: Political Recruitment in 20th Century Mexico*. Princeton: Princeton University Press, 1979.

———. "The Making of the Mexican Constitution." In William O. Aydelotte, ed., *The History of Parliamentary Behavior*, 186–224. Princeton: Princeton University Press, 1977.

Soldatenko, Michael. "The Mexican Student Movement of 1968: Myth, Repression, and the Petty Bourgeois." M.A. thesis, University of California at Los Angeles, 1977.

Spota, Luis. *Palabras mayores*. Mexico City: Editorial Grijalbo, 1976.
──────. *El retrato hablado*. Mexico City: Editorial Grijalbo, 1975.
──────. *Sobre la marcha*. Mexico City: Editorial Grijalbo, 1976.
Stevens, Evelyn P. *Protest and Response in Mexico: 1968–1980*. Cambridge: MIT Press, 1974.
Story, Dale. *The Mexican Ruling Party: Stability and Authority*. Politics in Latin America (A Hoover Institution Series). New York: Praeger, 1986.
Székely, Gabriel. "The Mexican Economic and Political Situation." In House of Representatives, Committee on Foreign Affairs, 98th Cong., 2d Sess., *The Mexican Economic Crisis: Policy Implications for the United States*, 257–74. Washington, DC: Government Printing Office, 1984.
Taylor, George Rogers. *The Transportation Revolution, 1815–1860*. New York: Harper and Row, 1951.
Tello, Carlos. "La crisis en México, saldos y opciones." *Universidad de México: Revista de la Universidad Nacional Autónoma de México* 40:415 (August 1985): 3–10.
Tirado Jiménez, Ramón. *Asamblea de barrios: Nuestra batalla*. Mexico City: Editorial Nuestro Tiempo, 1990.
Townsend, William Cameron. *Lázaro Cárdenas: Mexican Democrat*. Ann Arbor, MI: George Wahr, 1952.
United States v. Rafael Caro Quintero et al. "Memorandum in Support of Further Cross Examination of Witness Harrison; Memorandum of Points and Authorities; Declaration; Exhibits." CR 87-422-ER, U.S. District Court, Central District of California, vol. 47, July 5, 1990, to July 9, 1990.
Urquidi, Victor L. "Economic and Social Development in Mexico." In Tommie Sue Montgomery, ed., *Mexico Today*, 77–87. Philadelphia: Institute for the Study of Human Issues, 1982.
U.S. Department of Commerce. *1986. United States Foreign Trade Highlights*. Washington, DC: Government Printing Office, 1987.
U.S. Department of Commerce. Bureau of the Census. *Current Population Report. P–20, No. 443. School Enrollment. Social and Economic Characteristics of Students. 1987 and 1988*. Washington, DC: Government Printing Office, 1990.
──────. *Highlights of U.S. Export and Import Trade*. Washington, DC: Government Printing Office, 1986.
──────. *Statistical Abstract of the United States, 1987*. Washington, DC: Government Printing Office, 1987.
──────. *Statistical Abstract of the United States, 1990*. Washington, DC: Government Printing Office, 1990.
Vaca, Agustín, Mario Aldana, Jaime Olveda, Alma Dorantes, Frida Gorbach, Pablo Yankelevich, Cándido Galván, Angélica Peregrina, and José María Muría. *Historia de Jalisco: Desde*

la consolidacíon del porfiriato hasta mediados del siglo XX. Vol. 4 of *Historia de Jalisco,* ed. José María Muría. Guadalajara: Estado de Jalisco, 1980–82.

Villarreal, René. "The Policy of Import-Substituting Industrialization, 1929–1975." In José Luis Reyna and Richard S. Weinert, eds., *Authoritarianism in Mexico,* 67–107. Inter-American Politics Series. Philadelphia: Institute for the Study of Human Issues, 1977.

Weldon, Jeffrey. "Machine Politics and Middle-Class Reform in Mexico." Senior Thesis, University of Washington, 1985.

Wilkie, James W., ed. *Statistical Abstract of Latin America, 1987.* Los Angeles: Latin American Center, University of California at Los Angeles, 1987.

———. *Statistical Abstract of Latin America, 1989.* Los Angeles: Latin American Center, University of California at Los Angeles, 1989.

Wilkie, James W., and Albert L. Michaels, eds. *Revolution in Mexico: Years of Upheaval, 1910–1940.* New York: Alfred A. Knopf, 1969.

Wilkie, James W., and Paul D. Wilkins. "Quantifying the Class Structure of Mexico, 1895–1970." In Wilkie and Stephen Haber, eds., *Statistical Abstract of Latin America, 1981,* 578–90. Los Angeles: Latin American Center, University of California at Los Angeles, 1981.

Wolfskill, George, and Douglas W. Richmond, eds. *Essays on the Mexican Revolution: Revisionist Views of the Leaders.* Walter Prescott Webb Memorial Lectures. Austin: University of Texas Press, 1979.

Womack, John, Jr. *Zapata and the Mexican Revolution.* New York: Vintage Books, 1968.

Woodside, Kenneth. "The Canadian-United States Free Trade Agreement." *Canadian Journal of Political Science* 22:1 (March 1989): 155–70.

Zaid, Gabriel. "La propiedad privada de las funciones públicas." *Vuelta* 120 (November 1986): 25–32.

Zeveda, Ricardo J. *Calles el presidente.* Mexico City: Editorial Nuestro Tiempo, 1971.

Newspapers and Magazines

El Financiero
El Gobierno Mexicano
El Universal
Excelsior

La Jornada
La Opinión
Los Angeles Times
New York Times
Novedades de Chihuahua
Proceso
Unomasuno
Wall Street Journal

Index